About the editors

Elizabeth Sidiropoulos is the national director of the South African Institute of International Affairs (SAIIA) and the editor-in-chief of the *South African Journal of International Affairs*. Her research focus is on South African foreign policy and the impact of emerging powers on Africa's global engagement. Before her current appointment she was director of studies at SAIIA and research director at the South African Institute of Race Relations, where she was editor of the highly acclaimed *Race Relations Survey* (now the *South Africa Survey*), an annual publication documenting political and constitutional developments, and socio-economic disparities in South Africa.

Thomas Fues, trained as an economist, has been with the German Development Institute (DIE) as senior fellow since 2004. His main research interests are global governance, rising powers, the United Nations and international development cooperation. Recent publications include articles on the G8/G20, the role of rising powers in the global system, and the UN development sector, as well as on human rights and global governance. Since 2009 he has headed the training department at DIE and he has worked for the German parliament, the Institute of Peace and Development (University Duisburg-Essen), the government of North Rhine Westphalia and the German Advisory Council on Global Change, as well as acting as a freelance consultant.

Dr Sachin Chaturvedi is a senior fellow at the Research and Information System for Developing Countries, a think tank sponsored by the Indian Ministry of External Affairs. Till recently he was Global Justice Fellow at the MacMillan Center for International Affairs at Yale University, USA, where he worked on issues related to global governance and access to innovation and technology. He is author of two books and has published several research articles in various prestigious journals.

DEVELOPMENT COOPERATION AND EMERGING POWERS

NEW PARTNERS OR OLD PATTERNS?

edited by Sachin Chaturvedi, Thomas Fues
and Elizabeth Sidiropoulos

Zed Books
LONDON | NEW YORK

Development Cooperation and Emerging Powers: New Partners or Old Patterns? was first published in 2012 by Zed Books Ltd, 7 Cynthia Street, London N1 9JF, UK and Room 400, 175 Fifth Avenue, New York, NY 10010, USA

www.zedbooks.co.uk

Set in FFKievit and Monotype Plantin by Ewan Smith, London
Index: ed.emery@thefreeuniversity.net
Cover design: www.thisistransmission.com
Printed and bound by CPI Group (UK) Ltd, Croydon CRO 4YY

Distributed in the USA exclusively by Palgrave Macmillan, a division of St Martin's Press, LLC, 175 Fifth Avenue, New York, NY 10010, USA

A catalogue record for this book is available from the British Library
Library of Congress Cataloging in Publication Data available

ISBN 978 1 78032 064 9 hb
ISBN 978 1 78032 063 2 pb

CONTENTS

FIGURES AND TABLES

ABBREVIATIONS

AAA	Accra Agenda for Action
ABC	Agência Brasileira de Cooperaçao (Brazilian Cooperation Agency)
AMEXCID	Mexican Agency for International Development Cooperation
ARF	African Renaissance Fund
ASEAN	Association of South East Asian Nations
BAPA	Buenos Aires Plan of Action
BLNS	Botswana, Lesotho, Namibia and Swaziland
BRICS	Brazil, Russia, India, China, South Africa
Cabei	Central American Bank for Economic Integration
Complant	China National Complete Plant Corporation
CPC	Communist Party of China
DAC	Development Assistance Committee
DBSA	Development Bank of Southern Africa
DCF	Development Cooperation Forum
DfID	Department for International Development (UK)
DIE	German Development Institute
DIRCO	Department of International Relations and Cooperation (South Africa)
DRC	Democratic Republic of Congo
ECDC	Economic Cooperation among Developing Countries
ECOWAS	Economic Community of West African States
FOCAC	Forum on China–Africa Cooperation
GATT	General Agreement on Tariffs and Trade
GNI	gross national income
IBSA	India, Brazil, South Africa
IDB	Inter-American Development Bank
IIDCA	India International Development Cooperation Agency
ITEC	Indian Technical and Economic Cooperation
MEA	Ministry of External Affairs (India)
Mercosur	Mercado Común del Sur (Common Market of the South)
MFEL	Ministry of Foreign Economic Liaison (China)
MFERT	Ministry of Foreign Economic Relations and Trade (China)

MoF	Ministry of Finance (India)
MRE	Ministério das Relaçoes Exteriores (Ministry of Foreign Affairs, Brazil)
NEPAD	New Partnership for Africa's Development
NSC	North–South Cooperation
ODA	Official Development Assistance
SACU	Southern African Customs Union
SADC	Southern African Development Community
SADPA	South African Development Partnership Agency
SEGIB	Ibero-American General Secretariat
SJA	San José Agreement
SSC	South–South Cooperation
SUSSC	Special Unit for South–South Cooperation (UN)
TCDC	Technical Cooperation among Developing Countries
UNCTAD	United Nations Conference on Trade and Development
UNDP	United Nations Development Programme
UNESCO	United Nations Educational, Scientific and Cultural Organization
USAID	United States Agency for International Development
WTO	World Trade Organization

FOREWORD

In recent years, there has been increasing concern with the limitations in the coherence and coordination of development finance and, especially, aid provision. There is a strongly held view that the 'quality' of aid has deteriorated, even as its quantity has risen, albeit remaining stubbornly below internationally agreed guidelines.

Aid flows declined following the end of the Cold War, before rising again following the Monterrey Consensus on Financing for Development soon after the 9/11 terrorist attacks. Further progress has been patchy, and it is widely recognized that there are huge shortfalls in the promises made at the 2005 G8 Gleneagles Summit.

The adoption of the Paris Declaration on Aid Effectiveness was a step forward in the improvement of aid effectiveness, because it has helped to put 'quality' issues at centre stage. However, the weaknesses of the current aid system are as much systemic as they are behavioural.

Further difficulties have emerged in recent years. First, there has been a regression to bilateral aid, undermining multilateral mechanisms which generally provide less tied aid at lower transactions costs and with fewer political strings attached. This reversion can be explained by the wish to ensure public accountability in the donor countries, but there are clear pitfalls in this strategy.

Second, few countries actually fulfil their agreed aid commitments.

Third, what counts as aid can be confusing, if not deceptive. For example, debt cancellation under HIPC (Heavily Indebted Poor Countries) or MDRI (Multilateral Debt Relief Initiative) is a bookkeeping exercise which does not bring any new financial inflows, but is generally counted as Official Development Assistance (ODA).

Fourth, regardless of the level of actual outflows, the loan component continues to dominate. For example, Japan receives interest on ODA loans of more than US$2 billion per year.

Fifth, the numbers can be very misleading: the Democratic Republic of Congo is recorded as having received US$5.4 billion in ODA in 2003, but actual net financial transfers came to only US$400 million.

These limitations have important consequences. It is widely known that the ongoing global crisis has worsened the fiscal constraint in the donor countries, limiting the availability of aid possibly for years to come.

At a more concrete level, the administration of aid flows and aid-financed projects imposes heavy administrative burdens on developing country governments, while their managerial capacity has been degraded by years of low growth and misguided adjustment programmes. There is also a mismatch of capabilities and procedures between donor and recipient countries due to entrenched North–South asymmetries. For example, in the North, development ministries focus almost exclusively on ODA while, in the South, overstretched planning and finance ministries are normally their counterparts. The two sides often have very different capacities, interests and approaches to development cooperation. The limited mandates of development cooperation ministries also constrain what they can do, leading to the loss of crucial opportunities for international development cooperation in areas other than ODA.

Recently, several emerging economies have been scaling up their development cooperation activities on the back of strong growth performances. Such cooperation has, through the efforts of the G77, an established set of norms and principles based on the notions of solidarity, mutual respect and shared responsibility.

Assistance provided by emerging economies has, in particular, focused on developing productive capacities in recipient countries, while the traditional donors have increasingly turned towards social policy financing.

Still, despite the potential gains of this expanding pool of development partners, such cooperation has, at times, itself been constrained by national strategic interests, the imperative to deliver gains for domestic firms, and other narrow foreign policy considerations.

Given these differences, and in light of the deep development challenges still facing these 'new' donors, there is an unresolved tension around the (understandable) reluctance by the emerging developing country donors to be limited by the same monitoring and accountability standards and mechanisms designed by, and for, the rich donor countries. This tension will not be resolved by attempts to impose the latter's standards on the new development partners.

Rather, the emergence of new development partners should be seen as the starting point for the gradual emergence of more comprehensive and balanced international development cooperation, bringing greater gains to aid-dependent economies, including key international development issues such as international tax cooperation, sovereign debt workouts and international economic governance.

One major challenge is to ensure that the G20 is more sensitive and accountable to inclusive multilateral institutions, and strives to ensure international cooperation and global policy coordination.

Drawing on the varied experiences of Brazil, China, India, Mexico and South Africa, *Development Cooperation and Emerging Powers: New Partners or Old Patterns?* is the definitive volume on the state of South–South cooperation at the beginning of the second decade of the twenty-first century. Going beyond the media debate, this book sheds light on the fast-changing political dynamics of their development cooperation policies, against the current norms underlying current (Northern) donor conventions.

I am confident that this book will prove highly useful to policy-makers, practitioners and researchers.

Jomo Kwame Sundaram

Assistant Secretary-General for Economic Development
United Nations Department of Economic and Social Affairs
New York

INTRODUCTION

Elizabeth Sidiropoulos, Thomas Fues and Sachin Chaturvedi

The seeds of this book were sown with a workshop in 2007 on the development cooperation policies of the five nations that the G8 group of developed countries called the 'Outreach 5' (Brazil, China, India, Mexico and South Africa) and which later christened themselves 'the G5'. All of them are now members of the G20, which has replaced the G8 as the premier forum on global economic governance. Debate on development issues, 'emerging donors' and aid effectiveness has, of course, moved on since then. So has the domestic development cooperation environment in the G5. We wanted to capture the thinking in these countries as their development partnerships expanded and took form in both substance and structure. We also wanted to offer some insight into how they perceived the global aid architecture – until now defined largely by the Development Assistance Committee of the Organisation for Economic Co-operation and Development (OECD-DAC) – to determine what potential might exist for greater collaboration between Northern and Southern actors on the development cooperation stage. (The 'donor' terrain in the twenty-first century includes an increasingly important private actor component; this volume will not focus on those actors.)

In addressing these themes the editors recognized the need to position the case studies in the context of the way in which South–South cooperation (SSC) in development aid has evolved and the lessons learnt from traditional forms of aid; always emphasizing that the definition of SSC is much wider than that of 'aid' as defined by OECD-DAC. The book is therefore divided into three sections: the first examines the various contours of SSC; the second explores lessons in development cooperation from the experiences of traditional aid donors; and the third focuses on five case studies of emerging development partners from the South. Against the background of the changes in the international system of development cooperation, the concluding chapter discusses the possibility for convergence or conflict in this transitional phase of the architecture of development cooperation.

One of the biggest risks facing the modern world is the gulf that separates 'haves' from 'have-nots', and a growing income disparity characteristic of it. The World Economic Forum publication *Global Risks 2011* highlights two different but connected global risks, one being economic disparity and the other worldwide failures in governance. It argues that while the growth of Asia and other developing regions is 'rebalancing economic power between countries, there is evidence that economic disparity within countries is growing' (World Economic Forum 2011: 6).

The first of these propositions suggests that shifts in global power are engendering changes to a system that had remained much the same since the end of the Second World War. This trend is already in evidence, although the nature of the emerging global problems demands improved cooperation, especially between regional and global powers, if they are to be managed successfully. With regard to the second (and more obvious) phenomenon, tackling economic disparities within countries requires not only interventions at a national level but also a global system that works within rules more equitable than those currently in place. The more interconnected the world, the more acute are feelings of relative deprivation, with their concomitant effects on general stability and security. Hence this latter problem also demands more effective global governance.

Over the past two decades the means of achieving development across the world have been much influenced by the extremely rapid economic growth of developing countries such as China and India. Their progress, and that of other developing countries such as Vietnam, has affected the development debate, especially as it concerns ways in which domestic reform can be crucial to unlocking economic potential. On the other hand, the need to combat transnational threats, including environmental challenges, illicit financial flows, the spread of infectious diseases, institutional corruption and clandestine trade, necessitates the creation of a cooperative global framework within which international policy regimes may function effectively. This in turn requires both local and global interventions.

Development aid from the affluent North has long been seen as the primary vehicle through which the South can be helped to reduce poverty and meet development goals. Of course, this lofty and altruistic objective was not the only (nor, often, the primary) driver of the development assistance rendered to the 'Third World' by the industrialized nations, even after the end of the Cold War. Nevertheless, although in geopolitical terms developed countries have been broadly successful in maintaining critical alliances with developing countries, development assistance as the main source of economic progress for the latter shows a very patchy record.[1]

Beginning in the 1990s the burgeoning economic progress, power and authority of a number of developing countries, led by China, have introduced more actors to the development cooperation stage, even though they may consider themselves 'partners' rather than 'donors'. The arrival of these competitors in the development aid scene has raised concerns among richer countries, although the latter have also seen potential for cooperation. On the other hand, many developing countries have welcomed the emergence of new sources of assistance or cooperation that are outside the established OECD-DAC fold, seeing them as offering not merely new opportunities but also greater political leverage for aid recipients.

Inevitably, the question arises of whether, even under the sway of these powerful global currents, the way the world operates will change very much. The developing South hopes it will; the North, for its part, would probably prefer that the global rules its nations have created will remain in place, albeit with some modifications. With reference to the subtitle of this volume – are we analysing the phenomenon of 'new partners' or 'old patterns'?

But what does a 'development partner' entail? This terminology is not the monopoly of the new or re-emerging development cooperation actors. It is also being used by traditional Northern donors. Among the DAC, the introduction of the term reflected a change in approach from one that was unequal and based on conditionalities to a more balanced engagement with recipients. Changes in terminology, though, do not necessarily transform power relations. Although a power balance may not be a prerequisite, meaningful partnerships require both sides to bring something to the table. At their foundation lie trust, transparency and respect for the partners' respective views. Often these principles are enunciated at the policy level but struggle to materialize at the practical level. This is not only so in the case of Northern donors, but also for Southern partners, as this book will reflect.

First, by studying five Southern countries that are emerging as partners in development cooperation, the volume seeks to determine whether their own shared experiences of poverty have led them to evolve a unique method of engaging with other countries in the developing world. Secondly, it analyses the new-found impetus of SSC in the context of the rhetoric of Southern 'solidarity'. Significantly, in the light of the transnational challenges alluded to above, it enquires whether SSC can contribute to the evolution of an internationally acceptable public policy framework that advances and protects the global commons.

Development cooperation is a key area of global governance, yet SSC lacks an institutional home at the global level. There are three strategic options available to emerging powers: first, reject any attempt at international coordination; second, remain a separate collective entity, either utilizing existing groupings, such as the Non-Aligned Movement or the G77, or establishing a Southern DAC; third, support the United Nations Development Cooperation Forum 'as the provider of a universal framework for policy coordination and harmonisation'. While the third option confers universal legitimacy, the UN system suffers from a fundamental weakness – the inability to monitor implementation of the norms it establishes. If the UN cannot overcome this paralysis, it risks becoming marginal in global affairs. Nevertheless, the outcome of competing aid regimes will not be determined solely by the OECD-DAC and the emerging powers. 'Recipient' countries can play an important role in determining outcomes: they can nudge donors towards greater coordination or forsake harmonization by encouraging competition.

Three aspects in particular should be stressed. First, South–South engagement (if not cooperation) is no longer a marginal exercise. Its volumes are growing. Consistently high economic growth rates, experienced by China and India in particular, and the extraordinary strides made by smaller developing economies have together changed global economic dynamics. Trade and investment flows from and within the developing world are increasing, while countries such as India, China and some Arab states are becoming bigger contributors to development finance. The North's growing interest in these developments indicates a degree of anxiety about what they may mean for its own engagement on this global terrain, which in turn has led it to examine ways to cooperate with the newcomers or incorporate their activities into existing systems.

Secondly, many emerging economies want to be rule-makers, not merely rule-takers, and increasingly are making their voices heard in global forums. In doing so, they have also 'shaken old ways of acting' (Severino and Ray 2009: 7) and eroded the West's exclusive competence on matters of development (Six 2009: 1117). It is not yet clear, however, what types of rules they would like to craft, nor is there coherence among emerging powers about their content.

Thirdly, the emergence of major developing markets has accelerated the divergence in interests between them and their poorer and smaller peers. The motivation for emerging markets to engage in technical exchanges or trade and investment will arguably be different from that of twenty or thirty years ago. As early as 1981 the Pakistani economist Mahbub ul Haq was asking whether SSC is not merely a 'passing fad', a 'romantic notion, based on an "idealised" South that does not exist'. If that suggestion is correct, modern shifts in the nature of development aid may have put paid to the supposition of Southern solidarity that continues to be attractive, powerful and sentimentally important.

The growing divergence of interests between emerging regional and global powers on the one hand, and the rest of the developing South on the other, is bound to have an effect on the notion of SSC as a tool of mutual benefit premised on equality between the parties. Development cooperation in the various forms it assumes among the new participants is clearly an instrument of foreign policy; indisputably it may be used as part of alliance-building and as a tool for advancing a country's 'soft' power, and hence its international standing. These aspects of realpolitik may not appear in marketing brochures, but such nations are in the business of asserting their leadership credentials, whether at the regional or global level. However, development cooperation, where emerging markets with clear internal developmental challenges provide help to or exchange experiences with other poor countries, is a powerful narrative of 'compassionate ethics', to borrow a phrase from Severino and Ray (2009).

This analysis may sound a sceptical note concerning the discourse around the emergence of new development partners from the South, and the added value that their activities may bring. It is not, however, intended to disparage the promoters of SSC, but rather to illustrate first that, as they engage more deeply in development cooperation, new entrants face obstacles similar to those experienced earlier by industrialized countries, and secondly, that SSC is not shorn of the imperatives of power politics; nor are smaller developing countries oblivious to this. As Agarwal sets out, some of the greatest barriers to trade are found among Southern countries. The manner in which some of the more systemically significant developing countries are behaving does not reflect an overriding focus on contributing to global public goods, unless such activity is of direct benefit to them. In and of itself this is not problematic. After all, the primary responsibility of powerful and weak states alike is to secure their country's security and welfare. It is, however, also incumbent on the more powerful to work towards structures that as far as possible provide for the global good; this is the concept of 'responsible stakeholders' used by Bob Zoellick in reference to the role that China should adopt as its power grows.

Chaturvedi's chapter on typologies of SSC explores its meaning and how it can be distinguished from North–South cooperation. He argues that the philosophy behind the two styles emerges from notions of mutual growth in the former and philanthropy in the latter. Nevertheless, while SSC is characterized in theory by mutual respect, equality and a 'win-win' approach, these ideas may be difficult to implement in practice. There is too little empirical evidence to allow for a thorough comparison of the two forms of cooperation. Additionally, SSC is not exposed to global scrutiny in the same way as are development aid flows from the OECD-DAC. Thus, it is crucial to build a database of development partnerships, which would improve transparency, although it would also have to be linked to an evaluation system. As Herbert and Mackie note in their chapters, the lessons from traditional aid partners are not only about volumes of aid, but also the efficacy of aid. Chaturvedi emphasizes that in the debate on effecting development, more focus needs to be placed on the 'low profitability of modern tradable items' as a factor limiting growth. This means making efforts to improve production practices. He cautions that 'political rhetoric on SSC may not survive long if [cooperation] fails to stimulate growth across the South'. Southern development partners need to consider their own benchmarks for effective and timely delivery, but they should provide a framework for the assessment of SSC.

Agarwal's chapter focuses on trends in trade and investment flows within the South. He makes a number of recommendations to improve and increase trade and capital flows between Southern nations, while addressing some potential negative consequences for smaller, poorer countries. Intra-South preference arrangements could stimulate trade, while obstacles – such as a perception that certain developing countries would benefit more than others from such preferences – could be surmounted through a system of financial transfers, perhaps leading to a new Southern trade organization. Capital flows between Southern countries could be enhanced through tax preferences, while technology transfers might also take the form of preferences, such as partial or full exemption from intellectual property arrangements or subsidization of licensing agreements.

In the second section of the book, Herbert and Mackie explore the experience of traditional aid. Its failings over the past sixty years lie in the perverse incentives it has created as much as in the underpinnings of donor–recipient relations that many in the developing world see as problematical. Herbert argues that although issues of governance are less important for new powers, these participants should also have an interest in improved governance in partner countries. Indeed, support from European or US agencies for civil society in developing countries has contributed to the widening of their political and social horizons over the last two decades.

In analysing perverse incentives as they have emerged in the implementation of traditional aid, Herbert cautions new actors in development cooperation about unintended consequences arising from 'a combination of selfish and altruistic [motives]'. Since some of the new participants are still in the process of designing more systematic processes and structures for disbursing cooperation, Herbert suggests that they should become more familiar with the complex reasons for ineffectiveness, so as to avoid the mistakes of earlier donors. Mackie's discussion of the policies of the European Union's aid providers, which he describes as a 'unique group of donors', emphasizes that aid effectiveness in Europe is driven by the political need for governments to justify Official Development Assistance (ODA) budgets to their electorates. His contribution also considers likely reactions in the EU to the way in which new donors engage. If a growing international consensus on promoting aid effectiveness collapses and other donors ignore or undermine the existing international aid regime, EU governments may well feel that they need not be constrained by it either. The EU's attempt to implement policy coherence for development should also be integrated into the development policy of newcomers in the field.

The last section of the book deals with the way in which, in this fluid global environment, five countries that could be characterized as emerging powers (some of them global, others regional) are moulding their development cooperation policies. They are Brazil (Saravia chapter), China (Zhou), India (Chaturvedi), Mexico (Romero) and South Africa (Sidiropoulos). As putative global powers they contribute to the reworking of SSC and also to the definition of what constitutes and promotes development. All consider themselves part of the Southern bloc (although Mexico is a member of the OECD but not of the DAC, and on accession to the former organization was compelled to leave the G77). None of them is new to the field of technical (or, for that matter, development) assistance. As their contributions in this area have grown, however, so have they sought to systematize their involvement, often exploring the paths that traditional donors have already trodden in addressing some of the challenges posed by this kind of cooperation.

Some, like Brazil, channel their development cooperation through an established agency; much of China's aid goes through its Ministry of Commerce, while India and South Africa are in the process of establishing specific agencies. Their activities are largely project related, but they are also increasing their contributions to multilateral organizations. With the exception of Mexico, which has observer status at the DAC, none of the countries considers itself bound by the various principles of aid effectiveness developed by the OECD and encompassed in the Paris Declaration on Aid Effectiveness and the Accra Agenda. The new participants share certain shortcomings, including institutional problems, inadequate systems for monitoring and evaluation, and a need for more transparency in the decisions, aid volumes and agreements with partners. They have all dabbled with trilateral cooperation and do not exclude collaboration with OECD partners in specific activities. China, for example, participated with the OECD in a study group that focused on its own experience of growth and poverty reduction. One of the study group's key findings was that rapid economic and social development in poor countries can happen in a context of globalization, when strong development-oriented leadership emerges, focused on development performance rather than on entrenched policies and interests; and that, as in the case of China's economic transformation, international assistance can support and speed up Africa's transformation and poverty reduction process, when conceived and designed in this transformation framework (China-DAC Study Group 2011).

The profile of these five nations as developing countries with major domestic socio-economic challenges but willing to share their experiences with others is a consistent theme in their narratives.

In the concluding chapter the editors argue that a key factor for the future shape of SSC and the rebalancing of North–South relations will be the nature of broad-based alliances in the developing world. As with the present global system, forged in the aftermath of the Second World War, so with alliances such as the Non-Aligned Movement and the G77: neither represent a twenty-first century reality. The shape of any new alliances is still unclear, but it will affect both the global South's view of itself and the way in which international norms and systems evolve and are met. The chapter assesses the opportunities for, and constraints on, bridging the gap between North and South. Progress in this direction will depend on the success of emerging powers and traditional donors in identifying a common ground. Considering the divergence between them in terms of interests, identities and their approaches to international relations, this may be very difficult to achieve. The recipient countries, however, could play a decisive role by insisting, as a group, that the benefits of development aid would be greatly improved if a single, coherent system were to be agreed.

Completed before the High Level Forum on Aid Effectiveness, held in Busan, South Korea, in November 2011, the book's contributions do not reflect the forum's outcomes. Busan was significant because it sought to bridge the divide between North–South and South–South cooperation. In doing so it also exposed the divergent views each side held on this issue. The outcome document notes that 'the nature, modalities and responsibilities that apply to South–South cooperation differ from those that apply to North–South cooperation', and that 'the principles, commitments and actions agreed [at Busan by the North] shall be the reference for South–South partners *on a voluntary basis*' (emphasis added). Thus, Busan recognized that a 'more inclusive development agenda', in which Southern development cooperation partners also participated, was on the basis of 'common goals and differential commitments'. Whether the mooted Global Partnership for Effective Development Cooperation will better integrate the two forms of cooperation (North and South) will be determined over the next few years.

This book is based on case studies conducted by experts from their respective countries on the basis of a common framework developed by the editors and discussed in various meetings of the group. Contributors to the volume include practitioners and researchers. The project work has been facilitated by the German Development Institute (DIE), the Research and Information System for Developing Countries, India (RIS), and the South African Institute of International Affairs (SAIIA).

The editors would like to express their appreciation to John Gaunt, a master wordsmith and editor, who turned their sometimes polyglottal prose into flowing English. Ambassador Thomas Wheeler, a colleague at SAIIA, was helpful in shepherding contributors and peer reviewers around the deadlines in the last phase of the project, for which we are extremely grateful, while Terence Corrigan helped with the finicky task of referencing.

This publication was made possible through the partial support of the Swedish International Development Cooperation Agency and the Danish International Development Agency, who support SAIIA's Emerging Powers programme. We are also grateful for the support provided by Deutsche Gesellschaft für Internationale Zusammenarbeit (GIZ) through the Managing Global Governance programme, implemented jointly with DIE on behalf of the Federal Ministry of Economic Cooperation and Development.

Note

1 Their success also depends on domestic policies. South Korea, which was the recipient of large amounts of foreign aid after the Korean War, became a net donor by 1994 and graduated out of the World Bank's list of aid recipients in 1995.

References

China-DAC Study Group (2011) *Economic Transformation and Poverty Reduction: How it happened in China, helping it happen in Africa*, Paris: OECD and International Poverty Reduction Centre in China.

Severino, J.-M. and O. Ray (2009) *The End of ODA: Death and Rebirth of a Global Public Policy*, Working Paper no. 167, Washington, DC: Center for Global Development.

Six, C. (2009) 'The rise of postcolonial states as donors: a challenge to the development paradigm?', *Third World Quarterly*, 30(6): 1103–21.

World Economic Forum (2011) *Global Risks 2011*, Cologne/Geneva: World Economic Forum.

PART ONE

SOUTH–SOUTH COOPERATION

1 | DEVELOPMENT COOPERATION: CONTOURS, EVOLUTION AND SCOPE

Sachin Chaturvedi

Introduction

The sharp economic growth across Southern economies and subsequent expansion in their cooperation has invoked a growing interest in understanding the nature of South–South cooperation (SSC). Some of the questions being asked include: is it a substitute for North–South cooperation (NSC)? How does SSC actually differ from NSC? The emergence of various Southern forums, such as the BRICS (Brazil, Russia, India, China, South Africa) and IBSA (India, Brazil, South Africa), has given further impetus to the debates on these issues. The manner in which negotiations on global trade and climate change have proceeded is also a clear manifestation of this new dynamic. So what exactly is meant by SSC? What are the elements that this concept captures and to what extent may it be distinguished from NSC?

Historically, South–South development partnership has been a much wider concept, which included trade, investment and technology transfer. More recently, enhanced flows of trade and investment within and between the nations of the South have given a major boost to growth: in the period 1996–2009, South–South trade grew at an annual average 12 per cent, which was 50 per cent faster than that between North and South (United Nations Conference on Trade and Development 2011). According to data from the United Nations Conference on Trade and Development (UNCTAD), South–South transactions now account for around 20 per cent of global trade and almost 50 per cent of developing country trade. South–South foreign direct investment accounts for almost 10 per cent of global flows and is growing at 20 per cent annually (ibid.). Clearly, development partnership has emerged of late as an important element of poverty reduction strategies, sometimes supplanting prescriptive neoliberal market-driven orthodoxies, which might suggest something of a retreat by the state. After a major decline in the early 1990s almost all 'traditional' donors have enhanced both their bilateral assistance programmes (OECD 2005) and their contributions to multilateral institutions. In recent years, apart from the rise in private aid flows, traditional donors have been joined by emerging economies outside the ambit of the Development Assistance Committee of the Organisation for Economic Co-operation and Development (OECD-DAC), which have greatly increased the resources allocated for development partnerships. Prima facie that signifies a tectonic shift (Kaplinsky and Messner 2008) in global power, carrying its own implications for the ground rules of the global aid architecture (Woods 2008).

Following on from this development there have been serious attempts to define the dynamics of global flows of development aid in terms of objectives or key drivers, volume and direction of flows, and the national and international institutional mechanisms governing them. Those efforts have further fuelled a long-standing debate on aid which is again under discussion in various forums, including those led by the OECD-DAC, where the implementation of the 2005 Paris Declaration on Aid Effectiveness is being assessed.

Although the entry of emerging economies into the arena of development partnership falls within the existing SSC framework, it is widely perceived as a threat to the dominance of traditional donors (Chahoud 2007). The emergence of new participants at the global level may herald major changes in the earlier model of North–South aid flows, which assumes some importance now that global assistance from non-DAC nations is around $14.5 billion (closer to $17 billion if ballpark estimates for Brazil, Mexico and Venezuela are added) (Kharas 2010). This amount has doubled in only three years (ibid.); in fact China has lent more money to developing countries over the past two years than has the World Bank: the China Development Bank and the China Export-Import Bank extended loans of at least $110 billion to other developing country governments and companies in 2009 and 2010 (Dyer et al. 2011) while the equivalent arms of the World Bank made loan commitments of just over $100 billion in 2008–10.

The idea of SSC is not itself new (Woods 2008; Das et al. 2008) but has come increasingly under the spotlight as a result of a gradual decline in North–South flows (ECOSOC 2008). The sheer volume of funding that Southern mega-economies now have available for SSC, and the pace at which this is increasing, are a new and recent phenomenon. There is a correspondingly greater scrutiny of the means whereby development aid can contribute to economic development, empowerment and sustainability. The new economic power deployed by the large newly developing economies may also reduce the level of SSC rhetoric to more sober and substantive operational debate,[1] a process likely to bring to a wider platform the kind of debates on SSC hitherto largely confined to dissenting voices or minority groups at international negotiations.

Ties between North and South have loosened over the years. As Rodrik (2009) points out, building a 'productivist strategy' has played an important part in the evolving South–South agenda,[2] while in addition a growing adoption of inward-looking policies by the North is contributing to the regionalization of SSC. In this context it is important to note the observation of Pakistani economist Mahbub Ul Haq:

> It is increasingly fashionable these days to talk about South–South co-operation. Is this another passing fad or is it a new trend, mirroring long-term realities? Is this just a by-product of the current disillusionment with the North? Is it merely a romantic notion, based on an 'idealised' South that does not exist? Or is there far more to it? Does it finally represent an effort by the South to de-link (however partially) their economic growth from the North and to get organised for collective bargaining in international forums? Are we witnessing here a fundamental break from the patterns of past development and a serious search for alternative development styles? (Haq 1981)

Those issues are still relevant after almost thirty years. In the light of such questions, it seems useful to analyse the purposes of SSC and examine the present position regarding aid or development partnership. Consistent and rapid economic growth in some emerging economies has raised expectations among their peers, particularly those with which they enjoy close ties, and it is worth analysing the evolution of SSC. This is the topic of the next section; the third section compares North–South flows with the dynamics of South–South cooperation while the fourth section briefly captures SSC's linkage with the North through triangular cooperation. The last section suggests ways of overcoming SSC limitations.

SSC and its evolution

Continued high growth in some developing countries and persistent patterns of low growth in the industrialized North pose a challenge to the conventional terminology used to classify countries against economic growth criteria. For example, the term 'South' emerged after the Second World War to signify a bloc of countries in which levels of economic development were far lower than in countries in the North; at this time also, 'West' and 'East' came to signify respectively capitalist countries, and the socialist and communist bloc. Most countries that belonged to neither East nor West ended up in the group called the South.

The idea of developing countries coming together emerged in March/April 1947, when pre-independence India hosted the Asian Relations Conference (see Chapter 7). Twenty-seven countries with 227 representatives, mostly still under colonial rule, were in attendance (Sharan 1997). The next such major meeting in Bandung, Indonesia, in 1955, included representatives from Asia and Africa, by then representing independent national governments. The agglomeration process was taken farther in 1960 when seven major Latin American countries came together through the Treaty of Montevideo to form the Latin American Free Trade Association. Around that time several other regional organizations sprang up, including the Association of South East Asian Nations, the Organization of African Unity and the Caribbean Community. Cooperation among the Southern countries was institutionalized through the Non-Aligned Movement (NAM) founded in Belgrade in 1961, when twenty-eight countries attended the first non-aligned summit. In June 1964, at the first ministerial meeting of UNCTAD in Geneva, an informal grouping of seventy-seven developing countries emerged, commonly known as the G77 (Panchamukhi et al. 1986).

Membership of the G77 has since increased to 130 countries plus China, but the original name is retained for historical reasons. The idea behind the G77 was to enable the South to articulate and promote its collective economic interest and enhance its joint negotiating capacity on major international economic issues within the UN system, and to promote SSC for development. Both the founding of the NAM and the establishment of UNCTAD were clear manifestations of the emergence of the South. One initial success came after several years' protracted negotiations to gain acceptance of the principle of differential treatment for exports from developing countries to facilitate market access in developed countries. This finally came about in 1971 with the emergence of the Generalized System of Preferences, which offered exemption from the rules of the General Agreement on Tariffs and Trade (GATT), now the World Trade Organization (WTO) (ibid.). At this time there was great enthusiasm in the G77 and some major initiatives to help develop the South emerged from it. They included a declaration on a 'New International Economic Order' submitted through UNCTAD and adopted by the UN General Assembly in 1974;[3] in essence it was a proposal for restructuring the global system to repair economic imbalances between the developed and the less developed world. It was followed a year later by the adoption, through the UN Industrial Development Organization, of the Lima Declaration and Plan of Action, which set out proposals for the industrialization of the developing world; finally came the establishment of the Common Fund for Commodities (1976), designed to increase food and agricultural sustainability and security. Some aims were perhaps overly ambitious: the Lima Declaration and Plan of Action on Industrial Development and Cooperation expressed its intention that developing countries should attain 25 per cent of world industrial production by 2000.

Despite major expansion of South–South linkages during the 1970s, the wider economic and financial crises of the following decade had a serious impact on SSC and indeed resulted in near-closure of regional and bilateral cooperation programmes across the South (South Commission 1990). The Uruguay Round of trade negotiations, which brought about the transformation of GATT into the WTO, and the debt crisis that began in Latin America, coupled with a commodity crisis with its accompanying decline in processing industries, adversely affected the solidarity and negotiating power of the developing countries. At the same time the North was attempting to institutionalize its policies and the G7 group of industrialized nations held meetings in 1983 and 1988 that heralded a growing influence on the part of multilateral, Western-dominated institutions such as the International Monetary Fund (IMF) and the World Bank. Nevertheless, SSC has remained a cherished goal of developing countries' foreign policies, though in practice this aspect has been largely confined to political speeches and has not percolated down to the agencies actually responsible for programme evolution and implementation (Thorsteins-dóttir et al. 2011).

A central issue is the definition of a theoretical basis for SSC. There have been a few attempts at this but it is nevertheless clear that the emergence of the OPEC Fund, a multilateral development finance institution fund established by the Organization of Petroleum Exporting Countries (OPEC), shattered many ideological positions in theoretical debates on development. According to Bhagwati (1986), the Fund signified, first, that foreign aid from the North is not automatically the best instrument for redistribution of income; secondly, it showed that efficient aid delivery need not mean falling into the trap of 'conditionalities'; and thirdly, that the route to success is through control of primary natural resources. These imperatives in the OPEC model posed a major challenge to the ideological hegemony that dominated developmental thinking in the 1990s and was best exemplified in the Washington Consensus.

Theoretical framework

The central elements of SSC are self-reliance and self-help. It is multifaceted, and strongly informed by the notion of developing the South through equitable access to trade, investment and technology within a multilateral institutional framework (G77 1964). SSC aims to discover and exploit so-called 'complementarities' in production, consumption, trade, investment and technological and development cooperation. These processes are interlinked and may in turn generate forward and backward linkages, which eventually may produce value chains across Southern economies; currently, China's linkages with the South-East Asian economies are a perfect example. The evolution of SSC is characterized by three fundamental principles: mutual respect, equality and a 'win-win' situation. The South Commission (later to become the South Centre), established in 1987 as a result of decisions at a Harare Non-Aligned summit meeting the previous year, in 1997 identified ten major areas of SSC interest: they were respectively finance, trade, industry and business, services, transport and infrastructure, food security, science and technology, environment, information and communication, and people-to-people contact.

Sauvant (1983) explains that self-reliance policy rests on strengthening autonomous capacities for goal-setting, decision-making and decision implementation. It introduces the idea of an indigenous capacity to deal with indigenous resources. The element of cooperation is critical to the extent that it enables a particular country to progress on its own, which in turn presupposes horizontal supportive flows in the form of trade, technology and investment. Later, debate arose over whether or not the South should develop its own development model; Haq (1981) contended that instead of importing development concepts from alien systems and cultures, the South should develop its own mechanisms centred on local skills and knowledge, so as to build development around people rather than try to marshal people around development.

Amin (1977) suggests that the litmus test for assessing self-reliance should be the extent to which it reduces global inequality. This may require division of labour at the global level between developing and developed worlds, but if so, the strategy should be self-determined so that an externally imposed scheme of development does not encourage the formation of a few elite groups in recipient countries. The four major goals of SSC accepted at the 1986 Harare summit indicate the framework (RCCDC 1987):

- to take advantage of existing complementarities within developing countries by developing direct cooperation (facilitating fuller use of installed capacities) and eliminating intermediaries from the North;
- to create new complementarities and interdependence (at various levels) through coordination of development planning and achieving better scale economies;
- to introduce some of the major principles of the New International Economic Order (for example, mutual benefit and solidarity) into transactions among developing countries' cooperating partners; and
- to strengthen the bargaining position of the South vis-à-vis the North through selective delinking and greater collective self-reliance.

Much of the theoretical impetus for SSC came from the structuralist school and from dependency theorists who elaborated their ideas in the Latin American context. Kay (1989) and Gore (2000) provide a broad perspective on these discussions. From these theories it emerged that external factors are not the only ones that set countries on a growth path: endogeneity,[4] which is the causal loop between independent and dependent modelling factors, is much more important.

In this context, the UN Economic Commission for Latin America, a regional commission set up in 1948, developed a structuralist model known as the centre–periphery paradigm. This *dependencia* (dependence) theory, enunciated by Raul Prebisch, described a situation in which resources flow from a 'periphery' of poor and underdeveloped states to a 'core' of wealthy nations, enriching the latter at the expense of the former. This articulation reinvigorated debate on possible ways forward for SSC, the central issue being the choice between centre–periphery development and a pattern of equal-partner participation (Panchamukhi 1986). The former implied that existing growth centres lead the process of economic development as Japan led growth in South Korea, Singapore, Hong Kong and Taiwan, and perhaps the USA may lead Latin America. The theory of complementarities indicates that countries at similar stages of development may also cooperate for productive purposes in a 'win-win' situation.

Development cooperation

Post-Second World War reconstruction efforts overlooked the needs of the developing world. Few economies from the South could participate in the Bretton Woods Conference of 1944, which laid out the parameters of the post-war economic system, because they were not yet sovereign states. At that time the primary concern of the developed world was to avoid the disastrous errors of the pre-war years: 'beggar-thy-neighbour' trading and exchange rate policies, competitive devaluations and inadequate arrangements for liquidity (South Commission 1990). Bretton Woods was the foundation of an inequitable global order in which the South had little say in its own financial and economic destiny. It was with high hopes that in the 1950s developing countries came up with the idea of involving the UN in the process of development assistance through a Special UN Fund for Economic Development (SUNFED).

The proposal was resisted through Western filibustering, and hence was only partially successful.[5] It was the result of work led by the leading Indian economist V. K. R. V. Rao in his capacity as chairman of the UN Sub-commission for Economic Development, in which he had proposed a mechanism centred on the UN Economic Development Administration. Later, Sir Hans Singer developed the idea further in the form of SUNFED (Singer 1995). For newly independent economies at that time the supply of foreign exchange was a major concern and SUNFED was widely regarded as a means of easier access to foreign funds. Within the UN system, this notion eventually gave rise to the Economic Cooperation among Developing Countries (ECDC) scheme under the UNCTAD umbrella. Technical Cooperation among Developing Countries (TCDC), which came into existence in 1974 and was the basis for the Buenos Aires Plan of Action (BAPA), which emerged from a TCDC conference held in that city four years later, worked through the TCDC Information Referral Services (Inres) database, which prompted initiatives such as capacity-building through matchmaking (CNM). The UN Development Programme administered the TCDC trust fund, which received substantial funding from the North for the promotion of SSC (from 1978 to 1998, TCDC received $16 billion) (UNDP 1999). These varied initiatives did not, however, match the original idea of SUNFED in the early 1950s, which developing countries wanted to be UN-led: in the event support to TCDC from the North came only after three decades, and by then was constrained within the mandate of ECDC and TCDC.

The need for foreign exchange for economic development became more evident when it was postulated on the 'two-gap' economic model, which rests on the theory that domestic savings are inadequate for development and can be compensated only by external resources (Chenery and Strout 1966). At that time lack of foreign exchange was a major impediment to growth,[6] and the two-gap theory implied crucial dependence on external sources of foreign exchange in order to supplement domestic resources: hence, the emergence of a theoretical rationale for development cooperation.

Over two decades in the 1950s and 1960s, several countries in the developing world achieved their independence and, having done so, embarked on initiatives to form partnerships with other developing countries. They were mostly modest in their objectives, confined to medical missions, educational support programmes, fellowships and sharing food grains. In a few countries major initiatives were taken; for example, the Kuwait Fund for Arab Economic Development was established in 1961, charged with extending grants, among other means of support for technical assistance, to Arab and other developing countries. India was another country to play a prominent role in early steps in the realm of development cooperation.

After the end of the Cold War in 1989 some earlier distinctions all but fell away. The East–West divide between Northern nations almost disappeared, while over the past decade economic growth in some Southern countries has been high enough to overtake that of many Northern economies. Consistently high growth in China and India has placed those countries apart from other developing nations, insofar as their growth rates are much higher than those of almost all Northern countries, but per capita incomes remain lower than in many other developing countries. By contrast with the 1970s and 1980s, when those large economies lagged behind their Western counterparts, from the mid-1990s onwards their new-found prosperity and the ability to generate surplus resources have given a totally new dimension to SSC. Historically, SSC evolved largely at the regional level, where large economies played an important role as regional anchors (as did China in South-East and northern Asia, India in southern Asia, Brazil in Latin America and South Africa in southern Africa). With today's intense globalization, however, trans-regional alliances such as India–Brazil–South Africa have taken shape (although not for the first time: it is sometimes forgotten that in the 1960s Egypt, Yugoslavia and India formed a tripartite trade expansion and economic cooperation agreement, albeit less than successfully).

Although China and India have a sizeable proportion of their own population living below the poverty line and many millions facing malnutrition, they are still involved in the development processes of other developing countries. This process is not confined to these two countries alone. Leaving aside questions of scale, Brazil, South Africa, Thailand, Indonesia, Malaysia, Venezuela and Colombia all are equally significant in offering aid, despite most of them enjoying modest per capita incomes. It is important to acknowledge that such economies may prefer to be called 'development partners' rather than 'donors', since the latter term is often linked with a colonial past and emerging economies prefer to avoid such terminology for political and diplomatic reasons. In the light of this it is perhaps not surprising that an OECD proposal for enhanced engagement programmes with a view to future membership of Brazil, China, India, Indonesia and South Africa in OECD Council meetings met with a lukewarm response from those countries in 2007 (O'Keefe 2007). Since then, the OECD has begun an 'enhanced engagement' process with all five countries.

Altruism and 'win-win': differences between NSC and SSC

This section explores the possible differences between North–South and South–South cooperation in their approach and outcomes. The philosophy behind North–South and South–South development co-operation emerges respectively from the notions of philanthropy and mutual growth. The concept of North–South flows derives its strength from the Western social commitment of altruism. In the case of South–South cooperation, the underlying principle is to support each other for a win-win partnership on all sides. Some major differences are evident and are set out in Table 1.1.

The Paris Declaration established certain criteria to guide North–South aid flows but SSC has no such global guiding mechanisms and is not exposed to global scrutiny. Several Southern governments, however, have identified key features of SSC; for instance, the Chinese government has laid down eight principles for its aid programmes (see Chapter 6). The Accra Agenda for Action adopted at the 2008 Third High Level Forum on Aid Effectiveness in Accra, with the aim of 'deepening' the implementation of the Paris Declaration, mentions the principles of non-interference in others' internal affairs, equality among partners, respect for independence and national sovereignty, cultural diversity and the identity of local content.

In the last few years OECD-DAC has worked extensively on developing and defining various concepts related to development assistance (see Table 1.2). Official Development Assistance (ODA) comprises grants or loans provided by the official sector for promotion of economic development and welfare (in this context, a concessional loan is considered welfare-enhancing provided 25 per cent of it is by way of a grant). Apart from financial flows, ODA also includes technical cooperation and export credits (Manning 2006). A discount of 10 per cent is used in calculating the 25 per cent minimum grant element required for a loan to be regarded as ODA (Manning 2008). Assistance to multilateral organizations is also separately accounted for. Furthermore, in most DAC publications a distinction is drawn between 'tied' and 'untied' aid. All official grants or loans in which procurement of goods and services is restricted to the donor country are classified as tied aid (ibid.). On the basis of various DAC reports a few key elements for capturing aid flow are identified in Table 1.2, covering both bilateral loans and grants. Activities such as technical cooperation, developmental food aid, humanitarian assistance, debt relief grants, aid to NGOs, and project- and programme-specific support are included as part of bilateral grants. Aid to multilateral institutions, particularly UN organizations, is also included.

TABLE 1.1 Comparison of North–South and South–South development partnerships

Indicators	Aid programme (North–South)	Development partnership (South–South)
Nature and purpose of support	ODA. Stated to be altruistic in nature	Mutual benefit and growth
Philosophical perspective	Framework approach	Ingredients approach
Participants	At least one participant has very high per capita income	Both partners may have very low per capita income
Level of development	Large difference in stages of economic development between donor and recipient	Both partners almost at same stage of economic development
Role of participants	Donor and recipient of ODA	Relationship of equality: both may contribute to the process
Conditionality	'Top-down' with policy conditionality and no predictability	Request-driven and generally free from conditionality of any kind, so largely within timelines
Flexibility	Multilayered time-consuming bureaucratic structures, hence added transaction costs	Highly decentralized and relatively fast with few implications for transaction costs
Priority sectors	Grant assistance and budget support for social sectors	Economic and technical cooperation largely confined to projects in infrastructure and productive sector investment
Adherence to global governance frameworks like Paris Declaration	Donors use guidelines of Paris Declaration, which they evolved as an instrument for effectiveness	Providers are out of the purview of any global arrangement such as Paris Declaration, in which they were not involved. Hinges on mutual trust of partner countries
Data, monitoring and evaluation	Peer-reviewed by DAC-OECD. Data compiled and periodically released by the national governments and DAC-OECD	No monitoring mechanisms beyond occasional reports of data and anecdotal detail

TABLE 1.2 DAC concepts of development aid

Bilateral grants	Contributions to multilateral institutions
Technical cooperation	UN and others
Developmental food aid	Private sector
Humanitarian aid	
Debt relief grants	Preferential access to markets
Aid to NGOs	Export credits
Administrative costs	Special themes
Project and programme aid	Collaborations in S&T
Bilateral loans	
25 per cent grant element (calculated at discounted rate of 10 per cent)	

Source: Manning (2006)

This approach, however, seems extremely limited when analysing development aid from Southern countries. For example, a sizeable amount of assistance is provided by major developing countries in supporting peacekeeping operations across the world, particularly in their own region. South Africa, for instance, has engaged in such efforts following requests from the African Union and spends a large proportion of its development assistance for this purpose. This expenditure falls outside the UN mandate, under which most developed countries finance peacekeeping operations. Similarly, China and India have taken intensive measures to promote production and trade from least developed countries (LDCs) that are not accounted for under the DAC definition; in 2008, for example, India announced a duty-free tariff preference scheme for imported goods from LDCs covering around seventeen commodities and 94 per cent of its tariff lines (Khatua 2010). China has done the same since 2006, with some 4,700 exports from African LDCs receiving zero-tariff treatment by 2010 (Ministry of Commerce (People's Republic of China) 2010).

A key question is how to redefine development assistance in such a way that those kinds of measures to provide access to regional public goods, which are essential for neighbouring countries, are not excluded. There may also be conceptual differences when aid flows from emerging economies are analysed. Some countries may use terminology completely different from that of the DAC (e.g., as

---

Box 1.1 DAC guidelines for evaluation of development assistance

DAC conditionality incorporates the following essential elements:

- Aid agencies should have an evaluation policy with clearly established guidelines and methods and with clear definition of its roles and responsibilities and its place in the institutional aid structure.
- The evaluation process should be impartial and independent from the process concerned with policy-making, and the delivery and management of development assistance.
- The evaluation must be as open as possible with results made widely available.
- For evaluation to be made useful, they must be put into practice. Feedback to both the policy-makers and the operational staff is essential.
- Partnership with recipients and donor cooperation in aid evaluation are both essential; they are an important aspect of recipient institution-building and of aid coordination and may reduce administrative burdens on recipients.
- Aid evaluation and its requirements must be an integral part of aid planning from the start. Clear identification of the objectives that an aid activity is to achieve is an essential prerequisite for ongoing effectiveness in evaluation.

Source: OECD (2005)

---

previously noted, many may prefer 'development partner' to terms such as 'donor' and 'recipient') (Li 2007). This goes beyond semantics, because most such economies possess limited resources and are keen to share the development burden, but may need or expect some degree of reciprocity. Das et al. (2008) very aptly remark that 'South–South cooperation cannot mirror North–South cooperation'.

The DAC's current framework for capturing aid flows focuses on supply-side statistics and overlooks demand-side responses, and even this narrow reading needs to be extended to incorporate elements of enabling and disabling policies adopted by various national governments. In the case of the Netherlands, for example, a policy coherence unit within the Ministry of Foreign Affairs and the Directorate-General of Development Cooperation scans all national policy documents and international negotiations by the Netherlands government to ensure compliance with development aid policy objectives. This is regarded as essential because a mere account of numbers without policy indicators may not be useful for aid recipient countries. Such indicators may also help in capturing demand-side responses: the European Commission has initiated a process to evolve synergies between policies outside the development cooperation framework that nevertheless have a strong impact on developing countries, and has introduced mechanisms to report periodically on progress made by the European Union on policy coherence for development in selected sectors (EU 2007).

The composition of SSC is such that most of it is 'in kind', so it is difficult to account for the exact value or quantum of the support extended, which in turn means that there is no standard accounting framework to capture this flow. The accounting problem becomes all the more acute when there are numerous focal points, while various government departments also have different modalities and mechanisms. The problem of accounting, in many countries, is all the more complicated for their having no separate budget heads for the development and delivery of services and products under SSC.

It is clear from Table 1.1 that there are major philosophical differences between North–South and South–South approaches. Western aid donors have largely followed a 'framework' approach, focused on economic systems and management, while the 'ingredients' approach regards an economy as the sum total of its ingredients or component parts. These differences are captured by Yanagihara in the context of Japan's development cooperation policies (2006: 70–6):

> The framework approach represents rules of the game according to which economic agents make decisions and take action in a given economy and an economy is conceived in terms of the functions of institutions and mechanisms. In contrast, the ingredient refers to tangible organisational units such as enterprise, official bureaus and industrial projects and their aggregations such as industries, sectors and regions. In essence, the framework approach is principle-oriented while the ingredient approach is result-oriented.

SSC indicates that the costs of delivery as a requirement for processing generally are extremely low, which has significant implications for the transaction costs of Southern development partnerships (Lim 2011). Since Southern endeavours are mainly project based, they tend to be either in the form of financial (loans and grants) or technical cooperation. There are few problems of intellectual property rights; hence technology transfer for the most part is readily accomplished. A further advantage of SSC is that it is free from any kind of macroeconomic conditionalities and follows narrowly defined timelines.[7] Data compilation, however, is a major challenge for developing countries. As the OECD's Task Team on South–South Cooperation pointed out, SSC 'as a historic modality ... suffers from a persistent lack of systematisation' (Task Team on South–South Co-operation 2010). The UN Special Unit for South–South Cooperation (SUSSC) in 2009 showed that there are very few countries in the South possessing databases on SSC disbursements. Most of them have information on numbers of projects, technical training and participants but not on net disbursements and regional distribution; few countries, apart from South Korea (which joined the DAC in 2010), Colombia and Turkey, have electronic data-collection systems. Recently the Thai Development Cooperation Agency was commissioned to evolve a definition of development partnership and its volumes.

There is, however, little scope to continue with two separate worlds of North and South, particularly when links between them have so greatly expanded. UNCTAD (1992) clearly expressed its intention regarding such ties in the Chitose declaration, which followed the Junior Eight summit in Chitose, Japan, in 2008:

> South–South cooperation, however, is envisaged neither as a substitute for North–South cooperation nor as an autarchic device. In practice, such cooperation could take the form of a triangular relationship with developed and developing countries from other regions, although it has its own rationale. Increasing complementarities suggest room for enhanced regional interaction. South–South cooperation would have the advantage of expanding market access, encouraging regional capital flows, and fostering the transfer.

This idea was further articulated by the former Algerian foreign minister, Sid Ahmed Ghozali: 'It is otherwise naïve to believe that South–South cooperation could replace, at least in the foreseeable future, North–South cooperation' (quoted in Bobiash 1992).

These views notwithstanding, in contemporary times SSC is emerging as a major policy option for developing countries. In this context, triangular cooperation is being seen as an opportunity to link North–South and South–South development cooperation. The possible convergence of these two separate streams of development cooperation, which have their own richness of experience, work programme frameworks and traditions, is a major challenge for the development community. The changing global economic dynamics may encourage shifts in principles, forms and practices as encouraged by the DAC members.

Emerging dynamics of triangular cooperation

The 2010 fifth G20 summit held in Seoul, South Korea, paid detailed attention to triangular cooperation mechanisms, as have the OECD's High Level Forum on Aid Effectiveness and the UN Economic and Social Council (ECOSOC), through its Development Cooperation Forum (DCF). A survey conducted by SUSSC in 2009, however, showed that very few countries from the developing world are geared to triangular cooperation, although some, such as Indonesia and Malaysia, have a structured policy framework and a long-term national strategy. The most encouraging aspect of the new trend lies in the fact that triangular cooperation is extending beyond pivotal countries such as China, India and Brazil; for example, cooperation between Zambia, Malawi and Mozambique or Zambia, Benin and Mozambique has demonstrated a high level of endogeneity, with partners bringing in their respective comparative advantages without institutional frameworks that act as 'donors'.

It remains true, however, that an explicit understanding between different participants is still hampering any kind of consensus. The OECD-DAC defines triangular cooperation as a partnership between a developed and a developing member in a third developing country (ECOSOC 2008); it is a term originating at the global level with the 1980 Independent Commission on International Development Issues chaired by former West German Chancellor Willy Brandt, which suggested the development of triangular cooperation schemes in the context of ECDC. With the adoption of BAPA in 1978, the TCDC also increasingly adopted triangular cooperation as a strategy. In both cases the proposal was for a partnership between a multilateral agency and a developed country. There is also some discussion about

South–South partnerships in a third developing country, as in the two African examples cited above.

The OECD Task Team undertook 110 case studies of experiences with pivotal and recipient countries; the German aid agency Deutsche Gesellschaft für Internationale Zusammenarbeit (GIZ) analysed the same cases. The result suggests that countries in Latin America are most active in these kinds of schemes, although only in projects up to $2 million. Larger schemes (i.e. more than $10 million) are to be found only in Africa. China, India and Brazil play a limited role in triangular cooperation per se but operate their own international projects. For example, India has its pan-Africa e-network initiative while Brazil and Colombia have collaborated on a district-level recycling capacity-creation programme that now involves fifty-six countries, although modestly funded. Among DAC members Japan, Germany and Canada have shown most interest, while of the multilateral institutions the World Bank, UNDP and the African Development Bank have led the way.

The future of triangular cooperation depends upon the likelihood and manner of convergence between framework- and ingredient-based approaches. Northern donors bring a great deal of expertise in policy formulation that can be adopted by aid recipients, while Southern donors have tended towards more cost-effective delivery. One should perhaps postpone judgement on the possible success of horizontal linkages established for implementing triangular partnerships. A major challenge in this regard would be management of transaction costs, in pursuit of which best practices now being documented by an OECD-DAC team, through its Working Party on Aid Effectiveness, may prove useful.

Overcoming SSC limitations

SSC confronts different sets of limitations. Some may be addressed through institutional arrangements and policy initiatives and, in this way, triangular cooperation may help to overcome some limitations (e.g. the problem of scaling-up projects to a more appropriate operational scale, which is frequently an issue in the South). SSC also faces major limitations arising from its own background. 'Sharing' and developing country solidarity aside, at some point realpolitik becomes a factor. As mentioned earlier, another contemporary criticism is directed to a lack of data on SSC from national governments; this may be due in part to the regional nature of many projects. Larger geopolitical and commercial interests clearly also play a part in the success or otherwise of SSC.

There are several examples of development partnership that could be ascribed to non-development motives. Bobiash (1992) notes that in the 1960s and 1970s both the People's Republic of China and Taiwan used aid to African countries as a key weapon in their efforts to maintain or expand diplomatic ties; in the decade 1961 to 1971 the Taiwanese 'Operation Vanguard' provided agricultural assistance to twenty-four African countries with the aim of eroding Beijing's diplomatic support from African countries in the UN General Assembly. China currently requires its aid partners to recognize its 'One China' policy, which insists on regarding Taiwan as part of mainland China. Bobiash also points out excessive engagement of India in the South Asian region, which may have a bearing on the foreign policies of Nepal, Bhutan and Bangladesh. The IBON Foundation think tank (2010) remarks on Venezuela's aggressive approach to SSC as informed by its anti-US strategy.

Similarly, Saudi Arabia directs more than half its assistance to other Muslim nations (only 14 per cent goes to non-Muslim countries) (ibid.). Bobiash cites a 1987 survey conducted on behalf of non-aligned and other developing countries in which almost 63 per cent of respondents placed 'promotion of trade' ahead of 'promotion of national development goals' (61 per cent) as the chief objective of SSC. Even today, leading developing countries are criticized for using SSC to facilitate access to market and investment opportunities in Africa and other developing regions. This is not a fair criticism, as SSC is a wider concept which embraces the idea of mutual gain. It is clear from the literature that SSC is a concept that encompasses not only aid and assistance, but also a range of activities such as trade, political and economic cooperation through various regional and global forums, and finally capacity creation through initiatives like TCDC. Its second important feature is that since SSC has been closely integrated into the foreign policies of several developing countries over the past forty years or so, it is given high priority at the political level. There are many realpolitik objectives to this, among which solidarity and a collective will to progress are only a part. However, there is no systematic analysis of the successes (such as IBSA and other recent initiatives) and failures (such as tripartite agreement between

Egypt, Yugoslavia and India) and possible lessons from these experiences. In the process, possible distinctions between SSC and NSC, and comparable experiences, may also be derived. There is a clear and urgent need to create a database of development partnerships, which may facilitate communication among Southern economies; and SSC may be further widened and deepened through exchange and sharing experience. At a technical level, this process may save many countries and institutions from reinventing the development wheel, to understand what is and is not practicable and to use fellow members' comparative advantage in delivering goods and services.

The larger issue confronting the international community, however, is the task of 'unpacking' various elements of SSC so that the aid component may be brought within a global framework of aid governance.[8] Leaving aside the governance issue and considering only the impact of SSC and other processes on recipients or partners, it becomes clear that the limiting factor on growth is not access to funding, but the low profitability of modern tradable items. All possible efforts should therefore be made to enable small developing economies or LDCs to establish and expand export earnings through improved production practices. This in turn points up the need for upgrading skills and technical training in those countries. Given the current recessionary tendencies in global demand patterns, however, there is a limit beyond which high-cost products and services cannot be absorbed by the market. It follows that subsidizing production strategies in LDCs may be necessary, and sources of capital should address this issue. This may have to be supplemented by other financial and trade strategies, such as opposition in the WTO to industrial subsidies. Dynamic links between investment, exports and modern manufacturing and service technologies to promote productivity gains are also important to economic growth, while policy support for the production of manufactures, and stress on the evolution of effective industrial policies, would be another measure to advance broader developmental concerns in the rest of the developing world. Political rhetoric on SSC may not survive long if it fails to stimulate growth across the South.

Notes

1 It is not very clear when flows between developing countries can be seen as 'South–South cooperation' and when they fall into the category of 'development assistance'.

2 This means adoption of explicit in-

dustrial policies, undervalued currencies and financial repression; but success of these policies depends on greater cooperation among economic interest groups along with the availability of sufficient policy space.

3 This was in direct response to the prevailing global policy regime in that period. This is very often referred to as LIEO (Liberal International Economic Order), which was being pushed by the Bretton Woods institutions, i.e. the World Bank and the IMF, along with the GATT. In most general terms, these norms involve a commitment to free markets, private property and individual incentives, and a circumscribed role for government (Gore 2000). Later this was labelled the Washington Consensus by Williamson (1990).

4 This largely is the growth strategy of import substitution and industrialization (ISI), articulated by structuralist economists like Singer (1989), in which they emphasize industrialization oriented towards export-led growth with efficient reduction in imports so as to carefully balance the foreign exchange requirements.

5 Eugene Black, the then president of the World Bank, did his best to kill the proposal. Eventually it came in the form of a concessional loan facility from the International Development Administration (IDA) of the World Bank in 1959. See Singer (1995) for details.

6 Easterly (1999), however, rejects the hypothesis, suggesting that the Financing Gap model has many simplistic assumptions.

7 Illustrating experience with traditional aid, *The Economist* (2007) points out that only about 65 per cent of aid actually arrives on schedule. Zambia was due to receive $930 million in 2005 but ended up with just $696 million. Vietnam, which was expecting about $400 million, got $2 billion.

8 In this context some proposals have been made but largely at the sectoral level: for instance, Pogge (2010) has suggested a Health Impact Fund, whereby national governments pool their resources for reflagging of aid flows and keep the wider global interest as a central focus.

References

Altenburg, T. (2007) 'Trilateral development cooperation with "new donors"', Briefing Paper no. 5, Bonn: German Development Institute.

Amin, S. (1977) 'Self-reliance and the NIEO', *Monthly Review*, 29(3): 1–21.

Ashoff, G. (2005) 'Germany's development cooperation policy since the early 1990s: increased conceptual ambitions in times of severe financial constraints', in P. Hoebink and O. Stokke (eds), *Perspectives on European Development Cooperation: Policy and Performance of Individual Donor Countries and the EU*, London and New York: Routledge.

Bhagwati, J. (1986) 'Ideology and North–South relations', *World Development*, 14(6): 767–74.

Bobiash, D. (1992) *South–South Aid: How Developing Countries Help Each Other*, London: Macmillan Press.

Chahoud, T. (2007) 'Talking of rogue aid: mirror, mirror on the wall … Moises Naim and the new donors', *World Economy and Development in Brief*, 3, May/June.

Chaturvedi, S. (2006) 'An evaluation of the need and cost of selected trade facilitation measures in India: implications for the WTO negotiations', ARTNeT Working Paper no. 4, Bangkok: Asia-Pacific Research and Training Network on Trade (ARTNeT), United Nations Economic and Social Commission for Asia and the Pacific (UN ESCAP).

Chenery, H. B. and A. M. Strout (1966)

'Foreign assistance and economic development', *American Economic Review*, 56(4): 679–733.

Dalgaard, C.-J. and H. Hansen (2001) 'On aid, growth and good policies', *Journal of Development Studies*, 37(6), August.

Das, S. K., L. De Silva and Y. Zhou (2008) 'South–South development cooperation: a major force on the international scene', Background note for the high-level symposium on 'Result-oriented development cooperation: pursuing national interests', 19/20 January, Cairo.

Dyer, G., J. Anderlini and H. Sender (2011) 'China's lending hits new heights', *Financial Times*, 17 January.

Easterly, W. (1999) 'The ghost of financing gap', *Journal of Development Economics*, 60(2): 423–38.

Economist (2007) 'Foreign aid: the non-aligned movement', 7 April.

ECOSOC (Economic and Social Council) (2008) Background study for the Development Cooperation Forum 'Trends in South–South and triangular development cooperation', United Nations Economic and Social Council, New York, April.

EU (European Union) (2007) 'EU report on policy coherence for development', Commission Working Paper COM(2007) 545, Brussels.

G77 (1964) *Joint Declaration of the Seventy Seven Developing Countries made at the Conclusion of the United Nations Conference on Trade and Development*, Geneva, 15 June.

Gore, C. (2000) 'The rise and fall of the Washington Consensus as a paradigm for developing countries', *World Development*, 28(5): 789–804.

GTZ (German Technical Cooperation) (2010) *A GTZ Glance at the 110 Case Studies of the Task Team on South–South Cooperation*, Eschborn: Strategic Corporate Development Department.

Haq, M. Ul (1981) 'Beyond the slogan of South–South co-operation', *World Development*, 8: 743–51.

IBON (2010) *South–South Cooperation: A Challenge to the Aid System? The Reality of Aid*, Philippines: IBON Books.

Jobelius, M. (2007) 'New powers for global change? Challenges for the International Development Cooperation: the case of India', Dialogue on Globalisation, FES Briefing papers 5, Berlin: Friedrich Ebert Stiftung, March.

Kaplinsky, R. and D. Messner (2008) 'Introduction: the impact of Asian drivers on the developing world', *World Development*, 36(2).

Kay, C. (1989) *Latin American Theories of Development and Under Development*, London: Routledge.

Kay, C. and R. Gwynne (2000) 'Relevance of structuralist and dependency theories in the neoliberal period: a Latin American perspective', in R. Harris and M. J. Seid (eds), *Critical Perspectives on Globalisation and Neoliberalism in the Developing Countries*, London: Brill.

Kharas, H. (2010) 'South–South development cooperation dialogue: lessons for development effectiveness', Paper presented at the South–South Development Cooperation Dialogue, Planning Workshop meeting, Korea Development Institute, Seoul, December.

Khatua, A. (2010) 'India's Duty Free Tariff Preference Scheme for LDCs', Presentation made at the High Level Meeting on Trade Capacity Building and Competition Policy from African LDCs, Lusaka, Zambia, 1–12 May.

Li, A. (2007) 'Emerging powers and their development policies: case study of China', Presentation made at 'Emerging powers and their development aid policies', organized by the South

African Institute of International Affairs, Johannesburg, 29 October.

Lim Wonhyuk (2011) 'Critical Reviews of Approaches to Development Cooperation', Paper presented at the conference on Emerging Asian Approaches to Development Cooperation, Korea Development Institute and the Asia Foundation, Seoul, 29 September.

Lipton, M. and J. Toye (1990) *Does Aid Work in India? A Country Study of the Impact of Official Development Assistance*, London: Routledge.

Manning, R. (2006) 'Development cooperation report 2006', *OECD Journal on Development*, 8(1), OECD Publishing.

— (2008) 'The DAC as a central actor in development policy issues: experiences over the past four years', DIE Discussion Paper 7, German Development Institute.

Ministry of Commerce (People's Republic of China) (2010) 'China–Africa common economic development', Beijing: Ministry of Commerce, english.mofcom.gov.cn/aarticle/subject/minister/lanmub/201102/20110207420940.html, accessed 29 October 2011.

Ministry of Foreign Affairs (Japan) (2007) 'Japan's Official Development Assistance White Paper 2007, Japan's international cooperation', Tokyo: Ministry of Foreign Affairs.

Naim, M. (2007) 'Rogue aid', *Foreign Policy*, Washington, DC, March/April.

OECD (Organisation for Economic Cooperation and Development) (2005) 'Managing aid: practices of DAC member countries', Paris: Development Assistance Committee, OECD.

O'Keefe, J. (2007) 'Aid – from consensus to competition?', Paper presented at 'Global impact: philanthropy changing development', Brookings Blum Roundtable Agenda, 3 August.

Panchamukhi, V. R. (1986) 'Complementarity and ECDC', in V. R. Panchamukhi et al. (eds), *The Third World and the World Economic System*, New Delhi: RIS Radiant Publications.

Panchamukhi, V. R. et al. (1986) *The Third World and the World Economic System*, New Delhi: RIS Radiant Publications.

Perry, A. (2008) 'Global business', *Time*, 26 May.

Pogge, T. (2010) 'The Health Impact Fund: better pharmaceutical innovations at much lower prices', in T. Pogge, M. Rimmer and K. Rubenstein (eds), *Incentives for Global Health: Patent Law and Access to Essential Medicines*, London: Cambridge University Press.

RCCDC (Research Centre for Cooperation with Developing Countries) (1987) *Challenges and Prospects of South–South Cooperation: Synthesis Study*, Ljubljana and Harare: Research Centre for Cooperation with Developing Countries and Zimbabwe Institute of Development Studies.

Rodrik, D. (2009) 'Growth after the crisis', in S. Michael and D. Leipziger (eds), *Globalisation and Growth: Implications for a Post Crisis World*, Washington, DC: World Bank.

Sauvant, K. P. (1983) 'Organisational infrastructure for self-reliance: the non-aligned countries and the Group 77', in P. Breda et al. (eds), *The Challenges of South–South Cooperation*, Boulder, CO: Westview Press.

Serageldin, I. (1995) *Nurturing Development: Aid and Cooperation in Today's Changing World*, Washington, DC: World Bank.

Sharan, S. (1997) *Fifty Years after the Asian Relations Conference*, New Delhi: Tibetan Parliamentary and Policy Research Centre.

Singer, H. W. (1989) 'Lessons of post-war development experience, 1945–88',

IDS Discussion Paper no. 260, Brighton: Institute of Development Studies, University of Sussex, April.

— (1995) 'Bretton Woods and the UN system', *Ecumenical Review*, Geneva, July.

South Commission (1990) *The Challenge to the South*, Oxford: Oxford University Press.

SUSSC (Special Unit for South–South Cooperation) (2009) *Enhancing South–South and Triangular Cooperation: Study of the Current Situation and Existing Good Practices in Policy, Institutions and Operation of South–South and Triangular Cooperation*, New York: Special Unit for South–South Cooperation, UNDP.

Task Team on South–South Cooperation (2010) *South–South Cooperation in the Context of Aid Effectiveness: Telling the Story of Partners in 110 Cases of South–South and Triangular Cooperation*, Paris: Task Team on South–South Cooperation, OECD.

Thorsteinsdóttir, H., A. K. Kapoor, S. Aly, S. Chaturvedi, N. El-Nikhely, M. G. Elwakil, W. Ke, Z. Jiuchun, V. Konde, L. Li, M. A. Madkour, H. Maram, T. W. Sáenz and M. C. de Souza Paula (2011) 'Introduction', in H. Thorsteinsdóttir (ed.), *Building Bridges: A Study on South–South Collaboration in Health Biotechnology*, IDRC & Academic Foundation, forthcoming.

UNCTAD (United Nations Conference on Trade and Development) (1992) *Report of the United Nations Chitose Forum on South–South Economic Cooperation with particular reference to Asia and the Pacific*, Chitose, Hokkaido, Japan, 11–15 May.

— (2011) *Strengthening Productive Capacities: A South–South Agenda*, Trade and Development Board, Multi-Year Expert Meeting on International Cooperation – South–South Cooperation and Regional Integration, Geneva, 23–25 February.

UNDP (United Nations Development Programme) (1999) *Twenty Years of South–South Partnership Building – an Assessment of Technical Cooperation among Developing Countries*, New York: UNDP.

Williamson, J. (1990) 'What Washington means by policy reform', in J. Williamson, *Latin American Adjustment: How much has happened?*, Washington, DC: Institute of International Economics, pp. 5–20.

Woods, N. (2008) 'Whose aid? Whose influence? China, emerging donors and the silent revolution in development assistance', *International Affairs*, 84(6).

World Bank (1998) 'Assessing aid: what works, what doesn't and why', Washington, DC: World Bank.

Yanagihara, T. (2006) 'Development and dynamic efficiency: framework approach versus ingredient approach', in O. Kenichi and I. Ohno (eds), *Japanese Views on Economic Development: Diverse Path to the Market*, London: Routledge.

2 | SOUTH–SOUTH ECONOMIC COOPERATION FOR A BETTER FUTURE

Manmohan Agarwal

Introduction

In the years before the banking and financial crisis that began in late 2007, developing countries had been growing rapidly. In Asia this was a continuation of a long trend, but it was new to countries in Latin America and sub-Saharan Africa, where economies had stagnated for a quarter-century. The growth was accompanied by rising investment levels and increasing integration into the world economy in manufactured goods, services and capital (see section on 'Recent economic performance'). Two features of this increased integration stand out. First, there was increased interaction between developing countries themselves (see section on 'South–South trade and investment flows'). Secondly, much of it was based on private (i.e. non-state) action. Increased human migration from developing to developed countries brought with it a substantial increase in inward remittances to the former, which in turn resulted in more manageable balance of payments deficits. In the past, large, unsustainable deficits had often resulted in restrictive policies that curtailed growth. More recently, however, deficits have been financed much more by private capital flows, while the importance of aid has declined sharply. Further, a greater proportion of these private flows has been by way of equity, not the debt which in the past resulted in continual debt crises in recipient countries.

The chapter then examines the future of South–South cooperation (SSC) in trade, investment and technology development. Though earlier attempts to foster preferential trading arrangements among developing countries failed, either at the regional level or more broadly in negotiations for a Generalized System of Preferences, conditions are now much more propitious, especially since the financial crisis has reduced growth in developed countries. Investment flows, particularly foreign direct investment (FDI), and increasing trade between developing countries that provides a larger market for their manufactures, indicate that recent increases in the growth rates of developing countries will be sustainable. A problem may, however, arise in negotiations for a system of preferential trade arrangements between so large a number of developing countries.

In this, the newly advancing countries of Brazil, Russia, India, China and South Africa (BRICS) could play a crucial role, providing a hub around which such preferences could be negotiated. Some BRICS have been very successful in improving their own living standards and have also implemented innovative programmes to reach their poor, such as Brazil's *bolsa familia* (family allowance) and India's National Rural Employment Guarantee Scheme.[1] Such experience could be shared among developing countries to improve their living conditions and income distribution. Experience from developing countries, also, could be used, not least to extend civil and human rights in developing countries; these rights are important for their own sake, though the jury is still out on their effect on economic growth.

Lastly, the chapter looks at SSC in emerging areas of global governance. Accession of some developing countries, including the BRICS, to the G20 group of major economies provides them with a new platform to influence international economic governance. Negotiations on climate change also provide considerable scope for SSC, because developing countries share a need for substantial capital transfers to access cleaner technology.

Recent economic performance

Growth and investment World economic growth declined in the wake of the oil price shock of 1973/74, but had started to pick up immediately prior to the latest financial crisis (see Table 2.1).[2] This mirrored events in the pre-oil-shock period, when world output experienced such rapid growth that it is often called the 'golden age of capitalism' (Marglin and Schor 1990). That increase was entirely due to much faster growth in developing countries, most notably in Latin America and sub-Saharan Africa. For almost twenty years from 1982, however, per capita incomes in sub-Saharan Africa declined, while those in Latin America fell in the decade after the 1982 regional debt crisis that began with Mexico's default.

There followed, however, a period in which all developing country regions experienced faster growth (see Table 2.2). Furthermore, in 2006/07 developing countries performed better than they had done

TABLE 2.1 Growth of GDP (average annual %)

	1990–2000	2001–05	2006–07
World	2.9	2.7	3.8
High-income	2.7	2.1	2.7
USA	3.5	2.4	2.5
Germany	1.8	0.6	2.6
France	1.9	1.6	2.1
UK	2.7	2.5	2.9
Canada	3.1	2.6	2.7
Japan	1.1	1.3	2.9
Australia	3.6	3.3	2.2
Developing countries	3.9	5.3	7.7

Source: World Bank, *Development Indicators*, Washington, DC: World Bank, various issues

TABLE 2.2 Growth in developing countries (average annual %)

	1990–2000	2001–05	2006–07
East Asia	8.5	8.3	10.4
China	10.6	9.6	11.8
Indonesia	4.2	4.7	5.9
South Korea	5.8	4.6	5.0
South Asia	5.5	6.5	8.5
India	5.9	7.0	9.1
Africa*	2.5	4.5	5.3
South Africa	2.1	3.9	5.9
Middle East	3.8	4.0	5.5
Saudi Arabia	2.1	3.9	3.8
Turkey	3.9	4.5	5.3
Europe/Central Asia	−0.8	5.2	6.9
Russia	−4.7	6.1	7.4
Latin America	3.2	2.5	5.6
Argentina	4.3	2.3	8.6
Brazil	2.7	2.8	4.3
Mexico	3.1	1.8	4.0

Note: *Africa comprises sub-Saharan Africa only. North Africa is included in Middle East

Source: World Bank, *Development Indicators*, Washington, DC: World Bank, various issues

TABLE 2.3 Investment rate in developing countries (% GDP)

	1990–2000	2001–05	2006–07
All	25.5	25.1	28.2
East Asia	35.9	35.6	38.3
China	38.8	40.5	43.8
Indonesia	27.1	23.6	24.8
South Korea	35.0	29.8	29.4
South Asia	22.9	26.6	33.3
India	23.7	28.4	36.4
Africa	17.7	18.8	21.4
South Africa	16.6	16.8	20.7
Middle East	25.7	25.6	27.0
Saudi Arabia	20.0	18.9	20.0
Turkey	24.2	22.3	22.9
Europe/Central Asia	23.6	22.1	24.0
Russia	24.8	20.8	22.6
Latin America	20.2	18.7	21.3
Argentina	17.6	16.4	23.8
Brazil	18.7	16.6	17.4
Mexico	23.1	21.2	24.0

Source: World Bank, *Development Indicators*, Washington, DC: World Bank, various issues

before 1973/74, despite the poor record of developed countries at the same time. This suggests that economic performance in the former was no longer so closely linked with that of the developed countries.[3]

Thus it can be seen that most developing country members of the G20, South Korea excepted, improved their performance from the 1990s onwards (see Table 2.2).[4] This growth was accompanied by rising investment and increasing integration with the world economy. Investment as a ratio of GDP increased in high-income countries in 2006/07, but was still lower than it had been in the period until the eighties; there is a longer-term decline in the investment ratio indicating a surplus of capital in these economies (Table 2.3). Also, while there has been a reversal of the decline in investment ratios that countries in Latin America and sub-Saharan Africa had experienced earlier, they still remain lower than those achieved in the 1960s and

1970s. Furthermore, investment ratios in these regions remain substantially lower than those of Asia, where, incidentally, ratios in South Asia are beginning to catch up with those of East Asia.

South Korea and Indonesia are striking examples of a reversal of investment levels, reflecting the continued impact on their economies of the Asian financial crisis of 1997/98.[5]

Increasing integration of developing countries into the world economy The increasing integration of developing countries into the world economy can be seen in the higher ratio of exports to GDP (see Table 2.4), and of inward and outward flows of FDI as a percentage of GDP (see Tables 2.5a and 2.5b). The export/GDP ratio has increased considerably for all developing regions, and all developing country members of the G20 except Russia. There has also been

TABLE 2.4 Exports of goods and services (% GDP)

	1990–2000	2001–05	2006–07
All	23.3	30.5	33.9
East Asia	29.4	39.4	47.6
China	21.8	29.7	41.1
Indonesia	31.1	33.6	29.9
South Korea	31.7	39.5	44.6
South Asia	11.7	16.6	21.5
India	10.3	16.1	22.0
Africa	27.8	32.5	34.7
South Africa	23.9	29.1	30.9
Middle East	25.5	31.5	37.0
Saudi Arabia	37.5	47.8	63.6
Turkey	19.5	29.3	25.1
Europe/Central Asia	30.4	38.3	37.1
Russia	32.6	35.4	31.9
Latin America	17.4	23.4	24.9
Argentina	9.2	22.9	24.9
Brazil	8.6	14.6	14.3
Mexico	24.3	28.3	29.9

Source: World Bank, *Development Indicators*, Washington, DC: World Bank, various issues

convergence in these ratios between the different regions, but they still remain much lower for Latin America and South Asia. They have been increasing rapidly in South Asia, and are relatively stagnant in Latin America.

There is a significant difference between the absolute amount of FDI into developed and developing countries. As a percentage of GDP, however, flows are very similar. Inward FDI is much lower

TABLE 2.5a Inward flows of FDI (% GDP)

	1990–2000	2001–05	2006–07
World	1.74	2.18	3.42
High-income countries	1.66	2.05	3.41
US	1.33	1.04	1.54
Germany	1.52	1.25	1.55
France	1.77	2.99	4.90
UK	3.28	3.86	6.49
Canada	2.40	2.04	6.92
Japan	0.07	0.15	0.17
Australia	1.87	1.68	4.10
Developing countries	2.10	2.68	3.45
East Asia and Pacific	3.33	2.86	3.52
China	3.86	3.19	3.63
Indonesia	0.78	0.32	1.56
South Korea	0.73	0.78	0.31
South Asia	0.48	0.91	2.06
India	0.43	0.93	1.96
Middle East	0.86	1.60	3.97
Saudi Arabia	0.38	−0.11	−0.96
Turkey	0.46	1.46	4.19
Africa	1.46	3.22	2.91
South Africa	0.60	2.06	0.98
Europe and Central Asia	1.77	3.03	4.99
Russia	0.76	1.61	3.71
Latin America	2.31	3.01	2.70
Argentina	2.68	1.95	2.38
Brazil	1.80	2.73	2.18
Mexico	2.32	3.24	2.35

Source: World Bank, *Global Development Finance*, Washington, DC: World Bank, various issues

for South Asia, although increasing rapidly; as a share of GDP it has quintupled since the 1990s (see Table 2.5a).

Outward FDI from developing countries is much lower than for the developed countries, but it, too, has been growing very rapidly, quadrupling in the past fifteen years (see Table 2.5b). Outward FDI is becoming important for almost all the larger developing countries except Saudi Arabia and Turkey. This suggests that in line with modern

TABLE 2.5b Outward flows of FDI (% GDP)

	1990–2000	2001–05	2006–07
World	1.79	2.16	3.66
High-income countries	2.05	2.55	4.36
USA	1.27	1.32	2.09
Germany	2.12	1.16	3.96
France	3.70	4.26	6.99
UK	5.74	3.96	7.66
Canada	2.47	3.75	3.83
Japan	0.65	0.82	1.42
Australia	0.84	1.04	3.02
Developing countries	0.31	0.45	1.22
East Asia and Pacific	0.35	0.35	0.85
China	0.37	0.26	0.59
Indonesia	0.24	1.20	0.92
South Korea	0.71	0.55	1.20
South Asia	0.03	0.26	0.91
India	0.04	0.31	1.08
Middle East	0.08	–	–
Saudi Arabia	0.00	0.00	0.00
Turkey	0.12	0.24	0.27
Africa	0.59	0.31	0.55
South Africa	0.85	-0.40	1.93
Europe and Central Asia	0.27	0.83	2.02
Russia	0.58	1.62	2.97
Latin America	0.41	0.51	1.13
Argentina	0.59	0.24	0.79
Brazil	0.18	0.37	1.57
Mexico	–	0.51	0.74

Source: World Bank, *Global Development Finance,* Washington, DC: World Bank, various issues

theories, firms in most large developing economies have progressed far enough to hold intangible assets, which can best be exploited through FDI (Dunning 2002).

South–South trade and investment flows

Past attempts to foster regional preferential trading arrangements There is a long history of attempts to foster South–South trade (SST). The import substitution strategy adopted by most developing countries in the 1950s and 1960s often resulted in balance of payments deficits, which compelled governments to impose stringent fiscal and monetary policies that in turn slowed growth. This unintended consequence of import substitution arose from slow growth in exports relative to imports. Manufactures from developing countries were not competitive in world markets owing to the absence of economies of scale; production was characterized by low-capacity plants serving small domestic markets. Moreover, import substitution strategies were often directed at the production of goods such as steel and chemicals, which did not exploit the low-wage competitive advantage of developing countries for more labour-intensive products, such as clothing and textiles. Hence exports tended to stagnate.

On the other hand imports, particularly of capital goods and intermediate goods for the new industries, rose. This brought with it periodic balance of payments crises, with consequent interruptions of the growth process.[6] Observers, in particular Prebisch (1959), one of the first proponents of enhanced SSC and of Southern preferences, argued that the integration of domestic markets of developing countries could help establish larger and more efficient plants which would result in more competitive manufactured goods. As a result the 1960s saw a proliferation of efforts among developing countries to negotiate preferential trade agreements, including in particular the Andean Pact and the East African Community.[7] Such agreements later were given legal cover under an enabling clause in the General Agreement on Tariffs and Trade (GATT) in the Tokyo Round negotiated between 1973 and 1979. This clause effectively gave developing countries exemption from the restrictions on regional trade agreements contained in Article 24. Negotiations were initiated for an even broader Generalized System of Preferences covering all developing countries, but neither regional nor global preferential schemes really took off.[8] Few of them proved sustainable and some were never implemented at all.

Major obstacles proved to be concerns about uneven benefits among partners and the damaging effect of lower tariff revenues (for most developing countries, import duties were a major source of tax income). Agreement on possible compensation mechanisms was also hard to find. Members sought to equalize benefits by allocating industries between different countries, although there was no mechanism for doing so and, in its absence, each country sought to maximize the flexibility of its own arrangements and was reluctant to surrender its right to establish a given industry.

The East African Community, which initially comprised Kenya, Uganda and Tanzania, was a good example of an arrangement that broke down through different countries' perceptions of benefits, which in turn depended on the indicators used. Kenya was more industrialized than Uganda or Tanzania and its exports of manufactures to those countries were larger than its imports. After integration the growth of manufactured exports from Uganda and Tanzania was higher than that of Kenya; but since these countries started from a much smaller base the absolute increase in exports was lower. Tanzania and Uganda believed that Kenya reaped the greater benefit from the arrangement, whereas Kenya saw itself at a relative disadvantage. Another region experienced similar problems; negotiations on the Andean Pact could only limp along because member countries could not agree on the allocation of industries between them.

The 1992 signing of the North American Free Trade Agreement between the United States, Canada and Mexico, with a possible extension to other Latin American countries, and the preferential arrangements in place between the European Union and many North African countries, seemed to presage a new age of preferential trading agreements between developed and developing countries rather than developing countries alone (Whalley and Perroni 2000; Bhagwati and Panagariya 1996). More recently, however, there has been an upsurge of preferential trading arrangements between developing countries. Examples of these are the Mercado Común del Sur (Mercosur) in South America, and agreements between the Association of South East Asian Nations (ASEAN) and China (2002), and South Korea and India (both 2009). Before considering the motivations for these new agreements, it is important to examine trends in South–South trade and capital flows.

Recent trends in South–South trade Recent years have seen a large increase in exports from developing countries. SST grew faster between 1997 and 2007 than did trade between South and North, or North and North (Table 2.6).

TABLE 2.6 Rates of growth in trade between regions, 1997–2007 (% annual): exports to

Exporting country	High-income	Lower-income
High-income	7.0	10.6
Lower-income	13.4	16.6

Source: World Bank, *Development Indicators 2009,* Washington, DC: World Bank

The shares of exports from both high- and lower-income countries to those of lower income have increased. Clearly this is because the rates of increase of exports to lower-income countries were higher, representing the continuation of a longer-term trend. The share of imports to all countries from developing nations has also increased, and the very rapid growth in the share of developing countries' imports from other developing countries (see Table 2.7) is particularly impressive.[9]

TABLE 2.7 Imports supplied by developing countries (%): imports by

	Developed countries	Developing countries	World
1970–72	14.8	24.8	18.2
1980–82	29.5	32.6	28.1
1991–93	22.1	38.5	26.7
2000–02	28.7	47.7	34.4
2006–08	31.3	57.3	40.4

Source: United Nations, *International Trade Statistics,* various issues

Between 1948 and 1972 developing countries' share of world exports declined sharply, from about 33 per cent to 10 per cent. It then fluctuated, depending on commodity prices – particularly the price of oil – but over the past two decades it has again increased steadily, from about 18 per cent in 1970–72 to 40 per cent in 2006–08. Over the past two decades Asia's share of world exports has risen from approximately 8 per cent to 14 per cent. Africa's share declined from about 8 per cent in 1948 to 1 per cent in 1997, but later increased to some 2 per cent following a surge in commodity prices. The share of Latin America also declined, from roughly 13 per cent in 1948 to a low of 4 per cent in 1992; but since then it has grown slowly but steadily to reach almost 6 per cent in recent years.

SST has grown especially quickly. While the volume of world exports rose by about 6 per cent a year between 1980 and 2003, exports from developing countries outpaced this with 7 per cent growth. The gap in growth rates increased in subsequent years. Almost 50 per cent of developing country exports in 2006–08 were destined for other developing countries, up from 30 per cent in 1988–90. In terms of the share of world exports, South–South exports were 9.7 per cent in 2007 compared with 3.5 per cent in 1990. All regions, except Europe and Central Asia, which experienced a marginal decrease from high levels, exported more to other developing countries (see Table 2.8). More than half of Asia's exports, which accounted for 16 per cent of world exports in 2009, went to the South; 39 per cent of Latin America's exports were destined for the South, while markets in developing countries accounted for 47 per cent of Africa's exports.

TABLE 2.8 Total exports from specified regions to developing countries (%)

	1990	2009
East Asia	40	57
Europe/Central Asia	39	38
Latin America	23	39
Middle East	32	49
South Asia	32	59
Africa	16	47

Source: United Nations, *International Trade Statistics*, various issues

There is a strong element of regional bias in South–South trade, reflecting considerable intra-Asian and intra-Latin American trade. There is, however, little trade between developing country regions; what there is reflects mainly the dominance of China.

South–South capital flows Private capital flows in the global economy have passed through three distinct phases. In the thirty years from 1950 almost all private capital flows were between developed countries. Flows to developing countries were much smaller and mainly directed to their natural resources sectors, or to financing imports of capital goods through suppliers' credits. Later, in the 1980s and 1990s, capital from developed to developing countries became more important, both to underpin exports and to service domestic markets. The rapid growth in capital movements to China from the early 1990s is an important example of this. Many other countries, however, ranging from Indonesia to Brazil, also received significant capital flows. The nature of these funds changed over time from commercial bank loans to non-debt-creating flows such as FDI and portfolio equity.

More recently, in the third phase, outward capital flows from developing countries have become important. There are estimated to be about 21,500 transnational corporations (TNCs) based in developing countries (UNCTAD 2009). The number of TNCs from BRICS on the *Financial Times* 500 list more than quadrupled between 2006 and 2008, from fifteen to sixty-two (Economist 2010). In the 2011 FT Global 500 rankings, there were sixty-nine companies from Brazil, Russia, India, China and South Africa (eighty-seven if the Hong Kong-based companies are included) (FT Weekend Magazine 2011). Brazil's top twenty TNCs more than doubled their foreign assets in 2008. Indian companies have also been acquiring foreign firms to gain access to technology, markets or brand names.

While capital movements from developing countries still represent a small proportion of global flows, they contain the potential to become much more significant and, in one important aspect, to contribute significantly to Southern growth. A significant feature of FDI from developing countries is that it is directed mainly to other developing countries and an important element of this phenomenon is that products developed by TNCs for their domestic markets frequently are more appropriate to market conditions in other developing countries as well. Products tend to be stripped to their basic elements in order to keep prices within reach of consumers in developing markets. For instance, General Electric in India has developed a hand-held electrocardiogram that has only four buttons and uses a printer similar to a portable ticket machine; the device costs a mere $800 against $2,000 for a conventional machine (Prahalad and Mashelkar 2010; Economist

2010). The Chinese company Mindray has also developed a number of cheap medical devices. Godrej & Boyce, an Indian company, has developed a refrigerator that runs on batteries and costs $70. In other developing markets, 'smart' telephones can be used as ATMs. FDI and portfolio inflows as a percentage of GDP for 1990 and 2007 in both low- and middle-income countries are shown in Table 2.9.

TABLE 2.9 FDI and portfolio flows to developing countries (% GDP)

	FDI inflows		Portfolio equity investment	
	1990	2007	1990	2007
Low-income	0.4	4.0	0.1	1.6
Middle-income	0.7	0.7	–	0.9

Note: Portfolio investments by way of bonds were negligible in 1990 and remained very small even in 2007
Source: World Bank, *World Development Indicators* (2007, 2009)

All regions experienced FDI growth.[10] FDI flows increased from and to developing countries in primary, manufacturing and services sectors between 1990 and 2007, with a sharp increase in flows from developing countries (see Table 2.10).

TABLE 2.10 FDI flows from and to developing countries (% of global)

	From developing countries		To developing countries	
	1990	2007	1990	2007
Total	1.1	11.8	18.7	24.3
Primary	1.6	3.9	16.6	20.5
Manufacturing	0.9	3.9	9.8	21.6
Services	1.2	15.8	17.9	25.3

Source: UNCTAD (2009)

Over this period the increase in greenfield projects is even larger than these figures suggest, because developing countries generally lag in other dimensions of FDI, such as reinvested profits. Between 2004 and 2008 the number of greenfield projects from developing countries as a share of the total increased from 12.8 per cent to 16.3 per cent, and to developing countries from 43.9 per cent to 47.8 per cent (UNCTAD 2009). Almost all regions and all three of the economic sectors mentioned above shared in this increase. These trends have continued in more recent years.

An important feature of these investments is that they are flowing to countries which have found difficulty in accessing existing private capital markets. While the needs of these countries for investment to accelerate growth are increasing, aid flows are stagnant, and unlikely to increase in the current economic situation in which developed countries' budgets are stretched to support their own financial systems (Agarwal and Lele 2009). Private capital flows, as noted, do not service many of the smaller, poorer developing nations, and the accumulation of large financial reserves by some Southern countries may provide a good opportunity for those which aim to diversify their foreign asset portfolio by investing in developing countries. Instruments such as Southern tax preference agreements may accelerate these trends.

The future of South–South cooperation

South–South trade contributes to high growth in developing countries In the short to medium term, developed countries are likely to face a prolonged period of slow growth. Governments of many European countries are cutting expenditures and raising taxes in response to market reaction to large budget deficits in Greece, Portugal and Ireland, and some other, larger economies. This fiscal retrenchment is reflected in the tone of the communiqué issued after the G20 meeting in Toronto in June 2010 and is likely to slow the recovery of many economies in the Eurozone. Severe deficit-cutting policies have been adopted by other developed countries (e.g. the United Kingdom) and the unwillingness of the US Congress to support President Barack Obama's fiscal plans will mean a contraction of more than 1 per cent in America's GDP. Furthermore, past experience suggests that large imbalances are corrected primarily through long periods of slow growth (Adalat and Eichengreen 2007), which would imply that the US economy is likely to grow slowly during its adjustment. Furthermore, consumers in the USA may also need to rebuild their assets, so that the USA may no longer act as consumer of last resort for the global economy.

In this context it is also important to recognize the possibility of a continuance of the stalemate over special safeguard mechanisms in the World Trade Organization (WTO) Doha Round, so that multilateral liberalization cannot be relied upon for export growth. The attention of policy-makers in developed countries is concentrated on turmoil in foreign exchange markets and the need to cut budget deficits to try to reassure markets, and although, fortunately, there has been no substantial increase in protectionism, the Doha Round seems to have fallen below the policy-makers' radar. In addition, the current US administration apparently no longer puts a high priority on trade liberalization, despite its previous global leadership in this regard.

Moreover, theoretical work on negotiations between two parties suggests that outcomes that are either good or bad for all the participants alike make agreement more difficult (Sen 2010). The fact that the current crisis is bad for all negotiating parties at the Doha Round suggests that there will be little if any progress in the near future, and perhaps even in the longer term as well.

Meanwhile, developing countries have moved away from their earlier inward-oriented strategies and are relying more on exports to provide the momentum for growth. For all developing country regions the share of exports of goods and services, as noted earlier, has increased substantially: indeed, considerably more than for the world as a whole. Trade among developing economies has been growing rapidly, ushered in mainly by their faster growth and helped to a certain extent by preferential economic agreements between them. A feature of these agreements, in contrast to those of former years, is freer investment flows. Enhanced productive capacity of companies in developing countries and relatively high levels of innovation should in turn lead to a large increase in cross-border investments between developing countries.

Fostering South–South trade This process of expanding SSC can be further fostered by schemes of mutual preferences among Southern countries; by linkage to other bargaining issues (especially climate change amelioration measures); tax preferences for South–South FDI; and intra-South financial transfers to facilitate preferential trade and economic cooperation agreements. Such broad cooperation among developing countries would avoid some of the inefficiencies likely to accompany the current ad hoc proliferation of bilateral and regional preferential trading arrangements.

There is considerable scope to expand trade among developing countries through tariff preferences, since their tariffs generally remain much higher than those of developed countries. Average tariff rates levied on primary products are 15 per cent in low- and 11.3 per cent in middle-income countries, and on manufactured products respectively 12.3 per cent and 8.1 per cent. Also, tariffs are often higher on goods in which developing countries specialize. Such high rates clearly provide possibilities for negotiated preferential tariff cuts.

Since the 1990s developed countries have used bilateral trading arrangements, which concentrate on goods of interest to them, to stimulate their trade. Developing countries thus far have generally followed the same route, but have not focused on Southern preferences. Furthermore, all countries have abandoned the import substitution model. Not only have they placed greater stress on trade and private capital flows, but market forces have been allowed to determine the allocation of industries so that there is no need for negotiating on placement of industrial locations, which has been a major stumbling block in the past.

High tariffs and dependence on market forces rather than trying to allocate industries make for a more hospitable climate for SSC; in this respect South–South trade is very different from North–South trade. In addition, more sophisticated products from developing countries are usually first exported to other developing countries, while their exports to developed countries tend to be less sophisticated. An important hurdle in achieving preferential arrangements would probably be a perception of sharply unequal benefits for different countries. For example, China, as an established and dynamic exporter of manufactured products, would be seen as a large beneficiary, as would India and Brazil in their own regions. One way in which benefits might be more widely distributed would be a system of financial transfers to be agreed when a given country joins the system of preferences (Agarwal and Whalley 2010).

Those transfers might take the form of an upper bound on any tariff revenues lost from Southern preferences, and would be negotiated as a 'one-off' side payment on accession to the scheme, rather than as an amount to be renegotiated annually. This mechanism stands in sharp contrast to an absence of side payments in the WTO, but given the existence of large funds reserves, especially those of China, such transfers might be feasible and attractive. SSC could also grow sequentially, perhaps building initially on an India–China–ASEAN arrangement that other, smaller developing countries could then access. Alternatively, BRICS could provide the basis around which preferences were built. Early entrants would probably receive better terms, as they did in the WTO, which would tend to accelerate the organization's growth.

Such an arrangement in some ways would mirror the open regionalism structure of the Asia-Pacific Economic Cooperation forum (APEC), which does not commit to non-discrimination along the lines of a super-GATT or -WTO structure, primarily seeking to reach beyond WTO disciplines. It would also be open only to Southern developing countries. The opportunity to foster SST through Southern preferences might involve the creation of a new Southern trade organization. Members would commit to preferences to each other and – in the extreme case – to zero tariffs, and removal of other trade barriers, including a cessation of all anti-dumping and countervailing duty investigations and measures against one another.

A substantial hurdle to enhanced SST, encountered in earlier negotiations for the Generalized System of Preferences, is the difficulty of reaching agreement between so many disparate countries. The establishment of BRICS, however, could help to overcome this problem: BRICS countries could conclude a preferential trading agreement which other developing countries could then join, which would reduce the need for negotiations among too many different countries. Benefits would be larger and perhaps more evenly distributed through much broader economic cooperation among developing countries, a structure that could be larger-scale than one that deals only with trade. There are complementary interests between developing countries in capital flows and technology, and a similarity of interests in the environmental area (see below).

As noted earlier, capital flows among developing countries could be further enhanced through tax preferences. FDI might be particularly important in promoting the production of goods appropriate to developing countries. There is now also considerable scope for cooperation in technology transfer. This could be in the form of preferences, in partial or full exemption from intellectual property arrangements, or in subsidization of licensing arrangements. By broadening the scope of SSC to include financial flows, technology transfer and cooperation, and joint action on climate change and other environmental issues,

Southern bargaining power can be extended to the mutual benefit of Southern economies.

Sustained growth demands high investment and increasing productivity. Reliance on debt capital is risky; throughout history heavy indebtedness has brought with it debt crises and subsequent periods of slow growth. Largely for this reason, in recent years developing countries have depended more on non-debt-creating sources of capital, particularly FDI; increasing flows of which among developing countries are, therefore, likely to help sustain future growth. As noted earlier, tax treaties and other measures to encourage FDI would also bolster growth. This is particularly true because technology developed in developing countries is more suited to their growth patterns. In short, SSC is likely to encourage trade, FDI flows and technology development, which together will help foster growth.

If it is true that civil conflict hurts growth, any relationship between political factors and civil liberties with regard to economic performance is much more problematical. There is consensus that political instability is bad for economic growth because of its deleterious effect on investment (Barro and Lee 1993; Feng 2003; Siermann 1998); but significantly there is disagreement on what constitutes political instability.

Instability has sometimes been measured against the number and frequency of regime changes; but should every change be considered a sign of instability that inhibits economic growth? In an established democracy one might anticipate changes in government after some elections. Analysts have sometimes contended that coalition governments create policy uncertainty, hence are a sign of instability, but countries such as Italy or Belgium, which have had frequent changes in coalition governments, do not seem to have performed badly economically (at least not until the European sovereign debt crisis). One might then argue that large coalitions in particular are so carefully crafted that any significant policy change could lead to their unravelling and considerable effort would then be required to put together another coalition. Coalitions, on that view, would provide policy stability. The question of policy stability might then be reduced to arguing that the more polarized the positions of opposing parties, the greater the degree of policy uncertainty, hence the lower the growth rate (Feng 2003). Internal political conflict increases the difficulties of reducing deficits, which in turn inhibits growth (Alesina and Drazen 1991), and polarization also leads to higher ratios of debt to gross domestic investment, which adversely affects growth (Alesina et al. 1992).

Many analysts, however, are less than impressed by stability in policies. They argue that developing countries need policy reforms to stimulate growth, and that a critical mass of reforms needs to be assembled; this leads them to advocate economic and social 'shock therapy'. It is difficult to implement reforms in democratic countries, where vested interests are able to block them, and this has led some analysts to argue that countries face a 'cruel dilemma' between democracy and economic growth (Bhagwati 1966).[11] Reforms are much more likely to occur in countries with authoritarian regimes, which are likely to undergo higher growth rates (Alesina and Rodrik 1992; Stallings 1990; Alesina et al. 1992). In more recent years, however, opinion seems to have shifted in favour of democracy (Bhagwati 1995, 2002; Feng 2003).

The difference of views has not so far been resolved by empirical research. A review of thirteen studies of the subject showed very mixed results (Sirowy and Inkeles 1990). Cross-country regression analysis often indicates that most of the common explanatory political variables are not robustly correlated with long-term economic growth (Levine and Renelt 1992). Surprisingly, however, analysts find a positive relationship between civil liberties and growth (Kormendi and Meguire 1985; Grier and Grier 1989; Barro 1991), but none between democracy and growth, despite the fact that authoritarian regimes are more repressive (Pourgerami 1988a, 1988b; Kormendi and Meguire 1985; Grier and Grier 1989; Feng 2003).

The past two decades have seen a resurgence of democratic values in the developing world. One consequence has been the need for governments to implement development strategies and programmes that improve the living conditions of the poor. The BRICS countries provide good examples of this. There has, for example, been a substantial reduction of poverty in China and India, while innovative programmes such as *bolsa familia* and India's rural employment scheme have improved the incomes and living standards of poor people (Agarwal et al. 2010). Developing countries can learn from each other's understanding of successful social programmes, but they are very unlikely to try to force better governance or observance of civil rights on other developing countries through conditional cooperation programmes, and have as yet shown no desire to interfere in the internal governance of their peer developing countries.

South–South involvement in institutional change

South–South cooperation and climate There are two main issues in climate change negotiations. One is the level of emission cuts to which each country commits itself; the second is the sources of finance available to developing countries for the adoption of measures to reduce emissions. The UN Kyoto Protocol of 1997 accepted a notion of common and differentiated responsibility similar to the 'special and differential' treatment accorded developing countries through GATT. Now, however, developed countries want developing countries, particularly those with heavy emissions, to commit to cuts in their emissions, and use the refusal by large developing countries to accept this to justify their own inaction. It is likely that fifteen to seventeen OECD countries are in violation of their Kyoto Protocol commitments, and the USA has in fact made no commitments at all.[12] At the 2009 Copenhagen Climate Summit President Obama was offering only a 17 per cent cut from 2005 levels by 2020, which would still result in higher emissions than in 1990, the benchmark for the Kyoto Protocol; moreover it is not clear whether the US Senate will accept even this weak commitment.

Allocating responsibility for action on climate change raises complex issues of fairness. Developing countries have common interests in a climate regime that reflects historical rather than annual emissions, as has been repeatedly pointed out by the UN G77 group of developing nations. Large developing countries are also under pressure from small island and coastal countries, which are most vulnerable to the effects of climate change. The negotiations are similar to those in the run-up to the Uruguay Round that spawned the WTO. Then a split among developing countries (Narlikar 2003) resulted in the inclusion of, for instance, the 1994 Trade Related Intellectual Property Rights (Trips) agreement, which has acted to the detriment of small developing countries in particular (Finger and Schuler 1999).[13]

Considerable funding will be needed for developing countries to adjust to the impact of climate change. Money will also be needed to enable them to adopt cleaner technologies. Until now, the only substantial funds available are for the UN's Collaborative Programme on Reducing Emissions from Deforestation and Forest Degradation

(UN-REDD), which has encountered implementation problems and is not yet in operation (Schmidt 2009).

It will be difficult to coordinate the different positions of developing countries to arrive at a joint negotiating stance, but there are two promising avenues for SSC. Policies adopted by developing countries to meet the challenge of climate change can be explicitly linked to other policy areas in a global policy regime. China and India have recently concluded a five-year pact which, among other things, commits both to a common negotiating position on the issue. Significantly, at the Copenhagen conference President Obama negotiated with Brazil, China, India and South Africa as a group in a tacit recognition of their joint bargaining power. The climate change issue could greatly enhance Southern bargaining power in other theatres, including trade, if the South can link concessions on climate to other negotiable benefits.

The second major element of common interest is an implicit threat of trade measures against non-participating non-OECD countries. The USA and the EU have implemented legislation which, in the event of non-participation, could mandate a border tax adjustment against developing countries, based on the carbon content of their products, in order to offset so-called 'leakage' of increased emissions outside the OECD as a result of OECD countries' commitments to reduced emissions. These measures are also fuelled by the competitive disadvantage accruing to OECD domestic producers resulting from these arrangements. Developing countries may need to agree to retaliate by taxing imports from developed countries on the basis of the latter's historical contribution to emissions.

Developing countries and the G20 Since they are now members of the G20, key developing countries can participate fully in decisions concerning the practices and institutions of international economic governance. This has been a long-standing issue and was a major feature of the proposals placed before the UN Conference on Trade and Development (UNCTAD) for a New International Economic Order in the 1970s (Bhagwati and Ruggie 1984). The developed countries stalled this demand at the time, after involving developing countries in prolonged and fruitless negotiations. It is still not entirely clear what prompted US president George W. Bush to issue an invitation to developing countries and expand the G7 to the G20, nor his successor to call for the G20 to become the major forum for steering the world economy.[14] While it is true that developing countries are increasing in importance, they are individually still too small to make a major impact on the world economy (Agarwal 2010), which makes the president's motivation difficult to establish.

This participation of developing countries is, however, likely to lead to a change in perspective at G20 summits. The main focus of the G7 was on macroeconomic policies, aimed at preventing undue misalignments of interest and exchange rates between them. Occasionally they dealt with issues of interest to developing countries: for instance, aid to Africa was a major feature of the Gleneagles Summit in 2005, but the pledges were not met. Undoubtedly the participation of developing countries will lead to a shift in emphasis at the G20 because their interest is on development more than macro-management, but as yet it is unclear whether or not they will succeed in ushering in changes to the operations of the three major international institutions involved in international economic governance: the World Bank, the WTO and the International Monetary Fund (IMF).

The fact that the communiqué from the 2010 Toronto G20 meeting put heavy emphasis on deficit reduction, despite caveats from most developing countries, reflects the latter's limited influence in matters of international economic governance. It is not even clear what changes they would consider desirable. For instance, Chinese policy-makers have called for a new international currency; but it is far from obvious how such an arrangement would be governed. Despite recent increases in their voting percentages at the IMF, developing countries may not wish that institution to control any new currency. More importantly, conditions the IMF attaches to its loans have been a major reason for the build-up of monetary reserves by developing countries, so as to obviate the need to approach the IMF for loan funds; but as yet there is no indication that the Fund will change its loan conditions. Hence, while issues and problems discussed in the G20 may change, substantive policy shifts seem less likely. Any such changes would require a determined, coordinated effort by developing countries. The chances of success would increase if they became more important participants in the world economy, an outcome that would be furthered by greater South–South cooperation.

Conclusions

The economies of developing countries have grown rapidly in recent years and there has been increasing integration with the global economy; growth in trade and FDI flows between developing countries has been particularly marked. The economies of the developed countries are likely to recover only gradually from the current North Atlantic financial crisis, and it is therefore likely that for developing countries continued growth based on greater integration with the world economy must rely on increased SST.[15] The benefits of this would be much higher, however, if integration were to be extended to capital flows, technology development and transfer, and climate change negotiations; in all of these there is scope for greatly increased cooperation.

Preferential trading agreements, which are facilitated by the relatively high tariffs on goods traded between developing countries, can further promote increases in SST. Any system of preferences must, however, extend well beyond previous attempts at Southern integration, with firm systems of bindings and other supportive arrangements to produce a new institutional structure. To achieve an equitable distribution of benefits financial transfers to some developing countries may also be required, without which China, and perhaps Brazil and India, may be seen as holding an undue advantage. Such financial transfers could potentially come from developing countries' own reserves, particularly those of China.

FDI among developing countries has also been increasing, fuelled in part by manufacture of products more suited to demand in the South, particularly from poorer consumers. Such FDI can be further promoted through favourable tax treatment of South–South capital flows. Production and marketing of goods and services more suited to developing countries increases scope for cooperation in development and transfer of appropriate technologies. Changes in the intellectual property rights regime may be necessary to encourage such technological exchanges.

An important feature of recent interaction between developing countries has been increased aid from larger to poorer developing economies (though such transfers have existed for some time on a smaller scale). Any financial transfers raise obvious questions as to the justification for taking public resources from countries that are still relatively poor. Equally obviously, the answers range from altruism to self-interest. Altruism springs from the perception that such transfers, together with policy advice, would help the people of recipient countries. Experience in Brazil and India particularly suggests that poverty programmes are more effective (i.e. corruption is reduced) when civil society is involved in their design and implementation (Agarwal et al. 2010). Such experiences can and arguably should be more broadly shared, the more effectively to tackle different aspects of poverty.

While such financial transfers can bring with them the risk of conflict between donor countries, this is probably lower than among traditional donors, because there appears to be a degree of specialization among the major donors. China, for example, has concentrated on primary commodities and infrastructure, South Korea on export promotion, Brazil on technology cooperation and India on private sector involvement. The less hostile attitudes of recipient countries would also diminish the possibility of conflict. Nor do financial transfers seem to be driven by a need for export markets – a major motivation for developed country donors in the 1960s, when aid terms were akin to suppliers' credits.

The current system of international economic governance includes developing countries, which are now G20 members. The UN has been only peripheral in the development of this system (the main institutional participants having been the IMF, the World Bank, GATT-WTO, the G7 and the Bank for International Settlements) and is likely to remain so. Developing countries that are not in the G20 can have their concerns addressed only through cooperation with developing member countries.

Developing countries should also cooperate more in negotiations concerning climate change because concessions in this area could be used as bargaining chips on other issues more likely to enhance their growth prospects. They particularly need to develop a strategy for collective retaliation if developed countries, acting singly or as a group, seek to tax exports from developing countries based on their purported deleterious environmental effect. Cooperation in this area could, however, extend to development of new low-carbon technologies: Brazil and China already lead in some aspects of the development and use of renewable energy.

Taken together, all these measures and initiatives offer opportunities for developing countries to think creatively of new forms of regional integration, which go well beyond those currently under discussion.

Cooperation across broader aspects of global policy coordination, which could include investment and preferences in taxes and tariffs, would strengthen the joint bargaining power of Southern countries and add new impetus to the search for better living standards for the poorer nations of the world.

Notes

1 Bhagwati (1966) has stressed the importance of combining growth and special programmes to make a major impact on poverty.

2 For a discussion of economic performance in the period before 1990, see Agarwal (2008).

3 Per capita incomes in developed countries grew by 4.3 per cent a year in the earlier period, whereas they grew respectively by 3.6, 2.3, 0.2 and 4.5 per cent in Latin America, sub-Saharan Africa, South Asia and East Asia. In 2006/07 per capita incomes in the developed countries grew by 1.5 per cent while they grew by 3.7, 3.4, 6.0 and 8.6 per cent respectively in Latin America, sub-Saharan Africa, South Asia and East Asia.

4 South Korea and Mexico are members of the OECD and Russia is a member of the G8. But their per capita incomes are much lower than those of the high-income countries and so are included in the group of developing countries.

5 For a more detailed discussion of the impact of the crisis on the economies of South-East Asia, see Agarwal (2009).

6 Prebisch's argument that industrialization was needed because earnings from exports of primary products would not cover the imports of capital goods needed for faster growth applied to manufactures also, though of course for different reasons (Lewis 1969).

7 For a discussion of many of these schemes, see Robson (1972).

8 The reasons for the failure are discussed in Agarwal (1989).

9 There was a decline in 1980–82,

and 1990–92, because the share in the earlier period was exceptionally high owing to the high price of oil after Iraq's invasion of Kuwait and the subsequent First Gulf War.

10 FDI inflows declined for a few years after 1995 in East Asia; but they had recovered by 2007. The increase in portfolio inflows, however, more than compensated for this decrease. Hence total equity inflows rose.

11 But in more recent writings Bhagwati (1995, 2002) has moved away from his earlier position.

12 Australia claimed large emissions from deforestation in its base-year figure for 1990, so it would be relatively easy to meet its cut commitments (Macintosh 2010).

13 The contrast could be that small economies may gain from an agreement on emission cuts, depending on how the agreement is structured.

14 Russia was not a member of the G7, which discussed economic matters, as it was not considered a complete market economy (Hajnal 2007). Since the Asian financial crisis there have been G20 meetings at finance minister level, but this was upgraded to leaders' level with the Washington Summit called by President Bush for November 2008.

15 The Growth Commission considers openness to be essential for promoting sustained growth (Growth Commission 2008).

References

Adalet, M. and B. Eichengreen (2007) 'Current account reversals: always a

62 | TWO

problem?', in R. H. Clarida (ed.), *G7 Current Account Imbalances: Sustainability and Adjustment*, Chicago, IL: University of Chicago Press.

Agarwal, M. (1989) 'South–South trade: building block or bargaining chip', in J. Whalley (ed.), *Developing Countries and the World Trading System*, vol. I: *Thematic Studies*, London: Macmillan.

— (2008) 'The BRICSAM countries and changing world economic power: scenarios to 2050', Working Paper no. 9, Centre for International Governance Innovation, Waterloo (Canada).

— (2009) 'Financial crisis, Asia and growth', Paper presented at a joint CIGI–South Asia Centre conference held at South Asia Centre, National University of Singapore.

— (2010) 'Developing countries – even China – cannot rescue the world economy', Policy Brief no. 18, Centre for International Economic Governance, Waterloo (Canada).

Agarwal, M. and U. Lele (2009) 'Shrinking aid, increasing private capital flows and rising remittances', Paper presented at a conference on an IRDC Project on Emerging Donors, York University, November.

Agarwal, M. and J. Whalley (2010) 'South–South trade and economic cooperation organisation', Mimeograph, Centre for International Governance Innovation, Waterloo (Canada).

Agarwal, M., H. Besada and L. White (2010) 'Social challenges and progress in India, Brazil and South Africa', *South African Journal of International Affairs*, 17(3): 333–60.

Alesina, A. and A. Drazen (1991) 'Why are stabilisations delayed?', *American Economic Review*, 81(5): 1170–88.

Alesina, A. and D. Rodrik (1992) 'Distributional conflict, and economic growth: a simple theory and some

empirical evidence', in A. Cukierman and Z. Hercowitz (eds), *Political Economy, Growth and Business Cycles*, Cambridge, MA: Massachusetts Institute of Technology.

Alesina, A., S. Ozler, N. Roubini and P. Swagel (1992) 'Political instability and economic growth', National Bureau of Economic Research Working Paper no. 4173, Cambridge, MA: National Bureau of Economic Research, Inc.

Barro, R. J. (1991) 'Economic growth in a cross-section of countries', National Bureau of Economic Research Working Paper no. 3120, Cambridge, MA: National Bureau of Economic Research, Inc.

Barro, R. J. and J.-W. Lee (1993) 'International comparisons of educational attainment', *Journal of Monetary Economics*, 32(3): 363–94.

Bhagwati, J. (1966) *The Economics of Underdeveloped Countries*, London: Weidenfeld and Nicolson.

— (1995) 'The new thinking on development', *Journal of Democracy*, 6(4): 50–64.

— (2002) 'Democracy and development: cruel dilemma or symbiotic relationship', *Review of Development Economics*, 6(2): 151–62.

Bhagwati, J. and A. Panagariya (1996) *The Economics of Preferential Trade Measures*, Washington, DC: AEI Press.

Bhagwati, J. and G. Ruggie (1984) *Power, Passions and Purpose: Prospects for North–South Negotiations*, Cambridge, MA: MIT Press.

Dunning, J. (2002) 'Global capitalism, FDI and competitiveness', in *Selected Papers*, vol. 2, Cheltenham: Edward Elgar.

Economist (2010) 'The world upside down', 17–23 April.

Feng, Y. (2003) *Democracy, Governance, and Economic Performance*, Cambridge, MA: MIT Press.

Finger, J. M. and P. Schuler (1999) 'Implementation of Uruguay Round commitments: the development challenge', World Bank Policy Research WP 2215, Washington, DC: World Bank.

FT Weekend Magazine (2011) 'FT Global 500, 2011', June.

Grier, K. B. and T. Grier (1989) 'An empirical analysis of cross national economic growth, 1951–1980', *Journal of Monetary Economics*, 24: 159–276.

Growth Commission (2008) *The Growth Report: Strategies for Sustained Growth and Inclusive Development*, Washington, DC: Commission on Growth and Development, World Bank.

Hajnal, J. (2007) *The G8 System and the G20: Evolution, Rules and Documentation*, Aldershot: Ashgate.

Kormendi, R. C. and P. G. Meguire (1985) 'Macroeconomic determinants of growth: cross-country evidence', *Journal of Monetary Economics*, 16(2): 141–63.

Levine, R. and D. Renelt (1992) 'A sensitivity analysis of cross country growth regressions', *American Economic Review*, 82(4): 942–63.

Lewis, W. A. (1969) 'Aspects of tropical trade', Wicksell Lectures, Stockholm: Almqvist and Wicksell.

Macintosh, A. (2010) 'Reducing emissions from deforestation and forest degradation in developing countries: a cautionary tale from Australia', Policy Brief no. 12, Canberra: Australian Institute.

Marglin, S. and J. Schor (1990) *The Golden Age of Capitalism: Reinterpreting the Postwar Experience*, Oxford: Oxford University Press.

Narlikar, A. (2003) *International Trade and Developing Country Bargaining Coalitions in the GATT and WTO*, London: Routledge.

Pourgerami, A. (1988a) 'The political economy of development: a cross-national causality test of development-democracy growth hypothesis', *Public Choice*, 58: 123–41.

— (1988b) 'Socioeconomic determinants of political democracy', *Atlantic Economic Journal*, 16(1): 93–4.

Prahalad, C. K. and R. A. Mashelkar (2010) 'Innovation's holy grail', *Harvard Business Review*, July/August.

Prebisch, R. (1959) 'Commercial policies in underdeveloped countries', *American Economic Review*, 49: 251–73.

Robson, P. (1972) *International Economic Integration: Selected Readings*, Harmondsworth: Penguin.

Schmidt, L. (2009) 'REDD from an integrated perspective', Discussion Paper no. 4/2009, Bonn: German Development Institute.

Sen, A. (2010) 'Renegotiable-proof agreements under asymmetric information', Paper presented at the joint CIGI–JUN–NIPFP conference on Growth, Inequality and Institutions, New Delhi, 22–24 March.

Siermann, C. L. J. (1998) 'Politics, institutions and economic growth', in UNCTAD (2009), *World Investment Report*, Geneva: United Nations.

Sirowy, L. and A. Inkeles (1990) 'The effects of democracy on economic growth and inequality: a review', *Studies in Comparative International Development*, 25(1): 126–57.

Stallings, B. (1990) 'Politics and economic crisis: a comparative study of Chile, Peru and Colombia', in J. Nelson (ed.), *Economic Crisis and Policy Choice: The Politics of Adjustment in Less Developed Countries*, Princeton, NJ: Princeton University Press.

UNCTAD (2009), *World Investment Report*, Geneva: United Nations.

Whalley, J. and C. Perroni (2000) 'The new regionalism: trade liberalisation as insurance', *Canadian Journal of Economics*, 33(1): 1–24.

PART TWO

LESSONS FROM THE EXPERIENCES
OF TRADITIONAL AID POLICIES

3 | SIXTY YEARS OF DEVELOPMENT AID: SHIFTING GOALS AND PERVERSE INCENTIVES

Ross Herbert

Despite the high hopes expressed about six decades ago, when a complex global industry was put together to deliver money and expertise from rich countries to poorer ones, the realities of the world have proved stubbornly resistant to good intentions.

In Africa, today the principal focus of development aid, nations that had been born democratic and debt-free quickly collapsed into ethnic factionalism, larcenous one-party regimes and repeated *coups d'état*. Debt mounted, economies shrank. Unsustainable budget deficits, hyper-inflation, corruption, fiscal mismanagement and collapsing industries were commonplace. With the passing decades came a succession of new theories about developmental challenges and strategies. Yet despite an estimated $1.8 trillion in development aid to Africa since 1950,[1] poverty continued to intensify while at the same time shrinking dramatically in the comparatively aid-free zones of East and South Asia.

Those in the aid industry framed the question around how to make aid more effective. Others were less polite, questioning why aid did not promote political stability or rapid socio-economic progress. In the 1990s, the debate gathered force with demands for visible results and greater emphasis on governance. Donors, projects, goals and complex administrative procedures had increased dramatically, adding to the burdens of poor and poorly governed states.

Former aid agency 'insiders' underscore that diagnosis, raising serious doubts about the integrity and rationality of aid administrative systems and the damage they can do to governance, dependency and democracy. The sharpest critics included Moyo (2009), Dichter (2003), Easterly (2006) and Calderisi (2007), all of whom argued that aid actively causes, rather than relieves, problems. Today, optimists continue to argue for more aid, but optimistic and pessimistic camps alike concur that, as presently administered, aid needs major change.

The durability of debate should not be mistaken for stasis. In some sense, calls for higher aid levels and calls for more effective aid stem from the same concern: that old formulas are no longer working. At the 2002 United Nations International Conference on Financing for Development in Monterrey, Mexico, calls for more aid and more responsible governance were heard in equal measure. Monterrey in turn led to the 2005 Paris Declaration on Aid Effectiveness, the 2008 Accra Agenda for Action and an organized multilateral process aimed at improving aid effectiveness.

The Paris Declaration centres on the instruments and practices of aid: the 'what' rather than the 'why'. It is arranged under five themes, respectively ownership, alignment, harmonization, managing for results and mutual accountability. There are also goals for improvement on twelve indicators, which signatories agreed to measure annually. The Declaration relies on a simple formula: identify problems, measure them and instruct donors and recipients to adopt more efficient practices. Its themes might suggest five discrete problems, but the reality is much messier than that. The same issues that contribute to a lack of recipient country 'ownership' also affect donor responses, hence the degree of donor alignment with recipient priorities and a lack of harmonization among donors. One can assume that the multiplicity of known problems recur owing to strong institutional and personal incentives that promote certain practices. For the Paris agenda to work requires a deeper understanding of those incentives, and the measures needed to counteract them.

The chapter investigates these issues through three sections: the purposes to which aid is put and the issue of prioritization; major administrative problems that contribute to aid ineffectiveness;[2] and incentives embedded in donor and recipient systems, which work to the detriment of effectiveness.

Purposes

The most obvious and sustained critique of the purpose of aid arises from its apparent inability to foster economic growth. Particularly in Africa, many aid-dependent economies stagnated from the 1960s until the end of the 1980s. Although growth has improved since about 1995, high population growth has ensured that the number of people in poverty has almost doubled since 1981.[3] Many studies have found that aid has had little or no effect on growth. There is substantial consensus around a study by Burnside and Dollar which found that aid did not produce growth in poorly governed countries but was positively correlated with growth in better-governed countries (Burnside and Dollar 2000).[4]

Aid agencies have broadly embraced the Burnside and Dollar logic that aid will probably have a more positive impact in better-managed countries; but this still leaves a fundamental problem. If aid works only in better-governed countries but is supposed to bring growth to the poorest countries – which also tend to have the poorest governance – the inference would be that aid should be curtailed in many of the places where it is most needed, or that it will be spent inefficiently in poorly governed states.

Aid has also generated unintended side effects. Even if pouring funds into an economy in principle should promote growth, there are attendant negative social, economic and political effects. First, aid projects and agencies that offer significantly higher salaries than are generally available in the host country can act as magnets for talent, drawing away the best elements of society from other economic activities. Secondly, aid changes the dynamics within society. By providing free external resources, it reduces the need for governments to justify themselves to taxpayers and in so doing weakens accountability and the political incentives to deliver substantive results to voters. By insulating governments from accountability, it hampers or precludes the social and political developments needed to resolve conflicts over resource allocations among competing social groups. Such competition is a necessary and normal part of the democratic process, but heavy dependence on aid can halt the formation of institutions of compromise, thus leaving societies more prone to conflict when aid flows eventually decline.

Over time, aid can shift governmental priorities because it is fungible: the more aid, the freer is the recipient government to spend its own resources elsewhere. Hence increased aid can have the effect of increasing spending on arms, or patronage and corruption.[5] Aid can encourage a dependency culture and undermine national strategic planning (see below).

Djankov et al. found strong statistical evidence that high aid levels sustained over long periods dramatically reduce the quality of public institutions. They concluded that aid was a much stronger negative force than the so-called 'natural resource curse' through which easy money from natural resources is thought to subvert governance (Djankov et al. 2005). Scrutinizing the period 1967 to 1999, Kalyvitis and Vlachaki found a strong negative correlation between higher aid and democracy (Kalyvitis and Vlachaki 2009). Deborah Bräutigam found a highly significant relationship between higher aid and lower-quality governance:

> Large amounts of aid and technical assistance enable bureaucracies to continue functioning without at the same time creating any incentive for them to cooperate with efforts to increase meritocratic appointments, reduce corruption in procurement and provision of services, or cut back on unsustainable numbers of public employees. (Bräutigam 2000)

Van de Walle (1999) noted that by lessening the pain of economic crisis and the stresses that normally characterize an uncompetitive economy, aid helps governments postpone some of the difficult strategic choices that arise from changes in global competition, oil price shocks and technological progress.

Although it is reasonable to judge aid based on its ability to promote growth, states are motivated by many other reasons that inform aid practices. The list of such purposes can be long, ranging from maintaining valuable diplomatic alliances to improving law enforcement, promoting gender equality, offloading surplus farm products and preventing illegal migration. This plethora of motivations affects decisions when conflicts and moral hazards arise, and certainly informs decisions on allocations of funding. The more purposes to which limited aid funds are put, the less likely it is that the volume in any one area will be big enough to make a measurable impact.

The composition of aid flows, at least since the mid-1990s, is another reason why aid has not shown a clear impact on growth. Most of it is palliative and aimed at delivering basic social services; much less is aimed at directly promoting economic growth and job creation. In important ways it therefore undermines more productive interests.

Killick observed that there has been 'a sharp rise in the share of total aid in those countries devoted to the social sectors with an almost corresponding decline in the share of aid for production services'.[6]

This tendency has been accelerated by the modalities of the International Monetary Fund's Highly Indebted Poor Country (HIPC) debt relief initiative. HIPC mandated that money that would otherwise have gone to debt finance must go to so-called poverty reduction programmes, which came to be defined mainly as social services. Leaving aside humanitarian and commodity aid, and aid identified only as 'other', aid (2007) allocations were 68 per cent to social and administrative sectors, 22 per cent to economic infrastructure, 7 per cent to agriculture and only 3 per cent to industry and other production (OECD n.d.). The effect has been a dramatic shift from aid that might promote productive enterprise towards social services. Humanitarian aid in 2007 was 315 per cent of 1987 levels, while aid categorized by the Organisation for Economic Co-operation and Development (OECD) as 'social and administrative' expanded 45 per cent in the same period. Meanwhile aid to economic infrastructure fell almost 40 per cent, to agriculture 68 per cent, and to industry and other production 75 per cent (ibid.)

Stress on social services and poverty reduction gathered momentum in the aid industry because aid had appeared increasingly ineffective in promoting stability or sustained growth. The use of basic social service delivery as the measure of success, however, left the causes of poverty untouched. People are poor because what they produce is insufficiently valuable to deliver high incomes, not merely because they lack primary schooling or health clinics. Global trade statistics paint the picture clearly. Africa's share of world trade has slipped steadily since independence in the 1960s and 1970s. As the World Bank observed, 'Africa's share of world exports has dropped by nearly two-thirds in three decades from 2.9% in 1976 to 0.9% in 2006' (World Bank 2008).

If Africa had maintained its global market share its exports would now be ten times what they are. Calderisi (2007) argues that this loss in market share is the mega-trend that should have been the prime target of aid agencies and recipient governments.

Some donors have begun to emphasize growth. The United Kingdom funds a research centre on promoting economic growth. The Millennium Challenge Corporation established by the United States Congress in 2004 gives grants to governments that meet standards of good governance and with plans deemed to offer measurable and realistic prospects of substantial long-term improvements, particularly in areas promoting or facilitating growth. For the first time in a quarter-century the World Bank's 2008 development report focused exclusively on the growth-oriented task of improving agriculture. The Danish Africa Commission, which undertook a re-evaluation of aid to the continent, has embraced the need to promote growth as one of its main goals.

How might a more growth-oriented aid policy appear? As an improvement on the Millennium Development Goals derived from the 2000 United Nations Millennium Declaration, the author has previously offered a growth-oriented set of targets. This priority list centres on helping improve the competitiveness of all aspects of each major industry value chain. Using business information transfer as a starting point, aid could assist in creating stronger industry policy advisory bodies to advise and assist members in opening new markets; provide the infrastructure needed (e.g. phyto-sanitary testing facilities to meet health standards for produce in rich countries[7]) and improve the poor state of services vital to business. These last include infrastructure, electrification, communications, effective commercial justice systems, laws to facilitate debt collection, and the simplification of land-use procedures and systems that ensure fair, corruption-free public tendering (Herbert 2006).

Another practical starting point in shaping growth-oriented aid policy is the World Bank's Cost of Doing Business research, which provides detailed rankings and procedural analyses of problems with various forms of regulation and justice vital to business. By demonstrating poor country performance relative to regional competitors, such rankings provide a much better prioritization for spending than the ad hoc approaches that are common in current aid allocation.

Processes contributing to aid effectiveness

A major aspect of the effectiveness debate concerns the fragmented way in which aid is dispensed, which affects how recipient countries engage with emerging donors. Over the past sixty years there has been a dramatic expansion in numbers of donors. The OECD recorded 263 multinational agencies dispensing aid in 2008, in addition to twenty-three OECD donors and twelve other national donors outside the OECD. There are now thirty-four health-related agencies on the multilateral donor list, more than half of them created since 1990. The chaos led Helmut Reisen, head of research at the OECD Development Center, to observe that there is no international aid system but 'a non-system. ... [that] does not result from coherent design, but is a child of spontaneous disorder' (Reisen 2009).

There has also been a dramatic expansion in the number of causes and recipient countries. Aid agencies typically tend to spread their efforts too thinly by trying to solve too many kinds of developmental problems in too many countries. Such fragmentation means that agencies do not realize the economies of scale and the greater depth of experience that they might achieve if they narrowed their field. The US Foreign Assistance Act, which stipulates the terms of international aid, specifies 33 goals, 75 priority areas and 247 directives (Herbert 2004). In testimony before the Senate, a former head of the US Agency for International Development (USAID), Andrew Natsios, noted that American aid is given out by twenty different government departments, which

> embarrasses the US government abroad with contradictory pro-gramming, endless transactional costs in program implementation, time delays, interagency fighting, and unclear decision making. For example, over the past 12 years two federal departments have writ-ten Memos of Understanding with dozens of countries to provide technical assistance without funds to carry out the programs, no staff, no field presence and no coordination with the Embassies or USAID missions. (Natsios 2009)[8]

The problem of fragmentation is not unique to the US govern-ment. In 2005, Canada spent $3.7 billion on aid in 142 countries with only 132 staff (7 per cent of the total) deployed in field mis-sions; the remaining 93 per cent work from Canada (OECD 2007). Luxembourg divided its 2004 aid budget of $141 million across thirty different programme sectors and eighty-seven countries. Inevitably, token spending abounds. In 2004, Ireland spent $5,000 on support to non-governmental organizations (NGOs) and the Netherlands $30,000 to promote tourism to developing countries. Easterly and Pfutze reasonably ask whether aid cut into such tiny fractions even pays for the cost of approving, reviewing and tracking the expenditure.[9] The aid industry as a whole is spread so thinly across so many fronts that it lacks the momentum to advance at more than a glacial pace in any one area.

Several administrative forms of aid are in frequent use. These include project aid, the most common, which requires separate project teams or project implementation units to operate essentially outside the administrative control of the recipient government. At a larger level there are sectoral approaches, variously referred to as 'basket funding' or 'sector wide approaches'. These stress improvement over an entire sector, such as primary education or health, sometimes with multiple donors agreeing to fund a common agenda; in the parlance of the Paris Declaration, they are forms of 'programme support'. At the largest and most direct level is budget support, also a form of programme support, in which funds are transferred directly to the recipient country treasury to be used to fund its overall budget priorities.

Project aid is proportionately more costly to administer than budget support. In an effort to measure progress towards the Paris goal of greater budget or sectoral support, the OECD produces statistics on 'country programmable aid' (i.e. total aid less schemes such as debt relief or donor-defined projects that cannot be allocated by the recipient country). In 2007, Country Programmable Aid (CPA) constituted 59 per cent of total aid, but if technical assistance, which is heavily donor controlled, is stripped out the figure drops to about 38 per cent (Kharas 2009).

Project-based aid imposes significant transaction costs on recipient governments which are not reflected in the CPA estimates. Every project requires the attention of recipient government officials and the more projects there are, the more officials are drawn from their core duties to project-related administration. According to the OECD's Development Assistance Committee (OECD-DAC) in 1996 there were 17,000 new activity commitments registered with DAC, with a mean size of $3 million. Ten years later, the number of new projects registered was 81,000, but the mean value had fallen by half. Based on a sample of thirty-three countries representing about one third of total aid, Kharas estimated that some 30,000 aid missions are dispatched to recipient countries each year. Although the sample found the number of missions declining by more than 10 per cent from 2005 to 2007, it still represented about one mission per recipient country per day. In some countries there are hundreds or thousands of projects, and dozens of donors. The transaction costs thus generated offer a plausible part-explanation for a fall in standards of governance in countries that receive high levels of aid over a sustained period. Kharas observes: 'An aid "industry" has been built around mechanisms to deliver aid projects rather than to deliver development results.'

There are several alternatives to project aid. Instead of narrowly defined projects, aid can also fund agreed sector-wide initiatives which, like the value-chain idea noted above, seek to address all the challenges facing a given sector of government activity. Sector support programmes are intended to encourage different donors with an interest in a particular sector to cooperate and thus ensure less repetition in analytical and project definition work, and more coherence in the aims of the aid.

The idea of direct budget support, embraced by the OECD-DAC Working Party on Aid Effectiveness and incorporated into the Paris Declaration, is to reduce project aid inefficiencies by routing funding directly to recipient country budgets. This is arguably more efficient and has the added benefit of supporting the relatively few developmental priorities of recipients rather than the many pet projects favoured by different donors. In theory, by eliminating the need for separate project administration staffs, budget support can channel more aid money in the desired direction. The number of projects would be reduced under budget support, hence it would cut the administrative burden on the recipient and, by bringing more resources into government, could promote stronger governmental project and financial management.

Problems associated with project aid are not confined to fragmentation and attendant transaction costs. The kinds of scheme targeted are frequently fundamentally flawed in their conception.

Donors are under substantial pressure to deliver quick results. There is therefore a tendency to approve spending ideas that can be expressed in short, sharp proposals, which in turn contributes to a pronounced trend for aid agencies and recipient countries to overemphasize matters common to developed countries but visibly absent from poor ones. This leads aid agencies to focus on hardware – buildings, computers, farm equipment – but frequently miss the essential connective tissue that allows products to move efficiently from raw material producer to processers, wholesalers, marketers and exporters.

Carl Eicher, a researcher into agricultural development with decades of experience in Africa, saw how the internal dynamics and misplaced presumptions of aid agencies led to a two-decade struggle to replicate Asia's 'green revolution' in Africa. He noted that the imperatives of demonstrating progress and moving money to meet spending targets had the effect of killing prima facie promising ideas. Significantly, the 'missing hardware' pattern led to almost complete neglect of the means to get goods to market, likely demand patterns and farmers' profits:

> Notable among these flaws is the priority given to front-loading research, extension, and education projects with new buildings, vehicles, and overseas training in order to achieve visible progress in four to five years, the time frame that most donors need to justify the preparation of a second five-year phase. The repetition of this cycle often leads to a large staff, a magnificent set of buildings, limited scientific capacity, and a bloated and fiscally unsustainable institution. (Eicher 2003)

Eicher's observations suggest that even if aid agencies embrace growth ideas there is no guarantee that what emerges will be tailored to the demands of global competition.

One antidote to this trend would be a shift from project aid to programmes designed to benefit an entire value chain, to ensure that none of the links in the chain is missing. An edict commanding value-chain analysis will not, however, solve the problem unless it addresses the perverse incentives that encourage and sustain simplistic supply-side approaches.

Such dysfunctional patterns have persisted for many years, despite numerous internal and external critiques, because many aid agencies continue to do a poor job of evaluating their performance. The World Bank, probably the wealthiest and best-staffed aid bureaucracy, notes that monitoring and evaluation of projects were rated as 'modest' or 'negligible' for two-thirds of projects since 2006 (World Bank Independent Evaluation Group 2008).

The shortcomings that Eicher identifies reflect a profound lack of clarity about where development starts and which motivations, attitudes, values, social conventions and other forces accelerate or impede it. While not always easy, an approach that seeks to take time to understand the impediments and politics within a sector before funding interventions is a necessity.

Politically popular but less effective forms of aid The political incentives at work within donor democracies ensure that three particular forms of aid, viz. food aid, tied aid and technical assistance, continue even though a variety of studies point to their ineffectiveness.

Food aid could be considered a sub-topic of poor programme selection but is treated separately because it is so egregious an example of inefficiency. Rich nations heavily subsidize their own agriculture and their governments often stockpile huge reserves that cannot be sold domestically. Under the guise of helping the needy, many governments donate this food to poor countries. This may seem good public relations but it results in crashing prices for food in the recipient country. It is rare that an entire nation has no food. Usually, one region experiences drought or crisis while other regions or neighbouring countries have surpluses to sell. Thus food aid helps those who are starving but cuts the income of people around the hungry region; while by depressing prices it frequently induces farmers to plant less the following year because they believe prices will remain suppressed. Unless managed as part of a well-coordinated agricultural system, such food aid can exacerbate the volatility of incomes for the rural poor (Levinsohn and McMillan 2007).[10]

To help both the recipient country and their own national industries, countries frequently insist (overtly or implicitly) that aid should be spent on products from the donor nation. The practice is widespread but also highly inefficient, and both the Paris Declaration and the OECD have called for its elimination. If each donor insists on its own national products the recipient can be left with a variety of incompatible equipment. The OECD estimated that tying can drive up costs in general by 15–30 per cent and up to 40 per cent for food aid (Jepma 1991). Because tied aid projects are often conceived and written as proposals by consultants or contractors who stand to benefit, self-interest can dominate developmental goals and reduce the extent to which such projects attract political and managerial support from recipient countries to sustain them over the long term.

Much of the aid discussed so far involves the transfer of money, or financial assistance, but a large portion of overall aid flows is by way of so-called technical assistance, which involves aid agencies paying technical experts to manage projects, build capacity or conduct evaluations. Many problems in poor countries are attributable to lack of capacity, and donors therefore deploy outside experts to advise on management, planning and evaluation. This practice has been condemned by many analysts and development institutions as another form of tied aid, with the bulk of funds going to selected consultants, often former aid agency managers, who are adept at preparing proposals and using official jargon but whose efforts are often very difficult to correlate with tangible progress. A review of technical assistance by the Johannesburg-based Action Aid International noted:

> Damning critiques go as far back as 1969, with the Pearson Commission noting that it was, 'little related to development objectives'. By 1993 the critiques had hardened, with then World Bank vice president Edward Jaycox describing it as 'a systematic destructive force that is undermining the development of capacity'. (Greenhill 2006)

By continually hiring foreign managers, aid agencies miss opportunities to develop a market for expertise in local economies. Because of the often fuzzy nature of 'capacity building', reviews of technical assistance frequently remark on the difficulty of demonstrating results or managing experts. Although technical experts are supposed to develop local capacity, in practice they report to the aid agency that pays the bills, which undermines the ownership and control of the project by the recipient government. Instead of fixing the capacity problem, technical support can actually make it worse.

Some analysts assert a positive role for technical assistance, however. Elliot Berg (2000) draws a distinction between 'hard' technical assistance in the form of engineering plans, which arguably has been more effective, and 'soft' assistance for matters such as governance or systems reform, which are often judged ineffective. Collier (2007) argues that the effectiveness of technical assistance depends heavily on the extent to which the recipient government commits to the kinds of reform that outside experts are there to deliver; if it has not yet developed a strong belief in the necessity of change, technical assistance will achieve little.

Incentives

If both donor and recipient governments embrace the goal of development, profess commitment to effective resource usage and supposedly organize themselves to fulfil these aims, why have ineffective practices continued for so long? The reason is that the motivations of individuals and organizations differ, often sharply, from official goals.

Bargaining positions and donor fragmentation Recipient countries want to maximize the overall volume of aid, a stance that boils down to accepting whatever initiatives and changes in strategy the donors propose. As Carole Lancaster put it in her study of experience at eight major bilateral donors:

African governments have typically been exceptionally eager to obtain as much foreign aid as possible and have rarely rejected donor-proposed aid programs. As a result, Africans have frequently ceded much of the responsibility for identifying, designing, and implementing aid-funded activities to the donors, which have for the most part gladly seized the initiative. (Lancaster 1999: 3)

Three forces contribute to this pattern of passivity. First, poor recipients feel themselves to be in a weak bargaining position vis-à-vis their affluent donors. Secondly, the extent of fragmentation and the difficulty of renegotiating with many donors impose practical limits on how many changes recipients have enough resources to bring about. Donors may be receptive to critiques from recipients in the long run, but in the short term their funds are fixed according to budgets and regulations drafted at their headquarters. By the time an agency arrives at its annual consultations with recipients, there may be little room for reallocation from one fund or cause to another. Thirdly, given donor pressures for good governance, a recipient could logically calculate that a vigorous effort to challenge the donor's plans could be seen as resistance to donor suggestions, hence a sign of lack of commitment to change.

Project funding and the weakening of planning processes Although donor-managed projects are thought to be more tightly managed and less prone to corruption than some alternatives, there are many ways in which they can be skewed to the advantage of recipient country officialdom. They may offer higher salaries or salary top-ups over normal government pay-scales (Knack and Rahman 2007).[11] Recipient government workers may profit by building into the scheme workshops that pay per diem, or by giving 'insiders' early warning of new jobs and supply contracts that can be filled by family or allies. The more projects exist, the more profit opportunities there are.

Donors tend to favour financing projects because ostensibly they allow more direct donor control of management. The considerable time and effort needed to establish a coherent sector-wide programme mean that projects can appear successful in the short term, even though in the long term work in a given sector remains divided and uncoordinated. This situation can be attractive to the extent that no one project or agency can be held to account for failure.

At a higher level, the desire to maximize aid and fragmentation come together to weaken recipient country planning. Making a rational choice among competing developmental priorities is arguably government's most important management task, given finite funding, heavy developmental challenges and political factionalism. Resisting such pressures requires robust political mechanisms, yet with so many funders with different and particular interests, it pays recipients not to choose between them. When aid maximization and coherence pull in opposite directions states lose, or fail to develop, the necessary disciplines of debate and management structure.

As a consequence of these kinds of pressures development plans in Africa have become 'wish lists' that offer no real sense of how to spend money to best effect. A 2008 OECD survey of progress towards Paris commitments found that only one recipient country in five had a sound, operationally sequenced plan for using aid, while fewer than 10 per cent had 'sound frameworks to monitor and assess development results' (OECD 2008: 10–11). Malawi offers a case in point. Confronted with a severe fiscal and economic crisis in 2004, it crafted an impossibly ambitious plan with 547 new initiatives costing roughly twice its national product. Instead of choosing the few schemes that might actually get funded, Malawi chose everything, so in the end it was external factors (i.e. donor preferences) which determined its recovery strategy (Herbert 2008: 309).

This pattern instils in the heart of government a system that ostensibly guides its actions but in fact does nothing of the kind. In turn this exacerbates donor distrust of recipient country planning, which reinforces a cycle of fragmentation, project aid and aid ineffectiveness.

Programmatic and neo-patrimonial political strategies In an idealized image of democracy politicians compete to win public support by presenting the best programmes. In many developing countries, however (as in some more developed ones), political control is maintained by buying votes, and the support of key ethnic and regional leaders, through patronage and government tenders. This pattern of garnering support through individual exchanges rather than more widely based policy strategies tends to foster larger, more highly regulated state structures that place patronage and politics above merit and efficiency, hence political elites that corruptly divert government resources into partisan campaigns and purchases of loyalty. This in turn brings institutional subversion of formal oversight and accounting controls.

Many observers have documented in detail how patterns of personalized rule have led to the degeneration and corruption of the state in the developing world, particularly in Africa (Van de Walle 2001; Sandbrook 1985; Chabal and Daloz 1999; Bayart 1992; Diamond 2008; Bratton and van de Walle 1994). Far from harming presidential interests, instability and corruption enable the creation of vast personal fortunes that gradually push aside national developmental goals. The state and its programmes are conceived of as funding streams to be diverted for private purposes. Once initiated at the top, such organized diversion of state resources often spreads throughout the body politic. Instances of grand corruption leak into the media and begin to animate political party competition; running battles continue sometimes for years as opposition leaders try to bring out the truth and governments try to conceal it.

Should aid form a substantial proportion of total government revenue, such political practices put recipient countries' politics in direct conflict with donors' goals. The link between diversion of public funds and decay in government performance can be very significant. In Uganda, Reinikka and Svensson (2001) found that only 13 per cent of central government funds allocated to schools for non-wage expenditures actually reached the intended recipient. The remainder was siphoned off by officials at various levels of government.

Neo-patrimonial politics has negative effects far beyond the amounts stolen. Costs for construction and maintenance of infrastructure and services escalate; officials over-regulate to justify bribes needed to speed approvals; and political loyalty displaces merit, which undermines capacity and effective management. Over time the purpose of government is turned on its head. A team that reviewed governance in Kenya for the African Peer Review Mechanism described this dynamic:

> National priorities are not the primary consideration where the Government frequently adopts externally driven initiatives that have the added attraction of financial resources to implement

them. Once the resources are depleted, the project is forgotten and Government moves on to new policies and starts exploring for new funding. Additionally, policies are usually unfunded in the National Planning process. Parliament or the Executive enacts laws without securing funding for their implementation. For instance, laws passed by the Parliament in the year after the national budget has been adopted would not be implemented unless funded from external sources. Without adequate resources for implementation, the laws will most likely be put on hold until the next fiscal year, or be simply forgotten. There is a risk that, with all the policy reforms taking place, new policies will arise that will lack a coordinated approach, leading to incoherence in implementation and expected results. (APRM 2006: 93)

Donor incentives and their signals to recipients

Aid donors have long been aware of the need to improve governance, but for the most part have relied on 'conditionality' and technical assistance projects to solve administrative, political and electoral problems. These interventions, however, have failed to overcome the underlying political strategies of recipient regimes and have suffered the same kind of supply-side problems that plague project-based aid. Elliot Berg (2000: 3) notes: 'Virtually all the major instruments devised by donors over the past 20 years to strengthen state capacity … have turned out to be ineffective, and creative responses to these failures have been few.'

Donor governments face a conflicting range of motivations and incentives for aid expenditure. Nations may be partly spurred by a desire to speed development and help the poor, but altruistic as they are, these are not the only, or the most important, motivations. Donor governments give aid for a variety of diplomatic reasons, 'hard' or 'soft'. Hard motivations include shoring up strategic alliances, slowing illegal immigration, reducing drug trafficking, fighting terrorism, maintaining control in a sphere of influence, gaining or sustaining access to natural resources or trade, and peacekeeping or averting crisis in a conflict zone. Soft motivations revolve around national prestige and rivalry. Aid is a way for small countries to win a seat at the same table as more powerful developed nations. It promotes a positive national image, affirms a sense of moral superiority and, by portraying the giver as a good global citizen, helps ameliorate trade tensions and counter the view that wealthy nations selfishly dominate world affairs. Competition for prestige and influence within a recipient country is a further, powerful force that contributes to a lack of cooperation between donors and a preference for individual projects that confer bragging rights on the donor.

Thus, all of these aims can, and frequently do, conflict with the imperatives of national development. Governance systems are the heart of the matter: economic development cannot come about without dramatic improvements to the quality and rationality of governance.

Where governance reforms bring immediate political costs but only uncertain long-term benefits, some elements in recipient governments will resist change and, in particular, any restrictions it brings on unilateral executive power. This creates a fundamental conflict for donors that offer aid in order to secure strategic influence. When recipients do not use aid for its intended purposes, donors have only two corrective weapons: moral suasion, and the threat to withdraw or reduce aid failing the necessary action. The latter course, however, is an aggressive act that undercuts the desired strategic friendship. Whenever donors have a strategic interest in good relations with a recipient government that is not fully committed to reform, there is a conflict between the respective logics of friendship and development.

When aid is given merely to buy friendship, trade access or security agreements, donors lack the leverage to promote governance reform. Rather than confront this conflict between developmental and strategic goals, most donors try to deny or conceal it. Kenya provides a stark example of this. Officials in the government of Kenya created fake purchases in a fraudulent company for acquiring a wide variety of goods, amounting to about 16 per cent of government spending in 2003/04 (Wrong 2009). Despite ample evidence of such fraud, aid to Kenya dramatically and steadily expanded from $320 million in 2003 to $951 million in 2008 (OECD n.d.).

Conflicts between strategic and diplomatic goals encapsulate a certain lack of integrity that lies at the very heart of the donor–recipient relationship. Recipients have strong incentives to withhold information on non-performance and manipulate development plans to maximize revenue. For their part, donors with a strategic incentive to continue with aid frequently feel compelled to suppress issues of non-performance, in that way avoiding the clear conflict between strategic and developmental goals. In effect, there is a tacit agreement between donor and recipient to paper over the inconvenient cracks of corruption or other violations of development agreements.

This pattern of untruth sends powerful signals to recipient governments. One aid minister from an African country recently observed after an aid effectiveness conference: 'donors always lecture and complain about problems, but in the end they still authorise the money. It is like they are saying it is okay.'

Where there have been cuts in aid to corrupt governments they have mostly taken the form of delays in disbursement rather than permanent cuts or withdrawals. In deals with donors on five separate occasions over fifteen years, Kenya promised the same reforms to maize marketing systems. Each time its government reneged on the arrangement; each time, aid money continued to flow (Collier 2007: 109). Recipient nations have learned to play the conditionality system game and recognize the personal and institutional incentives operating on the donor side:

> Recipients are aware of the donor's incentives. Surprisingly enough, the impoverished recipients are in the driver's seat during negotiations over disbursement of aid loans. The threat that the country department will not disburse the loan if conditions go unmet is not very credible. The borrowers know that the aid lenders care about the poor and that aid lenders' budgets depend on the lenders' new lending. The borrowers can also threaten not to service their old debt unless they get new loans, so disbursements are made anyway. (Easterly 2001)

As has often been observed, strategic alliances should be approached with great care, because they frequently end with democratic donors aligning themselves with repressive regimes. When an oppressive regime loses power, the people will extract revenge on donors who propped it up. This pattern held in Côte d'Ivoire, Rwanda, Democratic Republic of Congo and Iran, and is visible today in Ecuador and Venezuela and potentially many other nations. The greater this risk, the greater the incentive for donors to prevent regime change.

All governments avoid criticism where they can and most suppress or restrict performance information to some degree. Unlike domestic government services in donor countries which are easy for voters to observe, aid activities occur far away. The only entity in a position to know whether aid is managed well or not is the donor agency itself.

The World Bank's Independent Evaluation Group (IEG) noted that

> In fiscal 2007, over two-thirds of projects rated moderately unsatisfactory or worse by IEG had been reported by the Bank as moderately satisfactory or better just before they closed. Such a wide disconnect – about twice as large as in fiscal 2005 and fiscal 2006 – means management is less likely to identify problem projects and take timely remedial action. (World Bank Independent Evaluation Group 2008: xiv)

Self-preservation is evident in Bank evaluations. Although it conducts several types of performance review, its most visible public statements rely on a performance measurement based not on ratings attached to individual project performance, but on overall country programmes: this is a judgement on whether all loan projects are successful when taken as a whole. According to the Bank, over the past ten years 60 per cent of country programmes were adjudged 'moderately successful' or better in meeting their goals, but as noted above, since 2006 monitoring and evaluation have been 'modest or negligible' for two-thirds of projects. Precisely how country programmes can be judged successful even though project-level monitoring and evaluation are weak or absent is not clear; but it does suggest that the desire to burnish institutional reputation is a powerful factor in the design of monitoring systems. As the Bank itself noted: 'It may not necessarily be policies and procedures, but rather a lack of incentives and priority that is constraining the design and use of M&E systems' (ibid.: 23).

Aid effectiveness could be much improved through enforcement of detailed performance reporting and independent auditing requirements. Aid agencies could be overseen by independent boards (as they are in Denmark), subjected to independent financial and operational audits, and required to publish all project evaluations, financial reports, strategic plans and reviews online.

Even if aid agency heads were bound by corporate-style disclosure rules, however, subordinate staff would have strong career-preservation incentives to suppress information about poor performance. This tendency has led to increasingly cumbersome rules and reporting regulations, but little progress. More regulation – driven by donor staff insecurity – leads to greater passivity in recipients. Instead of taking the initiative, thinking through what works and does not, and resisting donor agendas, recipients are encouraged by a complex rules framework to remain passive and follow the guidance of donors.

In an interesting twist, Wane compared pre-project assessments of the design quality of World Bank projects with post-project assessments of effectiveness, across a range of well- and not so well-governed countries. He concluded that Bank staff work harder and deliver better-quality projects when they confront a more capable, well-governed country across the bargaining table (Wane 2004). Such countries are more likely to reject poorly conceived deals than are poor countries. Knowing that money is going to weak projects can add to the motivation to suppress performance information, and undercut the ability of donors to call recipient governments to account for project failures.

Any solution to these problems would need dramatically more transparency within donor operations and within recipient country ministries; and it would demand systems that enlighten recipient country citizens on how much donor money is pledged and how it is used.

However, an additional factor at play is that donor agencies, like all publicly funded institutions, receive periodic allocations and must compete with other agencies for a share of available resources. If an agency does not spend all its allocated funds it is easy for parliaments to conclude that the money would be better spent elsewhere. 'Use it or lose it' is the slogan in government as well as business. Berg (2000: 11) asked:

> Why, despite innumerable warnings and exhortations, do donors, in particular the World Bank, continue to overestimate local commitment and capacity, and continue to design overly complex projects? One reason is the enduring power of the pressure to spend, which inclines staff to take an optimistic view on these matters.

Donors constantly (and with good reason) talk of lack of capacity in recipient countries, but this contributes to an inability to see that the same phenomenon is pervasive in the aid industry. Carol Lancaster, former deputy director of USAID, argued that two major causes undermine aid effectiveness. The first relates to conflict over goals, the second to the

> lack of capacity on the part of aid agencies to undertake the kind

of interventions they have attempted with the amount of aid they have tried to disperse ... [T]he aid agencies themselves have often lacked the technical experience, local knowledge, staff and appropriate processes to manage such projects and programs effectively. (Lancaster 1999: 4)

Or as Berg (2000: 11) put it more bluntly, aid agencies suffer 'endemic hubris – a belief among many staff that all obstacles can be overcome with money, intelligence and effort, and that all of these will be forthcoming'.

This tendency contributes to projects being designed in isolation, with no substantial input from recipient governments and virtually none at all from business or citizens. It also contributes to poor quality in project and programme design. Because the position of a donor is itself a proclamation of competence, it is difficult for agencies and individuals to reflect on their own lack of ability, insight, local knowledge or even common sense.

Lessons for new donors?

Aid programmes continue to enjoy enough political support for donor countries to pledge long-term increases in spending, but a growing volume of research, and official policy statements, acknowledge significant problems with the way aid is administered. The Paris Declaration reflects concerns that aid is making no long-term impact, especially in the poorest and most aid-dependent recipients that practise neo-patrimonial politics.

Although a useful step, the Paris process has several drawbacks. It focuses on the administrative inefficiencies of aid without probing why they have existed for so long despite ample, well-publicized analysis of the problems. It also calls for greater effort to address the problems inherent in aid systems but offers neither diagnosis nor ideas about how to solve them.

Some solutions are straightforward. Reliance on superficial, activity-based measures of success can be replaced by assessments of long-term impact. A lack of staff objectivity in performance self-assessment can be balanced by independent evaluations and surveys. Too much stress on basic social services can be constructively complemented by emphasis on productive economic sectors, value chains, infrastructure, policies that are responsive to shifting competitive realities, and removing inefficient, costly or cumbersome regulation.

That said, many problems that were noted in the Paris process result from multiple, more complex forces. The most important lesson is that there are no magic bullets. The hardest challenge for any donor genuinely interested in accelerating poor country development is the incentive environment faced by recipient countries and created by the collective but uncoordinated actions of myriad donors. Moreover, development assistance puts donors and recipients in a relationship of shared responsibility that is inherently lacking in transparency and effective accountability. The two parties share control over development policy but each is reluctant to cede its power to the other.

Unfortunately, many newcomers have already followed in the footsteps of older donors in concluding that such problems are intractable and aid must continue despite its imperfections. Once they have begun to deliver assistance knowing its flaws, the incentive patterns described in this chapter assert themselves. Unless their management approach acknowledges that good intentions and management edicts are inadequate, new donors are likely to contribute to the perpetuation of an already overly complex and ineffective system.

Awareness of the complexities is crucial. Aid programmes may be supported by diverse interest groups but they are initiated at the highest levels of government for the prestige and political and diplomatic benefits they purportedly offer. Candour about the political imperatives behind donor aid decisions is vital. Whether or not new donors confront the same problems and perverse incentives in development assistance as their predecessors depends on how well they understand the problems and conflicts that arise from a combination of selfish and altruistic motivations. Two scenarios are possible. The first involves a mix of motives, which will put new donors firmly on the course followed by Western donors that articulate humanitarian goals but respond to the undeclared pressures of national and organizational self-interest. The second is the path of self-interested realists that use aid to boost diplomatic ties or secure trade or security cooperation with little regard for the long-term impact of aid on development, or the trajectory of recipient country democracy. Such donors may judge their overtures highly successful when measured against their diplomatic returns, even if they achieve little of enduring value in the recipient country. China perhaps best fits this description. It places heavy emphasis on delivery of infrastructure using its own companies, workers and materials and does not concern itself with the extent to which its efforts help prop up undemocratic or corrupt governments. It is true that aid-funded infrastructure might remain in service for many years and may facilitate some trade and growth. If, however, it does not alter the predatory patterns of neo-patrimonial governance in the recipient country, it will fall into disrepair and will not bring about a sustainable improvement in economic development. Challenging the patrimonial status quo is, though, exceptionally difficult; particularly if politicians in the recipient country see no need to change their practices.

Given the complexity of the challenges and the difficulty in counteracting the many negative incentives at work, it is quite possible that development assistance cannot mend the most fragile, uncompetitive and dysfunctional countries. Recipients lacking strong tax bases and competitive industries learn to use the aid system to advantage. By allowing them to postpone hard choices, aid may forestall thinking on evolving stable political compromises among citizens, regions and ethnic groups. Paradoxically, reducing aid may therefore do more to bring about good governance than any effort to force the issue from the outside.

An approach advocated by the Washington-based Centre for Global Development and favoured by the Millennium Challenge Corporation is to bypass the minutiae of governance and make aid contingent on the achievement of better developmental results. In this way recipients are free to develop their own management schemes but earn more aid only if they significantly raise developmental outcomes. To be credible, however, such an approach requires donors with the political will to reduce aid to those countries which fail to make headway; while it offers little guidance when dealing with regimes that genuinely do not know how to improve their management, or are so politically or militarily fragile as to be unable to devote much attention to development efforts.

Greater transparency would promote both recipient country governance and the performance of development assistance. Long distances between donor capital cities and recipient countries, and the many layers of bureaucracy, limit the flow of information, which undermines the ability of donors to recognize and act upon problems. Citizens in recipient countries also have very little information about aid allocations or developmental performance and consequently lack the information necessary to inform their voting decisions. Programmes to provide recipient country citizens with information on their government's performance would foster democratic processes while creating more public pressure to improve service delivery.

Transparency troubles are linked to dysfunctional policy-making in other ways. In many poor countries, policy is formulated with little or no input from citizens, academics or business associations. In consequence, resources are seldom devoted to the problems identified as most important by those best placed to know. Without consultation systems governments are not subjected to critiques of their performance or priorities; a criticism that equally can be made of aid-funded development initiatives. Donors that involved citizens and business associations in planning, project design and evaluations could improve the accountability and effectiveness of donor and recipient governments alike.

Newer donors no doubt approach aid with the same meld of disinterested developmental aims and self-interested diplomatic objectives as older ones. They will face strong pressure to meet both sets of goals, but the desire to build diplomatic relationships will frequently undermine developmental effectiveness. They will also probably face many of the same administrative problems that affected their predecessors. To avoid compounding an already fragmented and inefficient aid system, they must be candid about the existing aid regime and recognize that their actions may contribute to making it more fragmented and inefficient.

For new donors wishing to build alliances through aid, there is a strong tension between, on the one hand, a desire to set themselves apart from other donor nations, and on the other the logic of cooperating with those older donors. Unless new donors enter with very large funding resources their contributions will be lost in the complex morass of Professor Reisen's 'non-system', to which many nations contribute but none can bring decisive change (Reisen 2009).

Notes

1 Based on net ODA from 1950 to end 2008, based on OECD-DAC data. Djankov et al. (2005) and Easterly and Pfutze (2008) put the amount at $2.3 trillion.

2 It is important to note that the exigencies of aid delivery in fragile or post-conflict states can be quite different from what prevails in countries not torn by conflict. Where government has

collapsed or lost most of its capability and staff, development agencies are forced to perform many functions of government directly. This chapter will not attempt to deal with this difficult area and focuses on the administration of aid in politically stable countries.

3 The proportion of sub-Saharan Africa living on less than $1.25 a day averaged 50 per cent of the population over the 1981–2005 period, with a peak of 58 per cent in 1996 and a decline subsequently. The total number of people living on less than $1.25 a day nearly doubled over 1981–2005, increasing from 200 million to 380 million. See Chen and Ravallion (2008).

4 This conclusion was contested by William Easterly and others, who found that a positive aid–growth relationship does not hold with a larger sample size or different indicators of governance. For an overview of the different approaches used to measure growth impacts of aid, see Wane (2004) and Clemens et al. (2004), who found a strong correlation between growth-oriented aid – two to three times the impact found in studies evaluating the relationship between aggregate aid and growth. They found that 1 per cent of GDP received in aid produces an additional 0.3 per cent growth in GDP. For a review of problems with the Burnside and Dollar approach, see Easterly et al. (2003).

5 Paul Collier estimates that 40 per cent of military spending in Africa is funded through the fungibility effects of aid. See Collier (2009).

6 Education is undoubtedly necessary to reach higher levels of economic sophistication but the emphasis has been overwhelmingly on primary education while secondary and tertiary education have seen declines in funding in many countries. Given the state of decay in infrastructure and business-related services, there are arguably

immediate growth and tax benefits to be had from funding productive sectors, but such spending need not come at the cost of withdrawing education. See Killick (2003). See also Herbert (2006); Rajan and Subramanian (2005); Calderisi (2007).

7 Cooperation in these areas could reduce costs if managed regionally. For example, aside from South Africa, few African states have more than a handful of technical staff available to manage the processes required to meet European or American agricultural safety standards. Centrally funded and managed testing facilities could improve efficiency and effectiveness in keeping pace with changing regulations.

8 Brainard (2007) contends that fifty different entities in the US government were involved in giving foreign assistance.

9 Luxembourg, Ireland and Netherlands figures from Easterly and Pfutze (2008).

10 For a review of the impact of food aid, see Levinsohn and McMillan (2007).

11 See Knack and Rahman (2007) on the dynamics and impact of donor incentives to poach top recipient government staff.

References

APRM (African Peer Review Mechanism) (2006) *Country Review Report of the Republic of Kenya*.

Bates, R. H. (1983) *Essays on the Political Economy of Rural Africa*, London: Cambridge University Press.

Bayart, J. F. (1992) *The State in Africa: The Politics of the Belly*, New York: Longman.

Bayart, J. F., S. Ellis and B. Hibou (1999) *The Criminalisation of the State in Africa*, Oxford and Bloomington, IN: James Currey.

Berg, E. (2000) 'Why aren't aid organisations better learners?',

Paper presented at the conference What Do Aid Agencies and their Co-operating Partners Learn from their Experiences?, Expert Group on Development Issues, Stockholm, 24 August.

Brainard, L. (2007) 'Organizing U.S. foreign assistance to meet twenty-first century challenges', in L. Brainard (ed.), *Security by Other Means: Foreign Assistance, Global Poverty, and American Leadership*, Washington, DC: Brookings Institution Press.

Bratton, M. and N. van de Walle (1994) 'Neopatrimonial regimes and political transitions in Africa', *World Politics*, 46(4): 453–89.

Bräutigam, D. (2000) *Aid Dependence and Governance*, Stockholm: Almqvist & Wiksell International.

Burnside, C. and D. Dollar (2000) 'Aid, policies, and growth', *American Economic Review*, 90(4): 847–68.

Calderisi, R. (2007) *The Trouble with Africa: Why Foreign Aid isn't Working*, New Haven, CT, and London: Yale University Press.

Chabal, P. and J.-P. Daloz (1999) *Africa Works: Disorder as Political Instrument*, Oxford and Bloomington: James Currey and Indiana University Press.

Chen, S. and M. Ravallion (2008) 'The developing world is poorer than we thought, but no less successful in the fight against poverty', Policy Research Working Paper, World Bank.

Clemens, M., S. Radelet and R. Bhavnani (2004) 'Counting chickens when they hatch: the short-term effect of aid on growth', Working Papers 44, Center for Global Development.

Collier, P. (2007) *The Bottom Billion: Why the Poorest Countries are Failing and What Can be Done about It*, Oxford and New York: Oxford University Press.

— (2009) *Wars, Guns and Votes: Democracy in dangerous places*, London: Bodley Head.

Diamond, L. (2008) 'The democratic rollback: the resurgence of the predatory state', *Foreign Affairs*, 87(2): 36–48.

Dichter, T. (2003) *Despite Good Intentions – Why Development Assistance to the Third World Has Failed*, Boston: University of Massachusetts Press.

Djankov, S., J. G. Montalvo and M. Reynal-Querol (2005) 'The curse of aid', Economics Working Papers Series, Department of Economics and Business, Universitat Pompeu Fabra.

Easterly, W. (2001) *The Elusive Quest for Growth: Economists' Misadventures in the Tropics*. Cambridge, MA: MIT Press.

— (2006) *The White Man's Burden: Why the West's Efforts to Aid the Rest Have Done So Much Ill and So Little Good*, New York: Penguin Press.

Easterly, W. and T. Pfutze (2008) 'Where does the money go? Best and worst practices in foreign aid', Brookings Global Economy and Development working paper series no. 21.

Easterly, W., R. Levine and D. Roodman (2003) 'New data, new doubts: revisiting "Aid, policies and growth"', Working Papers 26, Center for Global Development.

Eicher, C. K. (2003) 'Flashback: fifty years of donor aid to African agriculture', InWEnt, IFPRI, NEPAD, CTA conference on Successes in African Agriculture, Pretoria.

European Union Court of Auditors (2007) *Special Report No. 6/2007 on the effectiveness of technical assistance in the context of capacity development*.

Greenhill, R. (2006) *Real Aid 2: Making Technical Assistance Work*, Johannesburg: Action Aid International.

Hancock, G. (1989) *Lords of Poverty: The*

Power, Prestige, and Corruption of the International Aid Business, New York: Atlantic Monthly Press.

Hayter, T. and C. Watson (1985) *Aid Rhetoric and Reality*, London: Pluto Press.

Herbert, R. (2004) 'A new face for US aid?', *eAfrica*, 2, South African Institute of International Affairs.

— (2006) 'Towards an African growth plan', in SAIIA, *South African Yearbook of International Affairs 2005*, Johannesburg: SAIIA, pp. 119–27.

— (2008) 'Constraints on growth and state effectiveness – the case of Malawi', in B. H. Holger, G. Mills and G. Wahlers (eds), *Africa beyond Aid*, Johannesburg: Brenthurst Foundation.

Jepma, C. J. (1991) *The Tying of Aid*, Paris: OECD Development Center.

Kalyvitis, S. C. and I. Vlachaki (2009) 'More aid, less democracy? An empirical examination of the relationship between foreign aid and the democratisation of recipients', SSRN eLibrary, ssrn.com/paper=1002433.

Kharas, H. (2009) *Action on Aid: Steps toward Making Aid More Effective*, Washington, DC: Wolfensohn Center for Development, Brookings Institution.

Killick, T. (2003) 'Macro-level evaluations and the choice of aid modalities', Paper prepared for OED conference on 'Evaluating development effectiveness', July.

Knack, S. and A. Rahman (2007) 'Donor fragmentation and bureaucratic quality in aid recipients', *Journal of Development Economics*, 83: 176–97.

Lancaster, C. (1999) *Aid to Africa: So Much to Do, So Little Done*, Chicago, IL, and London: University of Chicago Press.

Levinsohn, J. and M. McMillan (2007) *Does Food Aid Harm the Poor? Household Evidence from Ethiopia*, in

A. Harrison (ed.), *Globalisation and Poverty*, Cambridge, MA: National Bureau of Economic Research.

Moyo, D. (2009) *Dead Aid: Why Aid is Not Working and How There is a Better Way for Africa*, New York: Farrar, Straus & Giroux.

Natsios, A. (2009) 'Foreign aid reform', Testimony before the US Senate Foreign Relations Committee, 1 April.

OECD (Organisation for Economic Co-operation and Development) (n.d.) *Statistics*, stats.oecd.org.

— (2007) *Canada Development Assistance Committee Peer Review*.

— (2008) *2008 Survey on Monitoring the Paris Declaration – Effective Aid by 2010? What It Will Take*, Paris: OECD.

Rajan, R. G. and A. Subramanian (2005) 'What undermines aid's impact on growth?', National Bureau of Economic Research Working Paper Series no. 11657.

Reinikka, R. and J. Svensson (2001) 'Explaining leakage of public funds', World Bank Policy Research Working Paper no. 2709.

Reisen, H. (2009) 'The multilateral donor non-system: towards accountability and efficient role assignment', *Economics Open Access Open Discussion E-Journal*, 18.

Sandbrook, R. (1985) *The Politics of Africa's Economic Stagnation*, Cambridge: Cambridge University Press.

Van de Walle, N. (1999) 'Aid's crisis of legitimacy: current proposals and future prospects', *African Affairs*, 98(392): 337–52.

— (2001) *African Economies and the Politics of Permanent Crisis 1979–1999*, Cambridge: Cambridge University Press.

Wane, W. (2004) 'The quality of foreign aid country selectivity or donors incentives?', World Bank Policy Research Working Paper no. 3325.

World Bank (2008) 'Why trade costs

matter to Africa', econ.worldbank.
org/, accessed 8 June 2009.
World Bank Independent Evaluation
Group (2008) *2008 Annual Review
of Development Effectiveness: Shared*
Global Challenges, Washington, DC:
World Bank.
Wrong, M. (2009) *It's Our Turn to Eat:
The story of a Kenyan whistle-blower*,
New York: HarperCollins.

4 | AID EFFECTIVENESS AND EMERGING DONORS: LESSONS FROM THE EU EXPERIENCE

James Mackie

In 2009 the twenty-seven member states of the European Union and the European Commission (EC) together provided €49 billion in Official Development Assistance (ODA) to more than 160 countries (European Commission 2009b). In total this represented some 42 per cent of the EU's gross national income (GNI). EU member countries constitute some of the world's oldest, and newest, development cooperation donors, with wide experience in the sector; and together account for more than 60 per cent of global ODA, as measured by the Organisation for Economic Co-operation and Development's Development Assistance Committee (OECD-DAC). Indeed, the group includes some countries with the highest ODA/GNI ratios in the world, even surpassing the UN target of 0.7 per cent; fifteen of them account for two-thirds of DAC membership.

It is instructive to draw on the experience of this unique group of donors and distil some of the lessons, both positive and negative, that it has learned. The purpose of providing such information in a book explicitly devoted to 'emerging' donors is partly to exchange experience and promote dialogue; but also to reflect on how the EU might react to the increasing role of new donors. The European development sector is generally somewhat defensive towards emerging donors in a field which it has long dominated. There is a sense that it has completed a long learning curve on the way towards discovering what works in development (or more often, what does not work), and that newcomers will simply ignore this accumulated knowledge. In practice, however, it is evident that new participants are interested in these lessons: the search for positive results is far from only a European concern.

It is important to explain some of the reasons why more established donors moved in certain directions in their attempts to improve the quality and effectiveness of aid. Starting with an introduction on the origins of the aid effectiveness debate, the chapter will therefore seek not just to outline some of the key steps EU donors as a group have taken to improve the effectiveness of their aid, but also examine the factors that impelled them to do so. Finally an effort will be made to draw some lessons that may be relevant for emerging donors.

Origins of concerns with aid effectiveness

The global debate on best practice and methodologies in development cooperation has intensified over the past two decades. It accelerated during UN conferences of the 1990s and discussions on the Millennium Declaration, and the Paris Declaration and Accra Agenda for Action (AAA) that arose respectively from the UN-sponsored Millennium Summit of world leaders in New York in 2000, and the Second High Level Forum on Aid Effectiveness in Paris in 2005. Debate in the EU development community has kept pace with that in the world at large.

While the effectiveness of aid is a vital concern for those involved, not least citizens and governments of developing countries, European and other donor governments' interest in effectiveness is arguably driven primarily by the need for domestic political justifications for ODA budgets. As ODA levels climb while national budgeting exercises become tougher, concern with effectiveness also increases. If politically acceptable justifications for development cooperation can be found, pressure on effectiveness may lessen.

Box 4.1 OECD-DAC definition of ODA (Official Development Assistance)

Grants or Loans to countries and territories on Part I of the DAC List of Aid Recipients (developing countries) which are: (a) undertaken by the official sector; (b) with promotion of economic development and welfare as the main objective; (c) at concessional financial terms [if a loan, having a Grant Element (q.v.) of at least 25 per cent]. In addition to financial flows, Technical Co-operation (q.v.) is included in aid. Grants, loans and credits for military purposes are excluded. Transfer payments to private individuals (e.g. pensions, reparations or insurance payouts) are in general not counted.

Source: OECD-DAC Glossary

Justifying development cooperation has always involved balancing self-interest and humanitarian concerns. On the one hand, governments argue that it is in their country's interest to provide aid to others because it promotes trade, security and political support on the international scene; on the other there are moral arguments, as a rule deployed mainly by socially or faith-based organizations, on the need to help others less fortunate. While governments by and large tend to rely more on the self-interest argument, no government with ambitions in international affairs wishes to be seen as lacking in generosity and compassion, or as unwilling to contribute to solving issues of global concern. Hence even those hard-nosed politicians driven primarily by realpolitik are not unmoved by the need to appear, to some extent at least, susceptible to the humanitarian argument.

Concern with effectiveness is thus intimately linked to political justifications for aid programmes. Unsurprisingly, the search for effectiveness is far from new. From the 1950s and 1960s, as development cooperation started to emerge as a new domain following the end of the Second World War and the beginnings of independence for former European colonies, economists and development specialists sought to understand how best to promote economic growth and reduce poverty. But the real concern with aid effectiveness as understood today and as promoted by the Paris Declaration is best traced to the post-Cold War years.

Among EU states, concern with effectiveness is clearly evident in debates from the early 1990s. The 1992 Treaty on European Union (the Maastricht Treaty) is an important landmark. With its 'three cees' of coordination, 'complementarity' and coherence,[1] it sought to improve the quality of EU aid as a whole by encouraging member states and the EC to work more closely together to improve the consistency of their external policies, and of those internal policies with external effects, so that they were more supportive of development. Sustained debate on effectiveness, however, began to intensify in the EU only in the late 1990s and became generalized in the early 2000s, in parallel with international discussion in the Rome (2003) and Paris High Level Forums.

There are a number of external drivers to this debate. The first is probably that with the end of the Cold War the main realpolitik rationale for aid – that is, as a reward for political support – fell away[2] (Stokke 2005: 46) more or less at a stroke. At first and very quickly this prompted a decline in global ODA levels from an average ODA/ GNI ratio of about 0.35 per cent in the 1980s to as low as 0.25 per cent in the late 1990s. This fall was exacerbated by other factors, such as a number of donors experiencing short but sharp fiscal deficits (Riddell 2007: 38). Moreover, a new element of competition for external assistance was introduced as DAC member countries felt politically compelled to support economic transition in central and eastern Europe. Hence in a short period a major and long-standing political justification for aid was removed, national budgets became tighter and demand for external assistance increased. The argument for aid had to be rebuilt virtually from scratch.

While these external drivers were felt primarily at a political and governmental level in DAC countries they also prompted a wider public debate, and in European and other DAC members an increased questioning of the value and effectiveness of development assistance. European civil society organizations, building on decades of practical experience in development in the 1970s and 1980s, began to invest more in advocacy programmes and more strongly to articulate the case for aid, specifically high-quality aid, to their governments. At an international level the case for more industrialized-nation support for development was also being argued in a series of UN forums (among them Rio in 1992, Beijing in 1995 and Copenhagen in 1995), where non-governmental organizations (NGOs) were increasingly vocal. The NGOs often worked with developing country governments and supported them in articulating their views on the importance of aid, and on the need for a stronger focus on poverty, and increases in the quantity and quality of aid.

European and other DAC governments thus came under pressure from several sides. Internationally they were being expected to increase aid levels while under fire for the quality of the aid they did provide; domestically they were faced by a strong NGO lobby in favour of aid and conversely by growing voter scepticism as to whether aid really worked. The term 'donor fatigue' became commonplace. As a result, donor statements increasingly stressed the need to reduce waste and make aid more effective and more targeted on poverty reduction. European governments, supported by development NGOs, typically explained to their voters that aid was worthwhile provided it was closely managed and that they were proposing to increase aid but only provided they could ensure its effective control.

The Millennium Summit in September 2000 can be seen as the culmination of a decade of intense international debate on aid with governments and NGOs strongly involved. The Millennium Declaration and its subsequent reworking into a set of so-called Millennium Development Goals (MDGs) was also a turning point in that it established the international political consensus and policy foundation on which to build a new period of growth in global ODA. It came, however, with a strong emphasis on the need to improve effectiveness. This latter point was not an argument voiced only by donor governments seeking to keep reluctant voters and taxpayers on board; it emanated also from developing countries at both civil society and government levels. The combined 'quantity and quality' message was repeated two years later in Monterrey at the 2002 UN Conference on Financing for Development, which re-established a consensus on the need for donors to reach the UN ODA target of 0.7 per cent of GNI but also stressed that along with this had to come improvements in effectiveness. The scene was thus set for the DAC to initiate a process of reflection on means to improve aid effectiveness. This formally kicked off with the Rome High Level Forum in 2003, and later that in Paris, which agreed the Paris Declaration that in turn became the most widely accepted basic text on aid effectiveness.

As the world moved into the new millennium, international affairs were shaken by the 9/11 attack on the New York World Trade Center in 2001. While this provoked the hard response of what US president George W. Bush chose to call a 'war on terror', it also prompted other reactions; certainly in Europe it led to renewed reflection on the role of 'soft' power and on the relationship between security and development. There were different points of view within the EU, perhaps best typified by the debate on EU High Representative Javier Solana's 2003 document *European Security Strategy* (European Council 2003). While its first version made an explicit link between development and security, it did so from the standpoint that development was not possible without security. Others, however, argued that the converse was also true, an opinion recognized when the security strategy was reviewed in late 2008 (European Council 2008). For EU development ministers, one of the first opportunities to react to 9/11 as a group was at the Monterrey Conference, in the run-up to which the view gained ground in the EU that reducing international disparities in poverty and development should be part of the European response to terrorism. Certainly EU ministers agreed that if the promise of the MDGs was to be realized they had a responsibility to make a strong statement in Monterrey on increasing ODA. The EC was asked to consult with each member state and prepare a common position. As a result, the EU was able to announce that as a group its members planned to achieve the UN 0.7 per cent ODA/GNI target by 2015, and that it was also setting itself intermediary targets so as to better monitor progress (European Council 2002).

Thus in the first years of this century ODA from Europe started to increase again, and until about 2006/07 the EU managed to stick to its targets for reaching the 0.7 per cent goal. The banking and financial crisis that began in 2008 inevitably had an impact upon this relatively good progress and DAC figures for 2009 show clear difficulties starting to emerge.[3] The slowdown was confirmed in 2010 with several EU governments announcing decreases in ODA as they sought to reduce budget deficits (although the new centre-right government in the UK stated that it would maintain UK commitments to increasing ODA, albeit with greater attention on how aid would help Britain). Overall, however, aid effectiveness is now solidly on the EU agenda, and indeed the financial crisis strengthened some arguments in its favour.

An issue that has further characterized EU thinking since the Cold War, and one in which Europeans often feel that they differ with a number of emerging donors, has been a growing preoccupation with human rights and good governance. The EU began to insist that human rights clauses be introduced into its international cooperation agreements in the mid-1990s at the time of the revision of the 1975 Lomé IV Convention between the EU and African, Caribbean and Pacific (ACP) countries. Again, this may be explained as a reaction to the end of the Cold War and a growing feeling among Europeans that during that time of muted hostilities, European aid money had been propping up oppressive regimes, in effect to buy loyalty. With the removal of the political imperative for aid, EU governments began to respond to internal political pressure, often mobilized by civil society human rights organizations. This was consolidated in 2000 with the EU–ACP Cotonou Partnership Agreement, signed in Cotonou, Benin, on 23 June 2000, with revisions in 2005 and 2010, and its 'essential element' clauses that made the derogation of human rights, the rule of law and democratic principles (and to some extent also good governance) grounds for suspension of the agreement. These clauses subsequently became standard in all EU international agreements. Such rights issues cannot strictly be grouped with the aid effectiveness agenda of the Paris Declaration and AAA, but in European thinking there is a clear view, symbolized by the reference to 'essential' elements, that without attention to these matters, development will not be possible. In other words, abuse will always undermine the potential effectiveness of aid. Developing country governments argue that this is political conditionality pure and simple, but most European citizens, if asked, would respond that without such conditions providing aid is by and large a waste of money. European governments therefore have little choice but to support that view. Of course, there is no consistent evidence to suggest that withholding aid in such circumstances has any effect on the abuses in question, but that is beside the point for many European voters.

The EU is thus now strongly wedded to principles of aid effectiveness and with that comes an interest in seeing that emerging donors also support the achievement of the MDGs. At the same time there is a recognition within the EU that putting aid effectiveness principles into practice is difficult, and carries a cost which should be shared between donors; furthermore that there is a continuing need for dialogue with development partners on how to improve and consolidate any gains.

At the same time the international environment is changing once more, with the EU having to recognize that it is no longer such a major player in international affairs. Indeed, it is unlikely to remain one of the largest global economic powers in years to come. The Chinese economy has already overtaken those of all individual European countries (though not the EU in total) and India is likely to do so in the coming decade. In such a context it will not be surprising if the case for the EU's continuing as the single largest contributor to global ODA comes under increasing pressure and the ability to demonstrate effectiveness becomes ever more important. On the other hand, if the growing international consensus on promoting aid effectiveness collapses and other donors are seen to ignore or undermine it, EU governments may well feel they need not be constrained by it either. There is therefore a potential danger that the quantity and quality of aid might decrease, should EU governments come to feel they are rowing against the international tide at the same time as they are trying to deal with growing domestic social and economic problems. On the other hand, that course of events of itself might become less of an issue if emerging donors step in to provide the higher levels of ODA that developing countries require.

Some key issues in effectiveness

The three key principles of the Paris Declaration and AAA (Accra Agenda for Action 2008) are 'ownership, alignment and harmonisation', accompanied by a further two: 'managing for results' and 'mutual accountability'. All these principles must be applied by both donors and partners jointly because their implementation depends on mutual cooperation and effort. Ownership by partner countries, for instance, requires the donor to relinquish, and the partner to assume, the initiative. Leadership by the partner country is essential; if it is not in evidence, donors will quickly fill the vacuum because they will be concerned that their assistance is not being used effectively. Action from one side only is therefore not enough. For some of the principles, though, there is much that donors can do unilaterally to move the process forward. Alignment and, particularly, harmonization require primarily donor action, even though partners must play their part. It is in these areas, therefore, that tangible action by the EU is most evident.

Internally, the EU enshrined its commitment to the Paris Declaration in very clear terms in its development policy statement, 'European consensus on development': 'The EU will take a leading role in implementing the Paris Declaration on improving aid delivery' (European Council, European Commission and European Parliament 2006: para. 32).

The EU also decided to go farther than the Declaration and set its own, higher, targets in four areas.[4] It is useful to highlight a few of these examples of measures EU nations would welcome if emerging donors were to pursue them as well. Furthermore, while some of the effectiveness issues the EU donor group picked up, such as donor fragmentation, are particularly relevant to the EU, others also apply to emerging donors. By and large these are associated, in EU eyes at least, directly with the quality of aid provided.

As a first example the EU has tried to improve the quality of its aid by seeking to reduce, and ultimately eliminate, 'tied' aid. Tying aid by stipulating that it be linked to goods and services provided by the donor country limits partner countries' ability to get the best deals on the open market. As with so many aid quality issues, poor practice is not too serious on a small scale but, as aid volumes increase, so too does the significance of critical issues in terms of negative impact and visibility. Such practices also undermine a donor's claim that it is acting in the best interest of the recipient rather than its own and, in terms of AAA principles, work against both ownership and alignment by blocking full partner control over purchasing. Tied aid is a good example of this. This type of aid was once widespread among EU donors. The EU has been engaged in an 'untying' process for some years (European Commission 2002) and has reached a point where on average only about 10 per cent of aid is tied, though this varies from zero in some member states to 20 per cent in others (Carlsson et al. 2009: 29–30).[5]

The imposition by donors of their own reporting, financial and other procedures, and failing to align them with those of partner countries while refusing to use the latter's systems, is another quality issue. Again, for one-off projects the impact is negligible, but on major programmes or multiple projects it creates parallel systems and duplication, which in turn impose a major burden on administration. This also implies wastage and ineffectiveness.

Harmonization is slightly different in this respect. Any particular donor's procedures are quite probably acceptable in themselves, though some may impose a greater burden on partners than others. Compelling partners to use specific procedures of individual donors can, however, rapidly become a problematic issue in a context of multiple donors. Donors therefore need to be sufficiently self-aware to realize they are not alone, and be open to adapting their practices and requirements to a common harmonized system even at some effort and cost to themselves. New donors must also be sensitive to the efforts that others may already have instituted to harmonize their practices, and ideally should quickly align themselves with those common harmonized approaches.

Another related issue is that of aid fragmentation (see also Chapter 3).[6] There are of course good reasons for growing aid fragmentation, relating particularly to visibility, accountability at home and a lack of confidence in partners. The problem is, however, heavily stressed in the AAA, which makes a strong plea for donors, under partner country leadership, to become proactive in establishing a proper division of labour between themselves, at sector and country level. Because the

EU comprises such a large group of donors, this is also an area it is better placed than many to address in a practical fashion. This is demonstrated in its internal Code of Conduct on Complementarity and Division of Labour from May 2007 (European Council 2007) and should give emerging donors pause for thought. The Code of Conduct encourages EU donors to work together to improve on three types of complementarity: respectively in-country, cross-country and cross-sector. At the same time partner-country leadership is vital because reducing fragmentation beyond a certain point could also result in a loss of choice for recipients and a converse danger of aid monopolies that might not work to the latter's advantage.

Although there is no unanimity on this in the EU, several member states and the EC have been keen promoters of budget support; which is the practice of channelling aid funds directly into the national budgets of partner countries. This ensures the use of partner-country procedures, enhances donor harmonization and reduces aid fragmentation should several donors participate. It is thus a powerful instrument for promoting effectiveness. The EC is one of the strongest proponents of budget support, with more than 40 per cent of the current 10th European Development Fund (EDF) being disbursed in this way (European Commission 2009b: 26). To increase predictability and encourage management by results (another Paris and AAA principle), the Commission has also, since 2008, established 'MDG contracts' with a number of partner countries. Full payment on these contracts is dependent on the partner's achieving certain agreed results from among the MDG targets; but they also provide for a minimum level of 80 per cent of funding over a sustained period of six years through budget support, so that the partner country has plenty of leeway to pursue its own policies for reaching the agreed objectives. Linking aid disbursement to results, in other words 'cash on delivery', is increasingly seen (Birdsall and Savedoff 2010) as one of the best ways of improving both results and recipient country ownership, as well as ensuring accountability.

The foregoing are a few examples of issues generally cited by EU donors when expressing concern about emerging donors entering the field. At bottom lies a perception that because existing donors have put some effort and cost into bettering their practices they do not want to see new donors arriving on the scene and taking advantage of the improved situation (or even worse, undermining it) by simply ignoring previous experience and doing what they like. For example, an EU group that has rather reluctantly agreed to use a recipient government's accounting system for a particular programme does not want to see a new donor join the programme and be 'allowed' to use its own methods at the expense of the group agreement.

One final issue is policy coherence for development (PCD). This is not a core subject of the Paris Declaration and AAA discussion, but is nevertheless increasingly recognized in the EU and the wider DAC group as a major factor in ensuring that development co-operation achieves its goals. For the EU this was an issue that arose in the 1980s, when NGOs and the general public pointed out that policies in sectors such as agriculture, trade or fisheries often had side effects in developing countries which directly undermined EU-funded development cooperation programmes and projects. This concern with policy coherence was written into the Maastricht Treaty and has been further strengthened in its latest iteration, the Lisbon Treaty. Some progress has certainly been made in terms of raising awareness and devising methods to promote PCD (Keijzer 2010). The institutional changes the Lisbon Treaty brought about, in particular the creation of the European External Action Service, in principle should also encourage more joined-up thinking in the conduct of EU external relations, including coherence with the EC's development programme (Koeb 2008). Whether this will have a wider impact on the external policy of EU member states is much less clear. PCD often works against perceived donor self-interest in other policy areas, and requires major political commitment as well as a sophisticated approach to international relations; not to speak of adhering to a long-term view that does not always sit well with the often short-term horizons of normal political processes.

Why should EU donors continue to be concerned by aid quality?

In October 2009 the EC published a report it had commissioned from external consultants entitled *The Aid Effectiveness Agenda: Benefits of a European Approach* (Carlsson et al. 2009). This study concluded that the 'major obstacles to increased cost effectiveness of aid are to be found in the proliferation of donors and implementing organisations and the ensuing fragmentation of aid' (ibid.: vii).

The authors further estimated that, for the EU group, potential savings from improvements in three areas (respectively: predictability of aid, reduced donor proliferation and further untying) could result in annual savings of somewhere between €3 billion and €6 billion. A further €1.4–2.5 billion could be added by reducing the fragmentation of EU aid into hundreds of small projects, and merging many of them into consolidated longer-term programmes. Set against a total €49 billion this represents a potential saving of around 10 per cent of EU aid.

In cost–benefit terms alone, therefore, these represent huge potential savings that partner countries and the EU could be making every year, thereby ensuring that available ODA funds can be stretched that much farther. Apart from this obvious immediate conclusion, the study is indicative of a number of other reasons why the EU is preoccupied with aid effectiveness. First, its publication illustrates a trend towards growing transparency on the part of official EU donors in response to demands for greater accountability, as much from external as domestic circles. The finding cited above is precisely the kind of conclusion that NGOs and members of the European Parliament monitoring the effectiveness of EU aid have long suspected, but find hard to demonstrate convincingly. Secondly, the amounts involved, though still small in relation to GNI, are becoming larger and therefore increasingly newsworthy, particularly in a period of economic downturn. EU aid has never been as extensive as it is now and, as the volume of ODA increases, so too does political pressure to reduce waste. Thirdly, the publication of such a report hints at the importance of public opinion in driving the European aid effectiveness agenda. The EU expects to come under scrutiny from its taxpayers and parliaments on the issue, all the more so as the sums involved increase; it is understandable that public attention and debate about the way in which ODA is delivered should then also grow. By publishing such a report the EC seeks to remain one step ahead of the debate.

Public opinion has thus been a major driver of aid effectiveness in Europe. Compared with many others, European society is open and has high levels of public education and awareness. NGOs and lobbying groups monitor official development aid closely, undertaking critical analyses and publicizing their findings on a continuous and systematic basis.[7] Given modern methods of communication and rapidly improving access to information, European donors must answer questions and accept accountability in a way they never have done before. This phenomenon is also rooted in the fact that over several decades much time and money have been spent by governments and NGOs on development education,[8] raising awareness of the importance of development assistance so as to sustain public interest and thereby increase political support for ODA budgets. European media have extensively reported on issues of poverty and humanitarian need around the world. Inevitably, therefore, Europeans raise questions about the effectiveness of aid and expect politicians to provide answers. Emphasis on effectiveness and a strong critique of waste and corruption have become core components of the political rhetoric of EU development ministers, as they struggle to maintain their international ODA commitments.

Lessons to be drawn

EU donors have a major stake in the current international aid architecture and in consensus on MDGs, ODA targets and aid effectiveness. They have contributed extensively to the definition and establishment of the aid agenda and have invested heavily in dialogue, monitoring and assessment processes to enhance quality and transparency. As a group they contribute 60 per cent of global ODA. They accept there is much farther to go and that agreed targets are not yet fully met, but there is also a view that the EU has already done much to demonstrate leadership and respond to the demands of developing countries for improving the system. In such circumstances member countries are not likely to walk away from the system, but it is also not a big step from there to contending that others should contribute more. The EU's commitment inevitably remains vulnerable to political change and continuing public support from voters. Hence in harsher economic and financial climes, and at a time when emerging economies are seen to grow faster than those of Europe, it would not be surprising to see EU governments argue that they will find it politically difficult to maintain their commitment to the 0.7 per cent ODA/GNI target and the Paris principles unless other donors, including those from emerging countries, also participate.

The lesson from the Paris and Accra dialogue on aid effectiveness is first and foremost that ownership by the partner country is vital, particularly if it is accepted that at some level all aid involves self-interest from the donor side. This needs to be countered through partner-country ownership. Secondly, alignment with partner policy in general, and in particular through the use of country systems, helps to increase ownership and reduce waste. Thirdly, harmonization on the donor side may require some effort, but at the same time reduces transaction costs on the partner side and helps to avoid duplication. Donor practices such as tied aid and fragmentation also need to be tackled. Fragmentation causes major difficulties in terms of effectively increasing the chance of denied ownership and of increasing transaction costs, duplication and waste. At the same time partners need to have their say in this issue because some degree of fragmentation creates choice, and if all aid came from one source partners would be faced with a monopoly that would also tend to reduce ownership.

The report of the latest Monitoring Survey of the implementation of the Paris Declaration in 2011 (OECD 2011) argues that progress is being made, but only the target of coordinated technical cooperation had been achieved by 2010. The report highlights two areas of particular progress: a tripling in the proportion of countries with sound national development strategies since 2005; and a rise in the number of results-oriented frameworks to monitor progress against national development priorities in developing countries. On the other hand, progress was weak in some areas, including donor use of country financial systems, donor communication of information on future aid to individual developing countries, and non-systematic capturing of aid for the government sector in developing country budgets and public accounts.

Although it is still too early to say whether the implementation of the Paris Declaration agenda has produced major improvements, the value of the individual principles is already well established. They have been extensively discussed between donors and partners and between official and non-governmental participants. There is little doubt that they constitute a very widely accepted standard of best practice on both sides of the international development partnership. Nonetheless, it is clear that it is vital to avoid too technocratic an approach to the problem: more effective aid, though necessary, is not sufficient to achieve development aims. Increasing calls for greater stress on development effectiveness are therefore important, but these pertinent reminders should not allow donors to sidestep or downplay the fundamental importance of better-quality aid.

The EU remains committed to the Paris Declaration and AAA principles and, as ODA levels rise, EU donors' interest in aid effectiveness will grow as they find it increasingly difficult to justify to voters the need for further increases. Paradoxically, while developing countries argue for higher volumes of aid, the higher the level the greater the demands for effectiveness and accountability. Equally, with larger amounts of aid comes greater pressure for recipients to adopt donor values and standards in areas such as democracy and human rights. Conversely, if European governments were once again to feel that they could justify ODA increases only in self-interest terms, there would probably be a return to such practices as tied aid and a consequent reduction in effectiveness.

Aid inevitably comes with strings attached and it is logical that development partners should look to diversify their sources of ODA, or seek other sources of development finance. From a developing country standpoint the arrival of emerging donors with different approaches to aid is to be welcomed, even though for the time being their ODA contribution remains small. Were it to substantially increase, however, the EU's current dominant position in global ODA would be challenged. This could well be to the advantage of partner countries, but if the EU experience is anything to go by, it also seems likely that as emerging donors substantially increase their ODA they will come under the same kind of domestic political pressure for improved effectiveness and accountability as is currently felt by EU governments.

Notes

1 Based on the Treaty these words have specific meanings in the EU context. Coordination refers to coordination between the aid programmes of the European Commission and the bilateral programmes of the member states. Complementarity also refers to this relationship but pushes it one stage farther by saying that these programmes should be complementary between each other. Finally, coherence refers to coherence between development policy and other EU policies in other sectors, for instance foreign policy, trade policy, the EU's Common Agriculture Policy, fisheries policy, etc. For more information, see www.three-cs.net.

2 Stokke (2005) provides a good analysis of the various factors that prompted rethinking on development aid among DAC donors during this period.

3 In 2009, total EU ODA reached 0.42 per cent of EU GNI whereas the intermediary target the EU set itself was to reach 0.56 per cent of GNI in 2010 so as to meet the 0.7 per cent by 2015 (European Commission 2010).

4 The four areas where the EU decided to push for higher targets than the Paris Declaration demanded are capacity-building through coordinated multi-donor programmes, the use of country systems, including through greater use of budget support, the avoidance of new programme implementation units, and the coordination of donor missions (European Council, European Commission and European Parliament 2006: para. 32).

5 As the authors also point out, European Commission aid is strictly speaking still more or less entirely tied

because its aid agreements, such as the Cotonou Agreement, specify that purchasing of goods and services can only be done from the countries signatory to the agreement; so in the case of Cotonou, from all ACP and EU member states, but not from others.

6 Here, for simplicity, we use the overall term of aid fragmentation, but Carlsson et al. (2009: 14) follow the World Bank in distinguishing between 'donor proliferation' as the number of donors in a country and the 'fragmentation of aid' as the number of donor-funded activities.

7 The regular publication of the Reality of Aid reports (www.realityofaid. org) is a good example of how NGOs monitor aid over sustained periods of years in an increasingly sophisticated manner.

8 The former EU budget line for Co-financing of NGOs (1976–2007 – superseded by a new budget line with somewhat different rules) traditionally set aside 10 per cent for the funding of development education work by EU NGOs in Europe, an allocation which in some years rose to around €20 million.

References

Accra Agenda for Action (2008) site resources.worldbank.org/ACCRAEXT/ Resources/4700790-1217425866038/ AAA-4-SEPTEMBER-FINAL-16h00.pdf, September.

African Development Bank (AfDB) (2010) *From Aid Effectiveness to Development Effectiveness*, Issues Papers for Roundtable Debates, Second Regional Meeting on Aid Effectiveness, 4/5 November, Tunis.

Birdsall, N. and W. D. Savedoff (2010) *Cash on Delivery: A New Approach to Foreign Aid*, Washington, DC: Center for Global Development.

Carlsson, B. T., C. B. Schubert and S. Robinson (2009) *The Aid Effectiveness Agenda: Benefits of a European Approach*, Study prepared for the European Commission by HTSPE Ltd, Hemel Hempstead, 14 October.

European Commission (2002) *Untying: Enhancing the effectiveness of aid*, Communication to the Council and European Parliament, COM(2002)639 final, Brussels, 18 November.

— (2009a) *A twelve point action plan in support of the MDGs*, Communication to the Council and European Parliament, COM(2010)159 final, Brussels, 21 April.

— (2009b) *EuropeAid Annual Report 2009*, Luxembourg: Publications Office of the European Union, October.

— (2010) 'EU official development aid reaches record €53.8 billion in 2010', europa-eu-un.net/articles/ en/article_10900_en.htm, accessed 2 January 2012.

European Council (2002) *Council Conclusions on the International Conference on Financing for Development* (Monterrey, Mexico, 18–22 March 2002), Barcelona, 14 March.

— (2003) *A Secure Europe in a Better World: European Security Strategy*, Brussels, 12 December.

— (2007) *Code of Conduct on Complementarity & Division of Labour in Development Policy*, No. 9090/07, Brussels, 15 May.

— (2008) *Report on the Implementation of the European Security Strategy – Providing Security in a Changing World*, S407/08, Brussels, 11 December.

European Council, European Commission and European Parliament (2006) 'The European consensus on development', *Official Journal of the European Union*, C46, 24 February.

Keijzer, N. (2010) 'EU Policy Coherence for Development: from moving the goalposts to results based management', Discussion Paper 101, Maastricht: ECDPM.

Koeb, E. (2008) 'A more political EU external action: implications of the Treaty of Lisbon for the EU's relations with developing countries', *InBrief*, 21, Maastricht: ECDPM.

OECD (Organisation for Economic Co-operation and Development) (2008) '2008 Survey on Monitoring the Paris Declaration', *Making Aid More Effective by 2010*, Paris: OECD.

— (2011) '2011 Survey on Monitoring the Paris Declaration', *Aid Effectiveness 2005–10: Progress in implementing the Paris Declaration*, Paris: OECD.

Riddell, R. (2007) *Does Foreign Aid Really Work*, Oxford: Oxford University Press.

Stokke, O. (2005) 'The changing international and conceptual environments of development co-operation', in P. Hoebink and O. Stokke, *Perspectives on European Development Cooperation*, London: Routledge.

PART THREE

NEW ACTORS, NEW INNOVATIONS

5 | BRAZIL: TOWARDS INNOVATION IN DEVELOPMENT COOPERATION

Enrique Saravia

Brazil's foreign policy drivers

I think President Lula will forgive me for saying this – he said to me, 'When I was leader of the trade unions, I blamed the government; when I became leader of the opposition, I blamed the government; when I became the government, I blamed Europe and America.' ... [H]e recognises, as we do, that this is a global problem. (British prime minister Gordon Brown, reflecting on the financial crisis one day before the London G20 Summit, 2009)

Emerging countries are today performing a transitional role in international development cooperation. The challenges presented by a rapidly evolving global environment over the past few decades centre on three main issues: overcoming financial crises, dealing with climate change, and eradicating poverty. These problems and the responses to them have been reshaping the political decision-making process and the nature of cooperative schemes themselves. As a result, current development cooperation structures represent a novel coexistence between old and new partners, and the development of old and new strategies based on old and new values. This transitional role applies especially to the G5 group of nations; its members (Brazil, China, India, Mexico and South Africa) share some special characteristics, among them a maturing political system doing its best to cope with enormous social, demographic and economic problems in their domestic affairs.

While G5 countries have been engaged in various forms of development cooperation for many years, their growing economic influence and a concomitant increase in the availability of development funds have prompted greater international interest in their activities over the past few years. At the same time, these countries have begun to examine their development assistance policies more closely, and to stress such issues as evaluation and monitoring procedures, and more clear direction in their programmes. They are evolving new principles suited to this task while also trying to develop new concepts of international cooperation; for example, by substituting the traditional dichotomy between 'donor' and 'recipient' with the idea of partnership directed to a common aim.

Hence, G5 nations are occupying a central position in the debate within the still somewhat exclusive G20. At the same time, in their own regions and among themselves they are playing a leading role in the promotion of South–South cooperation (SSC). Understanding global currents and their driving forces, representing their own national, and the broader Southern, interest, participating in decisions on international rights and obligations, dealing with the legacy of historical injustices, and defining innovative strategies to promote more equitable development, are often contradictory challenges.

The task of dealing with them falls primarily within the purview of national foreign policies. In this context, the action of former president Luiz Inácio Lula da Silva ('Lula') in calling on Brazil to help overcome the global financial crisis immediately before the 2009 G20 summit in London illustrates his country's active role in international affairs. The issue addressed by British prime minister Gordon Brown, citing President Lula's personal background, is this: what kind of global architecture in international development cooperation is Brazil designing? It is that question which this chapter tries to address.

The scenario outlined above, however, is necessary but not sufficient to answer the question. Brazilian foreign policy drivers are not led merely by government policies and governmental actions. In fact, Brazil's political stance in international development cooperation is shaped much more by state policies and institutions than by those of the government of the day. To quote José Saraiva, director-general of the Brazilian Institute of International Relations (IBRI), a private think tank:

> There are lessons in these fifty years that should serve as foundations for future ambitions. The major lesson is the national society strength to encourage a country that, calm and optimistic, uses peaceful means to [promote] its sovereign [interests] without ... violence and [with impeccable] respect to the [idea] of international [comity]. Brazilian foreign policy, being State policy, knew how to work with ... international society ... correcting distortions from within and ... outside the country. (Saraiva 2006)

It is important to stress that Brazil's foreign policy has been a real state policy since the times of Emperor Peter II, who ruled the country from 1840 to 1889. The main policy foundations were established by José Maria da Silva Paranhos, Jr, Baron of Rio Branco, minister of foreign affairs from 1902 to 1912. Brazil's foreign policy has been consistent from then on. All governments, both right- and left-wing, dictatorial or democratic, were respectful of those foundations. With very rare exceptions, Brazilian ministers of foreign affairs have been members of the permanent diplomatic service.

The most recent presidents, Fernando Henrique Cardoso (1995–2002), Luis Inácio 'Lula' da Silva (2003–10) and Dilma Roussef, who came to power in 2011, had career diplomats as foreign affairs ministers. Although the particular political emphasis differed depending on the president's ideology, the main trends were maintained.

Under President Lula, Brazil's foreign policy priorities focused first on South America, and particularly Argentina; secondly, on the twenty-three West African nations; and thirdly, on the emergent powers, namely China, India, Mexico and South Africa, considered as a bloc. Nevertheless, the traditional links with Europe and North America were preserved (Guimarães 2007). Consequently, Brazil's foreign cooperation is based on those policy priorities.

From the formal point of view, Brazilian policies for international cooperation are rooted in its 1988 constitution (Article 4, para. IX). It explicitly states that 'the Federative Republic of Brazil is governed in its international relations by the following principles: ... cooperation among people for the progress of humanity' (ibid.). Accordingly, national legislation[1] assumes that international cooperation programmes fall within the ambit of the Ministério das Relaçoes Exteriores (MRE: Ministry of Foreign Affairs, traditionally known as the 'Itamaraty').

MRE, responsible to the presidency for formulating and executing foreign policy, defines as its fundamental principles the peaceful solution of disputes, non-intervention in the affairs of other states and – mainly since the formation of the United Nations in 1945 – concerned but independent participation in international forums.

Through MRE, Brazil concerns itself with several areas of international cooperation, including humanitarian, military, scientific, technological and technical schemes. Given its increasing importance and the ready availability of structured information, however, this chapter concerns itself mainly with international technical cooperation for development, as defined by the Brazilian government through the Agência Brasileira de Cooperação (ABC: Brazilian Cooperation Agency) established in 1987 (see section on the agency below).

Brazil's international technical cooperation

The first initiative to implement an international technical cooperation system in Brazil had taken place in 1950 with the creation of the National Commission for Technical Assistance (CNAT). Its main task was to establish priorities between Brazilian institutions seeking technical cooperation from partners in the industrialized world. CNAT itself investigated legal issues related to Brazilian participation in technical assistance programmes in the UN and eventually in the Organization of American States. At that time, technical cooperation was strongly linked to domestic economic and industrial development policies. The USA, Japan, Canada and Germany were the main donors to Brazil; the country itself supported initiatives, through UNDP, other international organizations and non-governmental organizations (NGOs) (Vaz 2009: 204).

By 1969 the government had decided to centralize the main operational responsibilities for international technical cooperation in the Under-Secretariat of Economic and Technical International Cooperation (Subin), attached to the president's Secretariat of Planning (Seplan). The MRE's Division of Technical Cooperation was responsible for political aspects.

In the three decades from 1950 to 1980 Brazil was a net recipient of technical help and assistance. During the 1970s and 1980s, however, a strong effort was made to strengthen links with African countries. Indeed, the first agreements between Brazil and other developing nations were negotiated with Africa and Latin America, especially countries in the Southern Cone (essentially Argentina, Chile, Paraguay and Uruguay). After the Buenos Aires Action Plan was approved in 1978, Brazil intensified its activities in technical cooperation with other developing countries (TCDC). Before the Buenos Aires conference the country had approved only twenty-eight TCDC projects; by the 1980s the number had grown to more than six hundred, while at the same time there was a gradual reduction in multilateral and bilateral assistance received by Brazil (ibid.: 207).

The Brazilian Cooperation Agency The ABC was created in September

1987 by Presidential Decree number 94,973, as a department of Fundação Alexandre de Gusmão (Funag), a foundation linked to the MRE. In 1996, however, in what was seen clearly as a recognition of the new relevance of international cooperation for Brazil's foreign policy (ibid.: 209), it was integrated into the General Secretariat of the MRE and became a central operator of the country's foreign policy. Ten years later, the then minister of foreign affairs, Celso Amorim, stated explicitly, for the first time in Brazil's diplomatic history, that technical cooperation was an instrument of national foreign policy (Schmitz et al. 2010: 39).

The Brazilian government's intention was to establish a specialized agency for international technical cooperation combining technical functions and foreign policy. Its objective was to improve the management and coordination of technical cooperation received by Brazil from bilateral and multilateral donors as well as NGOs. Like several countries that had benefited from intensive international cooperation, Brazil had reached a stage of development that brought with it an increased demand for transfer of its knowledge, both from other countries interested in the Brazilian experience, and from international bodies. Over the past decade, ABC has assumed more importance as a participant in the international aid and development system. Its responsibilities are to negotiate, coordinate, implement and monitor Brazilian inward and outward technical cooperation programmes and projects, based on agreements between Brazil and other countries or international organizations.

ABC is organized into seven general departments. They are, respectively:

- technical cooperation between developing countries (CGPD);
- bilateral received technical cooperation (CGRB);
- multilateral received technical cooperation (CGRM);
- cooperation in health, social development, education and professional training (CGDS);
- donor cooperation in agriculture, energy, biofuels and environment (CGMA);
- general coordination of donor cooperation in information technology (IT), e-government, civil defence, urban planning and transportation (CGTI); and
- general coordination of donor or recipient TCDC: horizontal or South–South (CGPD).

Brazilian technical cooperation framework[2]

Concept and pillars ABC's policies are aligned with MRE's foreign policy and the national priorities for development that are defined in Brazil's national plans and programmes. Brazilian international technical cooperation is set against two different principles: received cooperation and horizontal cooperation. The former covers bilateral and multilateral technical cooperation and seeks to acquire the expertise provided by international agencies (multilateral) and more developed countries (bilateral) to accelerate Brazil's own development. The latter also refers to technical cooperation implemented by Brazil with other developing countries, aiming to strengthen political and economic ties with them.

Thus the Brazilian government considers that technical cooperation received from abroad should contribute significantly to its social and economic development and help build autonomy in relevant fields. Similar principles hold for technical cooperation offered by Brazil to other countries. ABC defines the national TCDC mission as intended to strengthen partnerships between Brazil and developing countries through the generation, dissemination and utilization of technical knowledge, for human resources training and for the development and consolidation of their institutions. Inherent in the idea of 'partnership for development' is a belief that partnership must include sharing both effort and benefit. Proposed initiatives are evaluated against their probable effects on recipients and the likelihood of improving standards of living, promoting sustainable development and contributing to social improvement. Prescribed procedures are laid down in order to improve the quality of project negotiation, evaluation and management.

Through both the 1995–2003 government of President Fernando Henrique Cardoso and the subsequent Lula administration, Brazil's foreign policy has been characterized by three major premises. They are:

- promotion of regional integration for achieving economic and social development, peace and stability in its neighbourhood;
- support and promotion of multilateralism on a global level, being actively engaged in international organizations such as the UN and its different agencies, in the World Trade Organization (WTO), and sharing OECD activities as a so-called 'outreach country' in the

context of the Heiligendamm Process (which formalized dialogue between the G5 and the G8); and

- promotion of SSC, as reflected in initiatives such as the Brazil–Africa Forum, regular meetings with Arab countries, an increased number of Brazilian embassies in Africa, and the launch of a dialogue forum between Brazil, India and South Africa (IBSA) (Souza 2009).

It is worth stressing that Brazil has its own special expertise arising from its domestic experience in combating underdevelopment, hunger and health problems: for example, its *bolsa família*, initiated by President Lula da Silva in 2004, which developed into an effective programme of income transfer to the poorest families in exchange for keeping children in schools and having regular health check-ups. Brazil also has the advantage of historic post-colonial and cultural affinities with the developing world, especially South Africa, the Caribbean and Portuguese-speaking countries in Africa and Asia (ibid.).

From formulation to implementation The basic tool for formulating a request for technical cooperation is a document submitted as a *Projeto de cooperação técnica* (PCT: Technical Cooperation Project), which should contain all the necessary information concerning the scope of the work, starting with accurate identification of the problem and the strategies, objectives and results that demarcate future implementation and subsequent monitoring and evaluation.

PCT may be seen as a major driving force in the development of Brazil's technical capabilities, through access to, and incorporation of, knowledge, information, technology, experience and practical application on a non-commercial basis and in all working areas. Through it, the definition of instruments and mechanisms to implement international cooperation receive special attention from the outset. Financial assistance, technical support, personnel training, technology transfer and donation of equipment and materials, among other mechanisms, have been and remain widely used in the application of schemes under the cooperation umbrella.

The main instrument for defining proposed interventions and for planning cooperation is the project plan, embodied in a document that contains the means and ends of the initiative as well as the rationale for the scheme (i.e. its logical framework, assumptions, risks, responsibilities and so on). The plan is, therefore, the main instrument for proper management of the work, and its structure and methods receive special attention from international organizations and bilateral agencies. In the case of international technical cooperation, which is marked out by the promotion of knowledge transfer without any commercial connotation, the stress is on expert advice, staff training and support for the infrastructure available to the recipient institution.

Finally, there are two ways of effecting an international technical cooperation project: international implementation (direct) and national implementation (indirect). Although ABC is not forthcoming on the finer details of each modality, it does indicate that national implementation is the preferred course whenever projects are totally or partly funded from the federal budget.

Monitoring The key instrument for supporting international technical cooperation initiatives is *Sistema de Informações Gerenciais de Acompanhamento de Projetos* (Sigap: management information system on project monitoring). It aims to organize information related to monitoring of international technical cooperation projects from the perspective of strategic decisions.

Through Sigap, issues of daily project implementation are addressed using the administrative module (Sigap Data Transmission). This channel handles monthly data on implementation agencies, consultants' registration and staff contracts, as well as on such matters as travel costs, the budget status of the project, and the position as regards suppliers of goods and services.

Selection criteria[3] TCDC constitutes both an instrument of external policy and an auxiliary tool for promoting social and economic development in recipient countries. It aims to strengthen political, economic and trading relations between these countries and foster the transfer of technology and experience on a non-commercial basis.

The following guidelines for TCDC have been adopted by the Brazilian government:

- to emphasize projects that are in line with national development programmes and priorities;
- to give priority to schemes with high multiplier effects and which can be sustainable beyond project termination;

- to give priority to projects that may present greater impact by avoiding fragmentation and dissipation of effort; and
- to give preference to projects in which counterpart resources are clearly defined by the partner country.

Technical cooperation projects are characterized by joint execution of an agreed work plan. This is usually reflected in a range of activities that aim at the transfer, absorption and/or development of specific experience. In this regard TCDC projects envisage the implementation of activities to ensure the flow of experience, or the generation of information, essentially by means of:

- consultancy services;
- personnel training;
- research; and
- improvement of the executing agencies' infrastructure as required for the execution of the work plan. This includes, for example, the procurement or leasing of equipment and written material.

These operational mechanisms, however, are not necessarily included in each and every technical cooperation project. Inclusion depends on the nature and importance of project objectives.

The project document, which constitutes the main instrument for assessing the feasibility of implementing the programme put forward by the partner institutions, should contain information concerning:

- the proposing institution(s);
- existing national initiatives in related sectors, or the policies and programmes that indicate the priority given to this sector;
- planning of the scheme under review, including its objectives, expected outputs, activities to be carried out, work plan, technical cooperation requested; and the counterpart resources offered, including cost estimates.

Against these guidelines, as well as those of other relevant government policy frameworks, Brazil's TCDC is concentrated in the following areas:

- South American countries, especially the country members of Mercado Común del Sur (Mercosur);
- Haiti;
- African countries, especially members of Países Africanos de

Língua Oficial Portuguesa (Palop: the Community of Portuguese Language African Countries, comprising Angola, Mozambique, Cape Verde, Guinea Bissau and São Tomé e Principe), as well as East Timor;
- other Latin American and Caribbean countries;
- support to the Comunidade dos Países de Língua Portuguesa (CPLP: the Community of Portuguese Language Countries, comprising Palop members, and Portugal and Brazil); and
- increasing triangular cooperation initiatives with international organizations and developing countries (through their own agencies).

Brazilian technical cooperation initiatives

Brazil is still a recipient of bilateral aid from developed countries. According to ABC, Brazil receives approximately $100 million annually in technical cooperation from bilateral donors. Counterpart contributions from Brazilian partners provide an additional $100 million. Overall, bilateral activity in Brazil may be divided into six main sectors: the environment, primarily linked to protection of the Amazon forest (40 per cent), agriculture (22 per cent), health (12 per cent), industry (10 per cent), social sectors (10 per cent) and public administration (6 per cent). Brazil's major bilateral partners are Japan (representing approximately 56 per cent of technical cooperation in Brazil) and Germany (approximately 14 per cent). Both programmes are primarily project-based and span a range of sectors (Souza 2009).

Unfortunately, neither MRE nor ABC permits free access to annual information. Thus, according to an MRE publication of July 2007, the main sectors that benefited from Brazil's horizontal cooperation in the developing world were: professional qualifications (22.4 per cent); health (18.8 per cent); farming and cattle-raising (14.9 per cent); education (10.2 per cent); social development (6.7 per cent); legislative assistance (6.4 per cent); and the environment (4.3 per cent). Information on Brazil's main partners is available only at the continental level: main beneficiaries are Africa (52 per cent); South America (18.4 per cent); the Caribbean (15.6 per cent); and Asia and Oceania (9.9 per cent) (MRE 2007).

The most recent study on bilateral aid flows, published in 2010, was carried out by the Brazilian Institute for Applied Economic Research (IPEA) and the ABC. It estimates Brazil's spend at $362.2

million in 2009. Most of Brazil's aid has gone to international organizations (about 77 per cent in 2005–09); technical cooperation has been increasing, from 7.2 per cent in 2005 to 13.5 per cent in 2009 (ONE 2011). Other calculations place it at about $1 billion per year ($480 million for technical cooperation and $450 million for in-kind expertise provided by numerous Brazilian institutions) (Cabral and Weinstock 2010).

Technical cooperation between developing countries Brazilian SSC has consistently increased over time and now plays an important supporting role for the country's foreign policy. Whenever Brazil's president or foreign minister visits a developing country, new agreements are signed, particularly in IT, nutrition programmes, agriculture and biofuels. It seems likely that SSC will grow to become one of the main items on the bilateral diplomatic agenda of developing countries in the twenty-first century.

Latin America and Africa Brazilian development promotion in South America is divided into regional integration projects and bilateral development programmes. The former include, for example, the Mercosur Fund for financing projects to overcome imbalances between Mercosur member states, along with support for smaller countries; and Brazil's engagement in the Inter-American Development Bank (IDB) and the Unión de Naciones Suramericanas (Unasur: Union of South American Nations, integrating Mercosur and the Andean Community of Nations plus Chile, Guyana, Suriname and Venezuela), which was launched in 2008.

Of bilateral Official Development Assistance (ODA), 38 per cent goes to Latin America, mainly Paraguay and the Andean region. The projects are oriented towards infrastructure improvement and education (such as Brazil's *bolsa família* scholarship scheme, and literacy programmes) and health (mainly projects for HIV/AIDS prevention and treatment). Many of these bilateral projects are based on Brazil's own experience, including domestic programmes to combat hunger and poverty and improve access to education and health.

Haiti, where the link between security and development is a key issue, is an interesting case of Brazilian development cooperation in the Caribbean region. Apart from providing financial support and expertise in combating urban violence, Brazil supports basic education and developing programmes for the treatment and prevention of pandemics such as AIDS, while also providing crucial skills and technical personnel. The Brazilian embassy in Haiti plays an important part in coordinating and supervising development programmes in urban and rural areas.

Apart from technical cooperation at government level, Brazilian cooperation is also performed by non-governmental foundations and organizations engaged in programmes of international development cooperation.

A notable example of this is Viva Rio's project to combat youth violence in the shanty towns of Haiti. Viva Rio is an NGO based in Rio de Janeiro. Its main goal is to promote a culture of peace and social development through fieldwork, research and the formulation of public policy. Viva Rio has been working in Haiti since 2005. Their work has intensified since the earthquake of January 2010. After that disaster, the organization decided to proceed with a dual strategy: humanitarian assistance on the ground and mobilization elsewhere. This supports emergency aid and helps Haitians to take their first steps towards reconstruction. Viva Rio is sheltering 320 families (approximately 1,600 people) in Kay Nou (literally 'our home', and Viva Rio's community centre inside Port-au-Prince's deprived neighbourhood of Bel Air). Another NGO with an active international programme is the Rio de Janeiro-based Comitê para Democratização da Informática (CDI: Committee for Democratization of Information Technology), which aims to shrink the digital divide through a large range of promotional and educational activities.

Nevertheless, Brazil's representation among NGOs in the international development context is still relatively small, and it is looking to engage with more civil societies in this area (Souza 2009).

Another important aspect of Brazilian bilateral cooperation is assistance to Portuguese-speaking countries in Africa, where Brazil is mainly engaged in projects providing social development and information and skills for improving agricultural practices. Direct investments in the mining sector, in particular in Mozambique, are also increasing.

Educating and retraining demobilized soldiers is the aim of the Brazil Angola Education Centre as a contribution to Angola's efforts in social integration and national reconstruction. A professional training centre in mechanics, civil construction, electricity generation, clothing and IT was established and the methods employed in the Centre's training and operational activities were subsequently passed to the Instituto Nacional de Emprego e Formação Profissional de Angola (Inefop: Angola National Institute for Employment and Professional Education). The agreement for the programme was signed in 1996 and is being implemented by Brazil's Serviço Nacional de Aprendisagem Industrial (Senai: the Brazilian National Service for Professional Training) and Inefop. The total project cost is $1.8 million with ABC and Senai sharing the $1.3 million cost of Brazil's contribution. Angola's participation through its Ministry of Public Administration, Employment and Social Security (MAPESS) is $514,280. The government of Angola provided the facilities for the Centre and controls the project.

In addition, since 2007 Brazil has cooperated (via the Getulio Vargas Foundation) with the Angolan government in a project to train and organize public service staff. It includes the establishment in 2008 of the National School of Administration (ENAD) in Luanda, training administrative staff and programming and coordinating several courses and seminars, and preparing training modules and other teaching material.

India–Brazil–South Africa (IBSA) The IBSA dialogue forum comprising India, Brazil and South Africa is a noteworthy case of SSC between three emerging powers. The forum was launched in June 2003 with the aim of increasing trilateral cooperation in key areas such as energy and trade, and achieving greater impact by unifying the members' voices in the global arena. While the three countries have more differences than similarities, they share values and interests at the global level, such as promoting democracy, human rights, support for international law and multilateralism, and peace and stability. IBSA funds a facility for development cooperation supported by the UNDP. The fund is currently implementing two major projects: waste collection in Port-au-Prince, Haiti; and agricultural assistance to Guinea-Bissau (see also chapters on India and South Africa).

The debate on SSC South–South technical cooperation is one of the mainstays of Brazilian foreign policy. At first restricted to neighbouring countries, it was subsequently extended to Africa. In due course, Brazilian technical cooperation was made available to Central American countries and East Timor, the only Portuguese-speaking country in

Asia (with the exception of Macau, which is now an administrative region of China).

Solidarity with other developing countries is the driving force behind the programme. Brazilian technical cooperation is demand-driven and not profit-oriented. Its focus is capacity-building and it aims to help partners strengthen their institutions and human resources. Essentially, Brazil adapts successful practices developed at home, under quite similar socio-economic circumstances, to the conditions prevailing in other developing countries. In practical terms, Brazil sends to developing countries experts in a wide range of disciplines, offers scholarships and internships at its research institutes or universities, and donates reasonably complex equipment.

So far, ABC has coordinated or implemented 246 projects in areas in which Brazil can provide a concrete contribution, in particular agriculture, animal husbandry, biofuels (ethanol and biodiesel), education, health (mainly the battle against HIV/AIDS), electoral support (e-voting), urban development, IT (e-government), trade negotiations and sport.

Brazil is a substantial contributor to international funds, managed either by the World Bank or the IDB. Its transfers to the International Development Association of the World Bank, the IDB Special Operations Fund, the African Development Fund, the International Fund for Agricultural Development, the Andean Development Corporation and the Fundo Financeiro para o Desenvolvimento da Bacia do Prata (Fonplata: Fund for the Development of the River Plate Basin) in total amount to more than $1 billion.

Over and above this financial effort, in the past five years Brazil has channelled $55 million exclusively for capacity-building in developing countries. This figure does not take into account the value of training or information transfers and according to international standards should be multiplied by fifteen to arrive at a more realistic figure. In 2008 alone, $30 million was earmarked for the implementation of fifty-two projects in forty-six countries. Special attention is given to 'aid for trade' projects, aimed at capacity-building in such areas as trade negotiations, sanitary and phytosanitary measures, development of small-sized companies, business support services and banking.

In the particular case of technical cooperation, the ABC encourages other Brazilian institutions to discuss with their foreign counterparts the local circumstances, cultural environment and peculiar needs in order to tailor technical assistance more precisely.

TABLE 5.1 Brazil: technical cooperation agreements with developing countries

Africa	Portuguese-speaking African countries (Palop), South Africa, Algeria, Benin, Cameroon, Côte d'Ivoire, Egypt, Gabon, Ghana, Mali, Morocco, Namibia, Nigeria, Kenya, Senegal, Togo, Zaire, Zimbabwe
Latin America and Caribbean	Argentina, Bolivia, Chile, Colombia, Costa Rica, Cuba, Dominican Republic, El Salvador, Ecuador, Guatemala, Guiana, Honduras, Jamaica, Mexico, Nicaragua, Panama, Paraguay, Peru, Suriname, Uruguay, Venezuela
Asia and Middle East	China, East Timor, India, Iraq, Israel, Kuwait, Lebanon, Palestine and Saudi Arabia

Despite the progress achieved so far, there are still some obstacles to SSC expansion. This is particularly true given a lack of well-defined national policies for economic development, as well as the absence of institutional support structures in some developing countries. There is also limited documentation on SSC successes, or credible South–South project databases, or reliable records of South–South financial flows; and there is no standard methodology to ensure quantification of non-financial contributions that are typical of much South–South technical cooperation. For Brazil, in particular, where the legal framework in this area dates back to the days when it was a net recipient of aid, one of the most important challenges ahead is to gain approval from the Congress for specific legislation to regulate SSC in its different forms.

In spite of ABC's many achievements and successes there are some management and financial deficiencies that affect its performance as the main agency for Brazil's cooperation policy. The most important of these are, first, the planning process, bedevilled by ad hoc demands and undue concentration on too few institutions; secondly, difficulties posed by the need to coordinate a growing number of initiatives and demands within a largely uncoordinated system; and thirdly, unsatisfactory financial management.

As to the planning process, it is important to recognize that currently there are more than one hundred institutions running technical cooperation initiatives. Aside from ABC, the most important at the government level are Empresa Brasileira de Pesquisa Agropecuária (Embrapa: Brazilian Agricultural Research Corporation), the Fundação Oswaldo Cruz (Fiocruz: the Oswaldo Cruz Foundation, a public health institution associated with the Ministry of Health) and the Conselho Nacional de Desenvolvimento Científico e Tecnológico (National Council for Scientific and Technological Development). In addition, some state governments are involved; among them those of São Paulo, Rio de Janeiro, Minas Gerais, and Rio Grande do Sul.

The issue of coordination is somewhat simpler and concerns prestige and bureaucratic standing. Since the other ministries consider ABC to be only one arm of the MRE, they do not consider themselves obliged to establish coordination channels with it.

The third problem arises because there is no monitoring system in place; or at least, no centralized register of the resources devoted to international technical cooperation. In 2010, the government decided to establish, as a monitoring agency, Cooperação Brasileira para o Desenvolvimento Internacional (Coop-Bradi: Brazilian Cooperation Resources for International Development) with the aim of establishing through accurate quantitative accounting a list of projects and their cost 2005–09 (Schmitz et al. 2010). The study, carried out by ABC and the Office of the President, established that the total funding for the period was about $1.75 billion, divided between humanitarian assistance, scholarships for foreigners and technical, scientific and technological cooperation, and contributions to international organizations (Brazil 2010).

Brazilian triangular cooperation Brazil is one of the most active emerging countries in triangular cooperation. In a 2009 UNDP survey, Brazil appeared as a key pivotal country among all responding donors and international organizations on triangular cooperation (UNDP 2009: 145).

With regard to developed nations and multilateral agencies, Brazil has sought to expand trilateral cooperation in initiatives under way in Portuguese-speaking Africa and in East Timor, Latin America and Haiti. In one of Brazil's own domestic reforestation schemes it is in partnership with Spain. It is also associated with Canada in mass vaccination programmes; with the World Bank in school feeding; with the UN population fund in combating violence against women; with the International Labour Organization in prevention of child labour; with the Inter-American Institute for Cooperation in Agriculture; and with the IBSA Fund in the area of solid waste collection. Brazil and Canada (an important donor to Haiti) have signed several agreements to cooperate in that country's education, health and social development programmes, while it is cooperating with the USA to increase ethanol production in El Salvador, Jamaica and the Dominican Republic.

Brazil is associated with Argentina in a project in Haiti aimed at increasing food security for low-income families. Designed to promote organic farming in urban and rural areas, it involves drilling wells and the cultivation of vegetables ('truck farming'), and is an adaptation of Argentina's successful Pro-Huerta scheme.

Regarding specifically African initiatives, Brazil has negotiated a project, partly funded by Norway, to bring Angolan and Guinea-Bissau nationals to Brazil for training in public administration. A memorandum of understanding has been signed with the USA with the aim of eradicating malaria in São Tomé e Príncipe and providing IT for the National Assembly of Guinea-Bissau.

For Brazil, triangular projects are likely to grow, even though it harbours reservations (as do other developing countries) about retaining its independence and not being seen as an implementer of Northern initiatives by other Southern countries. Cooperation with Northern partners in such projects has a number of advantages, including allowing Brazil to increase its assistance to other Southern countries and facilitating technology transfers.

Conclusion

As Brazil understands SSC, it is not about imposing knowledge or information, even of the most advanced technology available. It is, rather, to share experience with partners in specific fields and is in that way a learning process as well as an aid process.

During the UN's World Urban Forum 5, held in Rio de Janeiro in March 2010, the vice-director of ABC affirmed that cooperation is concerned with promoting the spread of knowledge and that it necessarily demands deep involvement from the recipient partner. Technical assistance and information-sharing are its motive force.

Accordingly, as Brazil's minister of cities stated at the same event, cooperation needs to be understood as aiming towards an autonomous and independent future: it is necessary not to give a man a fish but to teach him how to catch fish. The best way to achieve this end is to establish a symmetry of means and ends, find common working methods and reinforce ways to work together, bound by a common purpose.

Notes

1 Law no. 10,683, 28 May 2003; Decree no. 5,979, 6 December 2006.

2 The main concepts of this chapter are extracted from official Ministry of Foreign Affairs documents, but the author is responsible for all the statements herein contained.

3 This topic was mainly extracted from ABC's Guidelines for Presentation of Project Proposals of Technical Cooperation among Developing Countries: TCDC.

References

BBC Brasil (2009) 'Brown cita críticas de Lula em entrevista com Obama', www.bbc.co.uk/portuguese/noticias/2009/04/090401_brown_obama_dg.shtml, accessed 13 February 2010.

Brazil (2008) The Brazilian Experience, Ministry of Foreign Affairs, high-level symposium 'Trends in development cooperation: South–South and triangular cooperation and aid effectiveness', Cairo, 19/20 January.

— (2010) Cooperação brasileira para o desenvolvimento internacional: 2005–2009, Presidency of the Republic, Instituto de Pesquisa Econômica Aplicada, Agência Brasileira de Cooperação, Brasilia: Ipea/ABC.

Bresser-Pereira, L. C. (1999) 'Reflexões sobre a reforma gerencial brasileira de 1995', Revista do Serviço Público, 50: 5–29.

Cabral, L. and J. Weinstock (2010) 'Brazil: an emerging aid player', ODI Briefing Paper, October.

CIDA-Canadian International Cooperation Agency (2005) Canada's Cooperation Strategy in Brazil 2005–2010, www.acdi-cida.gc.ca/CIDAWEB/acdicida.nsf/En/NIC-22312535-N32, accessed 30 January 2009.

CLAD (2008) 'Experiencias de modernisación en la organisación y gestión del estado', in Administration, LACFD (ed.), Sistema Integrado y Analítico de Información sobre Reforma del Estado Gestión y Políticas Públicas, Caracas.

Gore, A. (1995) Common Sense Government: Works Better and Costs Less, New York: Random House.

Guimarães, S. P. (2007) 'O mundo multipolar e a integração Sul-Americana', Comunicação e política, 25(3): 169–89, www.cebela.org.br/imagens/Materia/04NCT02 per cent20Samuel.pdf.

Marini, C. (2002) 'O contexto contemporâneo da administração pública na América Latina', Revista do Serviço Público, 53: 31–52.

MRE (Ministério das Relações Exteriores (2007) South–South Cooperation activities carried out by Brazil, Brasilia, Secretariat General for Cooperation and Trade Promotion.

— (2010a) Agência Brasileira de Cooperação, www.abc.gov.br/, accessed 13 February 2010.

— (2010b) O papel do Itamaraty, www.
mre.gov.br/index.php?option=com_
content&task=view&id=6&Itemid=
342, accessed 13 February 2010.

ONE (2011) The Data Report 2011,
s3.amazonaws.com/one.org/pdfs/
dr2011.pdf, accessed 30 October 2011.

Osborne, D. and T. Gaebler (1992)
*Reinventing Government: How the
Entrepreneurial Spirit is Transforming
the Public Sector*, New York: Penguin
Books.

Saraiva, J. (2006) Instituto Brasileiro de
Relações Internacionais, ibri-rbpi.
org/2006/09/22/o-ibri-e-o-brasil-
50-anos/, accessed 9 February 2010.

Saravia, E. (1989) 'The Brazilian privat-
isation programme', *School of Public
and Environmental Affairs Review*,
10: 18–24.

Schmitz, G. de O. et al. (2010)
'Cooperação brasileira para o desenvolvimento internacional: primeiro
levantamento de recursos investidos
pelo governo federal', *IPEA, Boletim
de Economia e Política Internacional*,
3, July, pp. 35–45.

Souza, S.-L. J. de (2009) 'Brazil as a

new international development
actor, South–South cooperation and
the IBSA initiative', www.nsi-ins.
ca/english/events/DAW/2_de per
cent20Sousa.pdf, accessed 30 January 2009.

UNDP (United Nations Development
Programme) (2009) *Enhancing
South–South and Triangular Coopera-
tion*, New York: UNDP.

Vaz, A. C. (2009) 'La experiencia de Brasil en la cooperación para el desarrollo: trayectoria e institucionalidad',
in C. Ayala Martinez and J. Perez
Pineda (eds), *México y los países de
renta media en la cooperación para
el desarrollo: ¿hacia dónde vamos?*,
Mexico: Instituto Mora/FLACSO
México/CIDEAL.

Viva Rio (2010) About Viva Rio, www.
vivario.org.br/publique/cgi/cgilua.
exe/sys/start.htm?tpl=home&User
ActiveTemplate=_vivario_en,
accessed 13 February 2010.

Wahrlich, B. M. D. S. (1983) *Reforma
administrativa na era de Vargas*, Rio
de Janeiro: Ed. da Fundação Getulio
Vargas.

6 | CHINA'S EVOLVING AID LANDSCAPE: CROSSING THE RIVER BY FEELING THE STONES¹

Zhou Hong

Introduction

China is far from an 'emerging' donor. Indeed, its foreign aid 'has as deep a history and as broad a range of experience as any established in the West' (Brautigam 1998: 4).

In August 2010, China celebrated the sixtieth anniversary of its foreign aid history. In April 2011 it published the first ever White Paper on development cooperation. From 2004 to 2009, China's foreign aid spending grew by 29.4 per cent annually.

But China defines its foreign aid as 'a model with its own characteristics' (State Council Information Office 2011) to distinguish itself from traditional donor–recipient relations. China's development aid is sometimes given by way of grants and interest-free or low-interest loans, but more often through aid in kind, rather than cash; through infrastructural projects, equipment and technology packages, teams of medical and other experts, training classes and scholarships. China also provides humanitarian aid and other financial assistance in the event of natural disasters. In recent years China has also written off considerable debt owed by friendly Heavily Indebted Poor Countries (HIPCs). The Chinese government White Paper on China's foreign aid indicated that China provided a total of ¥256.29 billion ($41 billion) by the end of 2009, of which ¥106.2 billion were grants, ¥76.45 billion were in the form of interest-free loans and ¥73.55 billion were low-interest loans. By the end of 2009 China had cancelled ¥25.58 billion in debts from forty-nine HIPCs (ibid.). Close to 40 per cent of China's recipients are least developed countries, 23.4 per cent are low-income countries; close to 20 per cent are mid-low-income countries.

Over the past sixty years, China has undertaken about two thousand development aid projects in more than one hundred countries and regions, among which more than two-thirds are in the least developed and other low-income countries. Africa took 45.7 per cent of the share, Asia 32.8 per cent, and Latin America and the Caribbean 12.7 per cent; these projects included railways, highways, power plants, water conservation schemes, farms, schools, hospitals and sports venues, all of them aimed at improving everyday life in recipient countries. In a wider context, from 1963 to 2009 some 21,000 Chinese medical personnel have given treatment to 260 million people in other developing countries, and from 1953 to 2009 China offered training to more than 120,000 people from developing countries (ibid.).

In terms of foreign aid, China enjoys twin status: first as a developing donor country and secondly as a recipient of aid for its own development. From this standpoint, it sees aid as falling into two categories. In financial transfers from developed to underdeveloped countries, the donor country 'assume[s] the responsibility of helping underdeveloped countries. Assistance should be provided selflessly, with no conditions attached. ... underdeveloped countries should make poverty eradication a central task' (Wen 2008).

Conversely, in financial transfers between developing countries, 'mutual [benefit] and cooperation' should be promoted on the basis of equal partnership. China also distances itself in principle from the aid programmes of OECD countries, which hold 'good governance' and 'conditionality' as prerequisites for assistance.

China's foreign aid record may be divided into three main periods. The first began with the foundation of the People's Republic of China in 1949; the second covers the period from the 'reform' and 'open-door policy' initiated in 1978, to the end of the last century; and the third started immediately thereafter. These distinct periods differ in policies, methods and management mechanisms, in response to shifts in the international and domestic operating environment. Policy fundamentals, however, remain unchanged.

First period: beginnings of China's foreign aid – internationalism and patriotism

China began to provide foreign aid at the beginning of the 1950s, when the country was under blockade and embargo by the United States and its allies. In line with its 'leaning-to-one-side' foreign policy, China entered into all-round cooperation agreements with the Soviet Union and other socialist countries, receiving economic aid from the USSR while at the same time adopting 'proletariat internationalism' and providing military and economic aid to North Korea, North Vietnam and Mongolia. Shortly afterwards, it initiated economic and technical assistance programmes for some friendly countries in Asia and Africa.

China's foreign aid is based on values of internationalism, especially with regard to those countries with similar histories: as then chairman of the People's Republic of China, Mao Zedong, put it:

China is a land with an area of 9.6 million km² and a population of 600 million, and it ought to make a greater contribution to humanity (Mao 1956) ... the people who have won their revolution should aid people struggling for their liberation. This is our obligation of internationalism. (Mao 1963)

Premier Zhou Enlai gave a more specific interpretation of the thinking behind Chinese aid programmes when he said:

The starting point of our foreign aid is, in the spirit of proletarian internationalism, to support fraternal countries in their socialist construction and enhance the strength of the whole socialist camp, support countries in their efforts to win independence, the newly independent countries in their efforts to develop their national economies by self-reliance and consolidate the fruits of their independence and enhance the anti-imperialist forces of the people of all countries. When we aid our fraternal countries and newly independent countries and they have become stronger, it would weaken the imperialist forces. This is [a] tremendous assistance to us. In the past, few people advocated for aiding other countries. That is entirely wrong. In the future, with the growth of our economy, we should conscientiously strengthen our foreign aid within our own capacity and strive to make greater contribution to internationalism. (Zhou 1964)

Mao and Zhou conveyed two principles behind foreign aid: first, that in order to help break down its own economic and political isolation from the West and having achieved its own degree of independence, China should support other nations similarly striving for their independence and the development of their national economies; secondly, that as an economic laggard, China's interests were identical with those of other developing countries attempting to establish a more equitable and reasonable world political and economic order. Aid to other developing countries was intended to improve China's own external conditions for development, and it was therefore in

China's national interest from both an international and a domestic perspective to enter into mutual aid programmes.

The eight principles of foreign aid There have been several step changes in China's foreign aid. The first came at the beginning of the 1960s when the USSR terminated its assistance to China and withdrew all its experts and specialists, in consequence of which economic, trade and diplomatic relations between the two countries were greatly reduced. During this period China's economic and technical cooperation with developing countries increased rapidly. In order to make foreign aid more effectively serve China's general international strategy and break the Western blockade and embargo, Zhou Enlai advanced eight principles for foreign aid when he met Ghana's president Kwame Nkrumah in January 1964.[2]

These eight principles were unique for their time and their application brought about some important results. Chinese aid enabled colonized countries to better understand China's own position, while China came to represent a source of development aid entirely different in its approach from that of Western donors. Some recipient countries went so far as to propose submission of the eight principles to the United Nations as a universal code of conduct in economic and technical relations among nations. Some also used the new principles as a basis to support the accession of the People's Republic of China to a seat in the UN (and as a permanent member of the UN Security Council), which until 1971 was held by Taiwan. In the words of Mao Zedong, China, after being isolated by the West for more than two decades, was 'carried into the UN by the poor friends' of the Third World.

Two fundamentals underpin the eight principles. One is equality and mutual benefit: China sees its foreign aid as mutual aid rather than unilateral philanthropy. The second is non-interference concerning the internal affairs of recipient nations, with no conditions attached. In line with the eight principles, China as a donor strictly respects the sovereignty of recipient countries, attaches no political conditions and demands no privileges in return. (The only exception to this rule is assistance to Taiwan, which China regards as a domestic issue.) In addition, China committed itself to providing equipment and materials of the best quality it could produce. Its development aid aims to build projects that require relatively low investment, achieve rapid returns and assist recipients to increase income. Furthermore the Chinese government requires that specialists implementing aid projects receive the same rewards as local personnel, with no extra benefits.

A Chinese aid project begins with a request from the potential recipient government to the Chinese diplomatic mission in its country. After feasibility studies and budgets have been drawn up through bilateral negotiations, proposals and budgets are approved by the responsible Chinese office and duly made public. Agreements on concessionary loans include amounts, purposes, maturity and repayment terms and methods (Davies et al. 2008: 15; see also Shi 1989: 17–18). The maturity of aid funds is usually five to seven years, but may be extended to up to ten years. If the recipient country finds difficulty in payment, the term may be further extended.

Foreign aid management under a planned economy The type of aid management was determined by the social system of the donor country and the principles, policies, forms and contents of its aid. In line with the requirements of its centrally planned economic system, China used methods such as the 'general consigning department system' and the 'construction department responsibility system'. Under those protocols, central government authorities were responsible for delineating foreign aid policies, while relevant ministries and commissions were responsible for their implementation and management. In this way the leaders of the Central Committee of the Communist Party of China (CPC) and the State Council (the chief administrative authority) exercised direct control over foreign aid decision-making, and ministries and commissions were held accountable for the management of programmes. Each province, ministry and commission had its special offices responsible for foreign aid. Directions from above percolated to the operational level, within this unified administrative network.

Such institutions also had their drawbacks, as was pointed out at the time:

> The construction department responsibility system and the general consigning department system alike all simply relied on administrative means to manage aid projects. The budgeted management of finance allowed all expenses to be disbursed as they [were] incurred. The amount of investment, the construction period and quality of projects had nothing to do with the economic interests

of executing units. This is unfavourable to fully motivate project units and people implementing foreign aid. These drawbacks were revealed all the more obviously toward the end of the 1970s. (Shi 1989: 89)

In 1971 China took its seat in the UN. This greatly raised its international standing and influence, which among other things led to more frequent requests for help from developing countries. In consequence the scale of its foreign aid expanded dramatically: between 1971 and 1975, China's foreign aid accounted for 5.88 per cent of the national budget, in 1973 reaching as much as 6.9 per cent (ibid.: 68). Such elevated levels created an imbalance between international and domestic interests and proved unsustainable.

In the light of this problem and prompted by the State Council, the Ministry of Foreign Economic Liaison (MFEL) called five working conferences on foreign aid, respectively in 1971, 1972, 1973, 1975 and 1977. The meetings called for more self-reliance on the part of recipient countries, for the prevention of unduly nationalistic tendencies among Chinese agencies, and for more practical and appropriate working methods in developing and implementing aid programmes. It proved difficult, however, for an administrative system created under the planned economy to reshape itself within the same structure. This problem could be addressed only after China embarked on its national reform programme.

Second period: Deng Xiaoping and foreign aid reform

In contemplating major reform, three fundamental issues must always be addressed: what to reform, what to retain and what to improve. The reform of China's foreign aid policy had to answer all these questions.

After its return to the UN, China established diplomatic relations with some Western developed countries and expanded its economic exchanges worldwide. China thus became both aid recipient and donor. As the world's largest developing country, it was itself in urgent need of capital for long-overdue infrastructure construction, while at the same time struggling to continue aid to friends and partners in other developing nations.

At that time, Chinese permanent delegations at the UN or those on foreign visits were reporting that the UN spent $25 billion on aid annually, about $5 billion of it as grants, and that aid projects involved all aspects of economic and social development. They suggested that China, as a developing country, should itself try to attract financial support from aid agencies. These reports received close attention from the high-level political leadership (Wang 2001: 172), and by 1979 China had begun to receive large amounts of multilateral aid; it then went on to receive bilateral aid from Japan, Germany and other developed countries. By the mid-1990s, China had become one of the world's biggest aid recipients (Davies 2007: 33).[3]

Nevertheless, it did not stop providing aid in its turn. The paramount leader of China at the time, Deng Xiaoping, proposed at a Central Foreign Affairs Work Conference to 'get a breath', which meant revising methods employed in foreign aid and ensuring that recipient countries truly benefited from aid programmes. Deng advocated the efficiency principle: 'spending less but doing more'.

One task facing Deng was to explain to his senior officials how to correctly understand China's poor economic situation and long-term commitments to its friends in the developing world. In May 1978 he spoke of China's role as a developing donor:

> We are now very poor. It is impossible for China to do much in displaying proletarian internationalism. China's contribution is still very small. When China has realised four modernisations and when its national economy has developed, we may contribute more to humanity, especially to the third world. (Deng 1993b: 112)

In October 1979 Deng explained China's policy change in foreign aid to Chinese provincial leaders but reconfirmed to them that 'when China's *per capita* income reaches $1,000 on average, we shall spend more on aiding the poor nations in the third world. But we cannot do it now' (Deng 1993c: 194–5).

Wastage and other problems in China's aid to Vietnam and Albania aroused suspicion within the ruling CPC and the general public, but Deng reaffirmed in November 1980 that foreign aid was an indispensable element of strategic expenditure. He stressed repeatedly that China would never forget the 'poor friends' of the Third World (Deng 1986).

Deng believed that aid should be provided according to principles of equality between the parties, and mutual help. This idea was expressed in the third plenary session of the 11th CPC Central Committee in

1978, when the session officially put forward the principle of 'actively developing economic cooperation with other countries on the basis of equality and mutual benefit and striving to adopt advanced technology and equipment of the world' (CPC 1982).

The conference also stressed that in modernizing socialism China must tackle the issue from both domestic and international points of view. In practice this meant using domestic and international resources, opening up domestic and international markets, and learning two kinds of skills – organizing domestic construction and developing foreign economic relations (ibid.: 5). This broad-minded approach was the foundation for China's reform and development of foreign aid.

According to Deng, the fundamental principles of Chinese aid during the reform period were not subject to change: 'the basic principles shall remain these Eight [principles]' (Shi 1989: 70).

In line with this spirit, the Central Committee and the State Council issued a document entitled 'Proposals on doing our aid work conscientiously and well'. This offered a full appraisal of the achievements of China's foreign aid since the founding of the 'New China'. It stressed that the eight principles, and professional perfection among aid workers, were unique in the world, were winning political kudos for China and reflected symmetry between internationalism and patriotism (ibid.: 69). In order to reflect Deng's concept of 'seeking truth from facts', the eight principles were refined into four by the Central Committee in 1983. These four are, respectively: 'equality and mutual benefit; seeking practical results; diversifying forms; and seeking common development' (Chen 1982).

Changes in Chinese aid policy China's general foreign policy, as well as that towards Africa and the developing world, has become much less ideological in nature, and terms such as 'mutual benefit' and 'win-win' have become common parlance (Li 2007: 13–35). Commensurate with this change, China's development aid has been drastically revised in terms of policy, methodology, management and organization, following the overall transformation of China's economy.

Throughout the period 1979–82, the catchphrases for reform were 'efficiency' and Deng's call for 'less but better'. China undertook smaller and more diversified aid projects, controlled foreign aid expenditure and limited the number of new schemes. In the interests of reinforcing the benefits accruing to recipient countries, China began to ask recipients to meet certain local fees by way of matching funds, and increased 'symbolic' interest rates on loans. Local costs of aid construction were often unpredictable, and the change was designed to put a ceiling or 'cap' on local expenditure, and to introduce to recipients the idea of 'economic accounting' as a first step towards self-reliance.

Aside from those changes, three other major policy adjustments were made. First, there was a pronounced move away from aid to production projects (e.g. factories) and towards landmark schemes such as conference centres, people's palaces, stadiums and hospitals. Such structures were easier to manage than manufacturing projects, although perhaps not all of them were beneficial in the longer term; hence the shift helped reduce China's financial burdens and enhance project sustainability. Secondly came a shift in emphasis away from larger schemes to small and medium-sized projects more accurately targeted to improving living conditions for local people (see below). Thirdly, new financial channels were opened through the provision of loans at concessionary rates.

Taken together, these measures greatly reduced China's total foreign aid expenditure after 1979, as against the early 1970s, without a commensurate lessening of contacts between China and recipient countries.

Changes in aid forms and methodologies To put into practice Deng's precept that 'specific methods [of aid] must be changed so that ... recipient countries really benefit' (Shi 1989: 70), China launched a series of reforms to the structure and methods of aid provision.

First, and aside from the shift of aid to small and medium-sized projects, it directed aid to projects more closely related to the production capacity and living standards of the local people by building large numbers of farms, schools, hospitals, stadiums, railways, roads, power plants and water conservancy facilities. Such schemes extended to supplying experts to pass on technical skills, and organizing training courses or study tours in China for specialists from recipient nations.

Secondly, China undertook post-construction co-management of its turnkey projects. During the construction phase of aid projects China was responsible for the survey, design and provision of all or part of complete sets of equipment and of building materials; for management of engineering, installation and pilot-production processes; and for all-round technical assistance and on-the-spot training in related technologies. Even so, it found that the equipment and technology were often so advanced as to pose management challenges to recipients (minutes of meeting with Tanzania–Zambia railway experts, 2008). From November 1982, therefore, China committed itself to post-construction technical cooperation with recipient countries, should they request it (ibid.: 221). In 1984, the Ministry of Foreign Economic Relations and Trade (MFERT) issued a document entitled 'Proposals concerning the consolidation of the achievements of aid-financed complete plants', proposing post-construction technical and managerial cooperation. This subsequently became a new form of aid, which was not regarded as interference in the internal affairs of recipient countries, but as helping recipients to stand on their own feet.

In 1992 the 14th CPC National Congress took a landmark decision to build a 'socialist market economy' and 'make [the] market display its basic role in the allocation of resources under ... [the] macroeconomic control [of] the socialist country' (Jiang 1992).

This decision initiated momentous changes. Within two years, the prices of some 90 per cent of all commodities had been set by the market (Li 2007: 1045). This irresistible force became an important factor behind reform of the foreign aid system, which apart from reflecting changes in China's domestic economy moved farther into line with the economic systems of recipient countries. In 1991, for example, the government of Mali announced the privatization of the China-aided Covatex textile mill, and in 1993, after due consultation, 80 per cent of the project's shares were transferred to Covex, a Chinese overseas project company, which in turn became responsible for repaying the debt owed by Mali to the Chinese government. Further fostering market-oriented reform, each government provided preferential treatment to the joint venture (ibid.: 21). While the scheme was not without some opposition, the introduction of market elements brought about improvement to the mill's economic performance, and also introduced to aid programmes the idea of management: cooperation through shareholding.

Soon afterwards, China opened a further aid channel: the provision of 'interest-subsidy' concessionary loans. To meet requests from some African governments, governmental funds were used to subsidize interest rates, to make commercial loans more attractive to both Chinese lenders and African borrowers. Later, joint venture cooperation funds were created to increase the funding available from China to Africa. In this way, relatively small foreign aid allocations leveraged additional market funds for international development.

These concessionary loans from China's EXIM Bank have, however, caused some controversy because, paradoxically, EXIM Bank implements national policy in the development sector and also operates according to market rules. It therefore tends to direct investment to large development projects, and to issue loans to areas offering substantial economic returns, such as energy, communications and information technology, which may conflict with the policy of promoting smaller projects noted above. Subsidizing interest rates is supposed to encourage market forces in the development aid process. Involvement of these forces was proposed and welcomed by recipient countries; employing aid money to leverage increased capital investment has been successful in China, where development has come to be understood as a process that must be approached in the round, demanding the coordination of many factors (including the market) and many areas (including broader social objectives), if it is to succeed.

It is not only market funds from China, however, but also the funds and resources of recipient countries which have been mobilized for development. At the 1993 Tokyo International Conference on African Development, African representatives had asserted that programmes to increase foreign trade and attract foreign direct investment (FDI) were more effective than traditional development assistance. At a conference in 1995 called to discuss new kinds of foreign aid, the CPC Central Committee concluded that profound changes were taking place in both internal and external foreign aid environments. China was building a socialist market economy and business enterprises were becoming the main drivers of economic activity. Financial organizations were also playing an increasingly important market role in developing countries, which were aiming to attract FDI so as to lessen the debt burden of their governments and increase income and employment. The Tokyo conference had encouraged Chinese enterprises to enter into joint ventures with those of recipient countries, further applying China's successful experiences in market-oriented reform (e.g. establishing domestic economic development zones). The CPC conference followed suit, deciding that the formation of joint ventures between Chinese enterprises and those of recipient countries was 'conducive to the combination of governmental aid funds and funds of enterprises to expand the financial sources and project scale, consolidating the achievements of aid projects and raising their efficiency' (Wang 2001: 168–9).

Changes in aid management During the economic reform process China's foreign aid system had undergone major adjustments both to the changing needs of foreign aid recipients and to China's own socio-economic reforms. At the outset China had begun to scale down foreign aid and change its methods and contents, thus reducing the government's workload. At the same time, the market mechanism transformed the ways in which the state could control the economy, the main participants in economic activity having become business enterprises that operated according to market rules and profit principles. Hence the executive branch in charge of foreign aid programmes was compelled to seek out enterprises willing to undertake projects, and the power and authority formerly held by the administrative network under a planned economy were broken. Foreign aid authorities began to experiment with methods that could tap the potential of the market, introducing the 'investment contract' and 'contract responsibility' systems. The main thrust of this reform was to shift the executive management structure of China's foreign aid to a more diversified system working with both public and private actors.

Investment contract system In order to overcome the culture of buck-passing and bad practice inherent in what had been called *Da Guo Fan* ('big rice bowl', meaning 'everyone eating from the same big pot'), MFEL had begun as early as 1980 to probe methods of integrating economic with administrative means in the spirit of economic reform (Shi 1989: 89). In December that year MFEL had issued provisional rules on trying out an investment contract system under which new projects would be contracted out by relevant departments of the State Council or by local governments. Investors in such contracts would enjoy a degree of autonomy within the framework of national foreign aid policy and the regulations contained in aid project agreements. The contracting department would be responsible for disbursing the costs according to the contract price, and within the regulatory framework.

The purpose of the reform was to simplify administration and delegate powers, thus offering incentives to executive units. In the early reform period, however, most Chinese contracting parties were operations that had simply been converted from government departments and provincial foreign aid offices; and more or less enjoyed monopoly status. Since the market system was not yet fully developed, they had not learned to operate according to market rules, which often resulted in an inability to control contract costs, hence a failure to realize real efficiency and equity.

Contract responsibility system In order to address such flaws in the investment contract system, a new system known as contract responsibility came into being in December 1983. China's financial and economic situation was changing for the better and there was new progress in economic and administrative reforms. More market rules were introduced and many contracting units were spun off from government departments and state-owned enterprises and institutions, to become independent international economic and technical cooperation companies with a legal persona, subject to market forces of profit and loss. China's foreign aid programmes also increased in scale. In December 1983, MFERT issued its 'Provisional rules on introducing the contract responsibility system into foreign aid projects', which replaced the investment contracting system. Under the new arrangement international economic and technical cooperation companies, or other state-owned enterprises and institutions with independent status, were required to bid for foreign aid projects, with the winners selected on the merits of price, contract terms and technical capabilities. At the same time, contracting parties were given greater autonomy. Their economic and technical responsibilities were clearly defined and standards for calculating costs specified according to the principle of more closely aligning responsibilities, rights and interests. The form and scope of contracts became more flexible, allowing surveying, design and engineering to be contracted out separately. General contracting for an entire project was also permitted (ibid.: 73).

After the establishment of the contract responsibility system MFERT assumed responsibility, within the central policy framework and against financial targets issued by the Ministry of Finance, for formulating foreign aid principles and policies. It exercised unified planning arrangements and mapped out foreign aid plans, compiled budgets, conducted negotiations and signed government aid agreements; it organized feasibility studies for aid projects, arranged bidding, allocated funds to successful bidders and maintained contacts with recipient countries. It also checked and supervised project schedules, represented the Chinese government in project handover ceremonies and formulated rules and regulations.

In their turn, contracting parties were made responsible for carrying out surveys, helping in consultations for project design, blueprints and estimates, and aiding the China National Complete Plant Corporation (Complant), part of the State Council's Commission for Large State-owned Enterprises, in its handling of engineering contracts. They were also responsible for project quality and scheduling while providing blueprints and related technical data to recipient countries. They were authorized to take decisions on engineering plans, managing foreign aid workers and disposing of income, within state regulations (ibid.: 90–3). In this way authority for administration, personnel and financial management of aid projects were all devolved to contracting units.

By introducing bidding procedures along market principles the contract responsibility system brought about dramatic adjustments and changes in China's foreign aid practices, as well as its organizational structure.

Organizational reform With the reduction in the scale of foreign aid, changes in the terms of its provision and the shift from the state to the market, the workload of the government was reduced and systems of management also underwent changes. As mandatory work fell away, departments concerned with foreign aid began to shrink. There was a major streamlining and simplifying of administration in 1982. The ministries of Foreign Trade and Foreign Economic Liaison and two commissions, the State Commission for the Management of Foreign Investment and the State Commission for the Management of Import and Export, were merged, while at the same time the former MFEL became a departmental unit under MFERT. Simultaneously, Complant was established to execute foreign aid projects. The Ministry of Economic Relations and Trade delegated part of its management powers to Complant in May 1985; other related government offices at central and provincial levels also delegated responsibility for foreign aid projects to international financial and technical companies affiliated to them (see Figure 6.1).

Further measures were introduced in 1992, when the State Council decided to initiate government reforms in accordance with the socialist market economy. Most of the departments previously responsible for

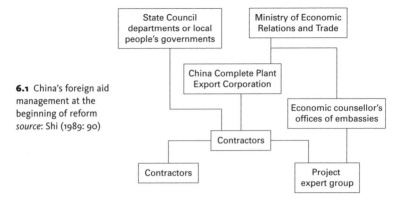

6.1 China's foreign aid management at the beginning of reform

source: Shi (1989: 90)

economic works were turned into industrial associations or companies (Li 2007: 935–6). In line with the policy of separating administration from enterprise, Complant was spun off from MFERT to operate as a business enterprise. Construction of complete plants provided under aid schemes began to be managed entirely by the new business enterprises, acting within the market system, while the foreign aid department of MFERT began to assume responsibility for formulating aid policies and overseeing the implementation of aid projects. In 1994, as a further spur to aid development and to meet a growing demand for concessionary loans, the EXIM Bank was established.

A flow chart of the entire foreign aid process covering proposals, study tours, consultation, policy decision-making, fund appropriation, acceptance of project proposals, bidding and implementation, with market forces and factors of recipient countries added, illustrates the scope of the structural change (see Figure 6.2).

In this chart, solid lines represent the policy formulation processes, dotted lines policy consulting processes, and dashes, foreign aid fund appropriation or project implementation. The chart illustrates how aid policy is based on demand from recipient countries and is directed through appropriate diplomatic channels and approved by expert groups, after field studies but before entering the finalization stage. In the policy decision processes, all ministries and commissions are guided by a consultative relationship. The private forces are integrated into a publicly managed process.

In tracking procedures for foreign aid funds appropriation, the degree of delegation of administrative powers and the important position of contracting units became even more marked.

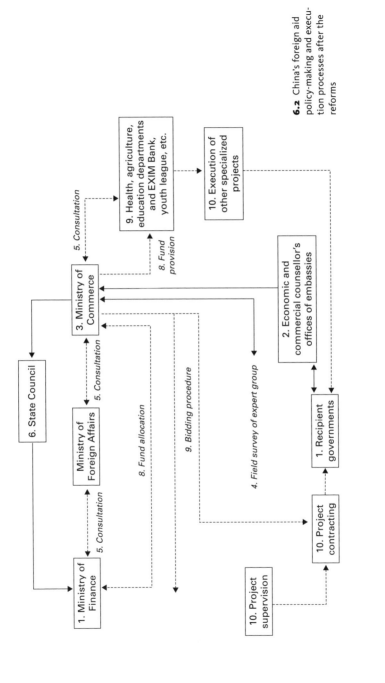

6.2 China's foreign aid policy-making and execution processes after the reforms

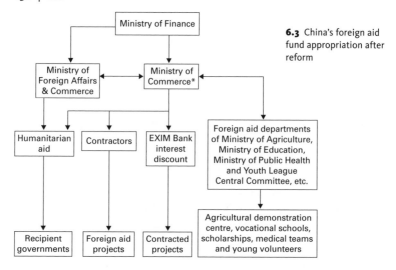

6.3 China's foreign aid fund appropriation after reform

Note: * Refers to the two departmental units in charge of foreign aid work under the Ministry of Commerce: Foreign Aid Department and International Cooperation Department. Following changes in the administrative structure new agencies are entrusted with works relating to foreign aid, respectively the statistic bureau, the China International Centre for Economic and Technical Exchanges (Cicete, in charge of aid in kind) and the Training Centre (in charge of organizing training).

The flow chart (see Figure 6.3) shows that foreign aid funds allocation by the Ministry of Commerce to the EXIM Bank and other ministries and commissions is merely transfer accounting enabling the authorities to monitor foreign aid statistics and not a charge on implementation. Despite its name, the China Development Bank is purely a commercial bank. All the ministries and commissions provide foreign aid within their own function and capacity, and therefore none exercises overall control or coordination. The task of coordinating market forces, however, is undertaken by a few departments in the Ministry of Commerce.

In 2008, by administrative order from the State Council, all the ministries involved in aid in China entered a coordination structure, with the Ministry of Commerce taking the lead. Foreign aid decision-making came to be made jointly by the Ministry of Commerce, the Ministry of Foreign Affairs and the Ministry of Finance, with coordination among twenty-eight agencies of ministerial level relevant to foreign aid. They operate according to a prescribed division of functions, in a consultative and coordinated fashion. The Foreign

Aid and International Cooperation departments of the Ministry of Commerce are also responsible for coordinating the actions of all the executive ministries, commissions and enterprises, but coordination remains at the level of maintaining accounts and inviting tenders. Figure 6.2 indicates the diversity of autonomous funding outlets.

Third phase: China's foreign aid in the new age

The growing importance of China's foreign aid attracts both praise and criticism. In a world where there are wide divergences in development paths and strategies, China stands for diversification between different cultures and civilizations, because it needs to defend its own development choices and is not prepared to commit cultural suicide ('culturocide') (Galtung 2006: 187). It follows that China's national interests and identity require it to support developing countries' defence of their own right to development choice. This position was reaffirmed by former president Jiang Zemin in July 1993:

> We must respect fully the rights of people of all countries in their free choice of social systems and development roads. ... The world is diversified. ... We must encourage different civilisations to exchange with and borrow from each other for common progress in the spirit of equality and democracy. (Jiang 2006: 109–10)

At the High-Level Meeting of Financing for Development at the UN in September 2005, President Hu Jintao reiterated that all development models should be tolerated and an effective coordination and cooperation mechanism to integrate resources should be established. China continues to call for political equality and mutual trust in development aid practices, while gradually extending aid volumes, bringing projects to the broad mass of the population, and more closely monitoring the quality of its aid. All these issues were touched on by President Hu when he announced 'five major measures' in 2005, and in the 'eight policy measures' he set out fourteen months later at the Forum on China–Africa Cooperation (FOCAC) meeting in Beijing.[4]

People-centred international development thinking and practices 'People-centred' projects have been a major focus for China's aid in the new millennium. Among President Hu's 'five major measures' (see People's Net 2005), two are directed at the general population of recipient countries. They are, respectively, providing anti-malarial drugs and other medicines; and helping to establish and improve medical facilities and training of medical staff. Former vice-premier Wu Yi declared: 'Cooperation in human resources development is an important part of China's foreign aid and an important way of personnel exchange in the new historical period.' Wu urged foreign aid organizations to optimize the effectiveness of staff training, pursue innovation in training methods and improve training results (Wu 2007).

People-centred foreign aid focuses on capacity-building. China has adopted 'inviting-in' and 'going-out' strategies in this regard. It sends people to China to study technology and management, and offers younger students Chinese government scholarships. Conversely, China has also sent out Chinese experts, technicians and management personnel to recipient countries. By the end of 2009, 107 schools had been built in Africa with Chinese assistance, and 29,465 African students had received Chinese government scholarships to study in China. At present, the Chinese government offers about five thousand scholarships each year to students from African countries. By June 2010, China had provided training programmes for over thirty thousand Africans, covering over twenty fields, such as economy, public administration, agriculture, animal husbandry and fishing industry, medical care and public health, science and technology, and environmental protection (State Council Information Office 2010). As an added incentive for such programmes, China believes that a common development path may serve to limit political and territorial disputes among developing nations.

A continual reform process

The economic reform process equipped China's foreign aid practitioners with the means to mobilize broad social forces. Nevertheless, managers of market-based enterprises within the contract responsibility system find difficulty in reconciling their narrower objectives with the political and strategic aims inherent in China's aid programmes. For example, during the time of the planned economy, the most highly qualified experts were selected by the aid authority as an important means towards a guarantee of project quality. People sent into the field were chosen for their morality, skill and physical fitness and won a good reputation for 'working selflessly and knowing no fatigue' (Kaplinsky et al. 2006: 8). Premier Zhou Enlai personally intervened in laying down the criteria for selection (Shi 1989: 268–9). China's 'soft' power derives not from the volume of foreign aid but from cultural factors such as project quality and, more especially, the moral standards, work ethic and professionalism of Chinese aid workers and managers. Under the contract responsibility system, however, aid experts and workers are employees of the contracting companies and the standards of selection necessarily differ. Although the State Council issued a document at the beginning of the reform process laying down standards for foreign aid workers, and the Ministry of Commerce organized rounds of training for people selected as aid workers, moral standards inevitably have weakened in a society undergoing such rapid market-oriented change.

Foreign aid reform and its implications for China's foreign relations

China's foreign aid, after adjustment in policies, methods, systems and organization, has become more complex and diversified in both structure and participation. Those changes in turn have brought about more subtle changes in its foreign relations.

New multilateral platforms Around the theme of 'development' China has built many new platforms for its diplomacy. The first workshop of China–Africa Economic Officials, under the auspices of China's development aid programme, took place in August 1998, when twenty-two participants from twelve African countries began to exchange views with their Chinese counterparts on how to manage the economy and promote development. The workshop is now held twice a year, and in 2002 was upgraded to ministerial level. Great numbers and higher levels of officials from other countries now come to China to acquaint themselves with China's experiences in poverty reduction, and to seek their own methods of poverty relief.[5]

As a recipient of Western aid China gained valuable experience in using aid funds for policy exchanges and human resources investment, as a means of accelerating development. One very early request from China to the World Bank was for training projects for Chinese officials. The first project-planning and management workshop for senior Chinese officials was held in Washington in 1980, and since then multilateral aid organizations have held several training classes either in China or elsewhere, for Chinese trainees. In this way China has accumulated knowledge of modern science and technology, of

market rules and of managerial skills (Zhou et al. 2007: 26, 243).
In passing on to third parties the knowledge and capability it has
acquired from Western aid donor countries, China has added its
own elements, including its understanding and experience of development (Chu 2006: 409), and has gradually established a new
development cooperation mechanism. In 2003 at the Second Ministerial Meeting of FOCAC, China committed itself to a three-year
programme to help train 10,000 Africans in various disciplines, and
set up an inter-ministerial mechanism for coordinating the human
resources development programme.

China has since participated in many more cooperation efforts,
joining the bidding for international aid projects and undertaking
large infrastructural schemes in developing countries, financed by
multilateral aid institutions. One of its aims is to concentrate on infrastructural projects in order to weaken the post-Cold War tendency of
Western donors to impose political conditions. Chinese aid personnel
are notable for their work ethic and are often seen as more appropriate development partners than Westerners insofar as they are more
responsive to local needs (see Davies et al. 2008: 36). China's foreign
aid has also met with approval from observers in the West; it has been
pointed out that China will 'turn its attention to long-neglected areas
such as infrastructure development and that its strategic approach will
raise Africa's status globally ... enabling African countries to better
integrate with the global economy' (Bates et al. 2006: v).

Market forces and China's international relations The shift from investment contracts to the responsibility contract system has introduced
market forces into China's foreign aid practice by way of contracting
enterprises which, through a market-driven selection process, have
been entrusted with aid project implementation. This has brought
them into direct contact with aid recipients. While these operations
are primarily instruments of China's aid programmes they also bring
with them additional capital, resources and skills and have facilitated
China's rise to its present position as an important global commercial
and development partner.

In addition, their managers and staff live cheek by jowl with their
peers in recipient countries, and in this way promote personal exchanges and foster mutual understanding. Their routine tasks do not
involve any kind of formal diplomacy, but they sometimes deal in

more complex economic matters than do diplomats proper. During project implementation there are many calls on their communications and negotiating skills. They frequently deal on the spot with sensitive business issues such as an absence of committed local co-financing, scheduling delays, conflicting local laws and regulations with accompanying contradictions and disputes, pricing of raw materials against specification, transport issues and the variable quality of local employees. All these matters may affect the project construction cycle. In some cases, project reports find their way into diplomatic exchanges between the top leadership of China and the recipient countries. Although contracted out to business enterprises, projects are *au fond* provided by the Chinese government and their effectiveness has a direct bearing on state relations, and the reputation of the donor country.

Contractors in their turn are regarded as representatives of China and are not permitted to bid for non-foreign aid schemes in recipient countries. At the end of a contract, however, by dint of their reputation and connections, they may become involved in competition for other development projects, or even stay on at the invitation of recipient countries. Their managers and representatives may become guests of the leaders of host countries as envoys of friendship, market pioneers and cooperative developers for recipient countries (Managers at Huawei in Ethiopia 2008). Such joint developments – of market-driven forces and cooperation partners – have helped expand exchanges between China and recipient countries while promoting the development of wider economic relations, including trade and investment. In strengthening its aid to Africa, China has rapidly developed broader economic relations with African countries. In 2008, China–Africa bilateral trade volume exceeded US$100 billion, of which US$50.8 billion is China's exports to Africa and US$56 billion is imports from Africa. Although China–Africa trade volume dropped to US$91.07 billion in 2009 as a result of the international financial crisis, China became Africa's largest trade partner that year for the first time. As the global economy recovered, China–Africa trade also maintained a favourable recovery and development momentum. From January to November 2010, China–Africa trade volume reached US$114.81 billion (State Council Information Office 2010). As Chinese aid volumes grow, so does debate and criticism. One of the more heated discussions is over the 'Chinese model' for foreign aid.

China's own development as a model Is there in reality a Chinese model? First, the term 'model' is not used in this context to indicate some kind of optimal solution for universal application. Until recently, Chinese aid enjoyed a good response, mainly because recipients see China more as a development partner than as a donor in the traditional sense. Daniel Large, a specialist in the study of Sino-African relations, holds that China's development programme is unique and for that reason its success has aroused extensive international attention, especially in Third World countries. It has become a source of ideas and development assistance quite different from the norm experienced in the immediate post-colonial era (Large 2008: 53). South African economist Stephen Marks believes that its most important aspect is that China did not develop by following the neoliberal policies of the 1990s Washington Consensus, but on the contrary by avoiding attaching conditions of good governance and human rights to its aid programmes. Such an approach is not only different from Western-centred ideology, but also produces results through 'avoidance of conditionality', thus shaking the foundations of the universal values propounded by the West, not to speak of disturbing the balance of national and strategic interests safeguarded by application of these values under the rules of a game hitherto dominated by the West (Marks 2007: 6–7).

Some international observers have noted, accurately, that China's external development policy is closely linked to its own development path (Berger and Wissenbach 2007: 13). China holds that as a 'developing donor' it has demonstrated many features that cannot be compared with Western practice. Having itself been colonized, China had to regain its national independence before launching on a course of development based on its own needs and characteristics. This proved to be a crucial experience, and one shared by many other developing countries with similar histories. As China can well understand the position of such countries, so its support to them is regarded as appropriate and well targeted.

China itself uses the term 'socialist market economy with Chinese characteristics' to describe its own development model. Its experience has led it to the realization that the cause of political independence must be coupled with independent economic decision-making; during its three decades of reform, the nation has been standing on its own feet while welcoming capital, technological and skills transfers from the developed world. The lessons from China's domestic development have left obvious marks on its external policy (ibid.: 13).

One lesson is never to surrender control of development decisions to donors. Foreign aid can only serve China as a window into foreign experience, not as a lever for domestic policy shifts (Davies 2007: 33). Nor should the effectiveness of aid to China be underestimated; with its reform-minded government, China has come to understand the importance of self-determination to developing countries, and in furthering international development it sticks to the principles of equality, mutual benefit, non-interference in internal affairs, and 'no strings'. It does not regard development aid as a tool for exporting its values, unlike some Western donors, which, one Ethiopian financial official has remarked, invariably impose on recipient countries standards and procedures conceived and evolved in Western capital cities. China, on the other hand, respects the choices of recipient countries and safeguards the norms of equality in interstate relations. As Chris Alden of the London School of Economics has observed, 'in this area that is tired of the preaching by Western society, China's foreign policy without strings attached has rapidly won friends in all political arenas' (Reference News 2007).

Many developing countries also welcome China's aid because they can learn from China's experience in acquiring funds, technology and expertise, and developing the markets they need for their economic development.

In sum, it is not only market elements introduced during the reform period which are embedded in China's aid programmes. There are also other characteristics of China as a developing country that stimulated its own development and also contribute to the enrichment of international development thinking and practice.

The 'China threat' in foreign aid China's development aid programmes are depicted in some quarters as a challenge to Western-style good governance, and the protection of human rights and democracy. It should, however, be noted that China has made headway in its own development without stressing such matters. More specifically, the question of Chinese aid raises the following issues:

- whether or not an aid agreement is relevant to the recipients and whether donors should pursue national and private interests when offering aid;

- whether conditionality is too low, thus postponing or obstructing necessary changes in governance on the part of recipient countries; and
- whether donors pursue hidden agendas and waste aid resources in areas that do not produce results. (Manning 2006: 371–85)

Does – or should – foreign aid serve the donor's interests? Almost no bilateral donor would deny that it does, one way or another, though it may define 'interests' differently. Some would assess economic development gains in recipient countries as a long- and short-term cost–benefit calculation to the donor; others may see the matter as a question of political influence. Comments on Chinese aid in particular usually come from one of two perspectives. The first is one of economic development, which focuses on the real needs of recipient countries and the acknowledgement of such needs; the other is political, informed by the intricate and long-term strategic calculation of donor countries. Comments on Chinese aid from recipient governments, business enterprises and the general public are by and large favourable, a view acknowledged by former US Under-Secretary of State and outgoing World Bank president Robert Zoellick: 'China's investment in Africa is probably very favourable as it can help African countries develop infrastructure facilities and utilise their own natural resources' (Reference News 2007).

As Zoellick admits, many resource-rich countries have developed rapidly as a result of using foreign aid, including that from China, to obtain and master the use of their natural resources (Hyden and Mukandala 1999: 19). On the other hand, criticism of China's aid has risen sharply of late. Aid, from one standpoint, is defined as 'a transfer of taxpayers' money from one government to another ... [S]uch transfers are thus a wholly political matter at both ends of the spectrum' (quoted in Riddell 1987: 4).

On this view, aid is provided for political and strategic interests and for maintaining an unequal state-to-state relationship, with the donor setting the rules of the game. Members of the OECD Development Assistance Committee spend on average only about 0.3 per cent of their GDP (roughly $50 billion) on foreign aid, but aid funding can account for 25–30 per cent of the budget of some developing nations, hence becoming a dominating financial force. For some underdeveloped countries, therefore, international aid is a far more important source of capital than the inflow of FDI. If conditions were to be attached to this funding, the imbalance of financial power could easily make aid an instrument of leverage in favour of donors, thereby surrendering economic and political dominance to them. To members of the 'realist' political school such as the late Hans Morgenthau, foreign aid is an element of foreign policy with a natural inclination to reflect state interests. The ultimate purpose of aid, humanitarian or economic, is to maintain the imbalance of international strength favouring donors (Morgenthau 1962: 301–9), and its rationale is to maximize the donor's national interest. On this logic, foreign aid should be directed towards primary production in developing countries, rather than in manufacturing industries that might in due course compete with those of donor countries; and aid projects must conform to the needs of the world market and the will of donor countries instead of those of recipient countries. Aid should result in long-term economic dependence on donor countries (Dos Santos 1999) and the maintenance of special political relationships (Payaslian 1996).

Since the turn of the last century, foreign aid has moved further: in becoming a tool for promoting Western concepts of democracy, human rights, good governance and security, it also reflects the existing global political imbalance. Olav Stokke of Norway's Fridtjof Nansen Institute has noted that foreign aid has been used as a lever by donors to push through objectives that the recipient government would otherwise not accept (Stokke 1995: 12). Owing to the imbalance of power in the donor–recipient relationship conditionality in aid programmes means, unequivocally, interference in another country's internal affairs. A fundamental UN principle guiding international relations among states thus comes under challenge, and a growing inclination in the West to propagate its values as universal carries with it a strong intent to deprive recipient countries of their freedom of action (Carothers 1999: 19).

Market-oriented transformation, economic restructuring, democracy, human rights and good governance have all been used as prerequisites for development assistance from the West (Stokke 1995: 12). Yet while themselves persisting in the principle of interference, some Western donors criticize China for non-interference, presumably because it may threaten their own position and degrade the standards they set (Carothers 1999: 19).

Some critics of Chinese aid regard China's different approach from the West's as a self-serving instrument of commercial ambition (Davies et al. 2008: 58; Berger 2006: 119; Karumbidza 2007: 91). This tends to overlook altruistic elements in China's aid programme. To cite one small example, while itself a major producer and exporter of tea, China has nevertheless passed on tea production and processing skills to Morocco, a potential competitor; moreover, although a large agricultural producer, it has established ten foreign agricultural demonstration centres; and as an emerging information technology country, has begun to build schools for IT training beyond its borders.

China sees many of its critics' arguments as spurious. Contrary to a common perception, there is, for example, little clear evidence that China exports cheap labour with its aid projects, and there is certainly no rule that stipulates that Chinese aid projects must use Chinese workers.[6] On the contrary it is noteworthy that twelve years after beginning its aid to Sudan, for instance, 90 per cent of the payroll in China's projects is made up of local labour. With Chinese help, Sudan has established its own oil companies and indeed an entire oil industry that has promoted urban construction and social development (Wang 2007). Moreover, far from supporting unequal competition through aid projects, there are indications that the Chinese government does not permit aid enterprises to compete in recipient countries' domestic markets. A further criticism, that China conceals information concerning its aid projects, again does not seem to be borne out by facts. It is true that there are some differences in definitions of foreign aid between China and the West, and China is still in the early stages of building a sophisticated statistical system. The first step was the publishing of the White Paper on China's Foreign Aid with basic but important information and statistics (State Council Information Office 2010). There is no indication of deliberate concealment of information.

Does 'no strings' aid serve to delay the reform and socio-economic development of recipient countries? The contrary is true. Many developing countries have found that they have spent twenty years trying out reform plans designed by Western donors[7] that promote what might be called Western liberal values of governance (Killick 1998: 4) without a concomitant plan for economic and social progress. It is admitted that aiding democracy 'cannot change the basic economic level or orientation of development of ... recipient countries' (Obiorah 2007: 38–9).

By contrast, China's aid policy represents an alternative to the model of 'votes before bread' (ibid.: 38–9); indeed, its success represents a road that stresses the converse. The aforementioned policy of aid in kind, closely related to improving the standard of living for the people, rather than financial aid per se, gels with China's comparative advantage as a developing country, and also with the needs of recipient countries; furthermore, it is less likely to foster corruption and mismanagement than the alternative.

Many criticisms of Chinese aid come from NGOs in Western donor nations and some recipient countries. In pursuing Western ideas and methods, such organizations show a propensity to demand political liberalization as a precondition for development assistance and to regard development aid as an 'interest-dominated model of politics' (Killick 1998: 98) which may be deployed as a means of changing domestic policies; while at the same time they overlook differences in history, social conditions and institutions that promote development and reform among recipient countries.

This position tends to mirror that of governments in Western nations that have created a political architecture according to which government is only one element of overall governance; within that context other social instruments and institutions may act independently of governments (Rosenau and Czempiel 1992; Kohler-Koch and Eising 1999; Marks et al. 1996). When the West uses the term 'governance' in relation to developing countries, it carries with it an implicit morality. 'Good' governance is often narrowly defined in terms of public sector management with, for example, respect for democracy and human rights (Neumayer 2003: 8), and thus acts as a measure for gauging government performance. On the other hand, 'bad' governance justifies intervention without regard for national sovereignty. In this way, international (and UN) norms of non-interference are broken and the right of sovereign states to independent development comes under threat.

Chinese aid offered unconditionally therefore poses a challenge to the principles of the prevailing aid regime. A report from the Washington-based International Assessment and Strategy Centre commented that 'China's ambitious, new high-profile role in Africa challenges [the USA] to think far more comprehensively about how it will engage China on African matters in the future' (Bates et al. 2006: 3). Such commentators consider that China's development model may come to dominate a field thus far largely in the hands of Western donors, and in this way undermine the West's 'soft' power. China has been under attack as an 'irresponsible player in international affairs', and for 'challenging current development paradigms' (Davies 2007: 16). At the extreme, some have called on the USA and the European Union to form a tighter 'concert of democracies' to limit China's influence (Campbell 2007: 126) or alternatively to try to make the Chinese shift the emphasis of their aid programmes from 'non-interference' to 'non-indifference' (Davies 2007: 96).

Although 'many of the fears about Chinese aid and engagement are misinformed' (Brautigam 2009: 307), China faces enormous challenges in its development aid. The Chinese development model, coupled with industrious labour, effective administration and active business involvement, is a very difficult one to copy or even understand. Sometimes even Chinese find it difficult to secure the right balance among the three elements mentioned above. Relatively strong administrative power can lead to efficient project management and implementation, but it can also become the source of waste and misuse. A hard-working labour force in China is partly a cultural and historical factor, and thus hard to emulate elsewhere. Traditionally, Chinese business is intuitive and creative, but severely checked by administrative power. More recently it has enjoyed much more freedom; yet a modern sense of social responsibility and a professional code of conduct are just beginning to be instilled. Even Chinese aid workers, who are now more skilled, having received a better education than those in the 1950s, 1960s and 1970s, are motivated by different factors today. China's image, projected by multiple actors, has become blurred and confused and the efforts of government agencies to mend it can produce adverse effects.

Conclusion

China's market-oriented economic reform and domestic development inevitably affected the policies, contents, methods and management systems of its foreign aid. It has been under constant adjustment in order to meet a fast-changing domestic and international environment. By adhering to a policy of non-interference in internal affairs and equality and mutual benefit in accordance with the eight principles, respecting the free choice of development direction by recipient countries, and providing them with whatever assistance is within China's capacity, foreign aid has stimulated exchanges and cooperation with recipient countries in political, economic, social and cultural fields. Owing partly to such exchanges and cooperation, the economies of some developing countries have begun to show sustained growth in recent years. Many countries have reoriented their foreign policies towards the East – China – rather than the West.

China believes it has found a way of meeting its international obligations by establishing markets and fostering the idea of first raising productivity and improving the material life of the people, before turning to issues of social equity and harmony. Its approach is designed to disseminate experience, create opportunities, improve living standards and promote balanced development on the basis of respect for sovereign independence. It is not designed to compel others to do what they otherwise would not wish to do.

Notes

1 This chapter is based on an earlier paper, 'China's foreign aid reform', in Yizou Wong (ed.), *Transformation of Foreign Affairs and International Relations in China, 1978–2008*, Leiden: Brill, pp. 185–237.

2 The eight principles are:

i) The Chinese government has always persisted in the principle of equality and mutual benefit in providing foreign aid, never regarding it as a unilateral charity but rather as mutual.

ii) In providing foreign aid, the Chinese government strictly respects the sovereignty of recipient countries, never attaches any strings, and absolutely demands no privileges.

iii) The Chinese government provides economic aid in the form of interest-free or low-interest loans and, when needed, the maturity term may be extended in order to lessen the burdens of recipient countries.

iv) The purpose of providing aid is not to create dependence of recipient countries on China but help them on to the path of self-reliance and economic independence.

v) The aid projects undertaken by the Chinese government require less

investment but achieve quick returns so as to help recipient countries increase income and accumulate funds.

vi) The Chinese government provides equipment and materials of the best quality it can produce and the prices may be negotiated based on the international market. If the equipment and materials fail to meet the prescribed standards and quality, the Chinese government ensures that they are exchanged for new ones.

vii) In providing any technical assistance, the Chinese government ensures that the recipient countries master the technology.

viii) The experts sent by the Chinese government to aid recipient countries enjoy the same benefits as the experts of recipient countries. No special demand and benefits are allowed.

3 In 1994, China obtained $3.225 billion in aid to become the biggest aid recipient country in the world (Davies 2007: 33).

4 These eight measures are:

i) Double the aid volumes of 2006 to Africa in three years.

ii) Provide $3 billion concessional loans and $2 billion preferential export buyer's credit in the three years from 2006 to 2009.

iii) Create the China–Africa Development Fund to encourage and support Chinese companies in investing in African nations, with the total funding amount up to $5 billion.

iv) Help build the African Union Conference Centre and support African countries in their joint efforts for self-improvement.

v) Exempt all the government interest-free loan debts that were mature before 2005 of all heavily indebted and the least developed African countries with diplomatic relations with China.

vi) Expand the categories of commodities exported by the least developed African countries at zero tariff from 190 to more than 440.

vii) Establish three to five overseas economic and trading cooperation zones in Africa from 2006 to 2009.

viii) Help train 15,000 African people in various professions, send 100 senior agricultural experts and set up ten speciality agricultural technical demonstrative centres, build thirty hospitals, provide ¥300 million free loans for use in malaria prevention and control, build 100 rural schools and increase scholarships for African students in China from 2,000 per year to 4,000 per year from 2006 to 2009.

5 *People's Daily*, 24 September 2004, cited in Li (2007: 23).

6 Martyn Davies pointed out that Chinese companies have no automatic preference for Chinese labour, but notes the lack of specialized skills in many African markets where aid projects are being implemented. According to our interviews, the import of Chinese labour is often welcomed in recipient countries (see Davies et al. 2008: 17).

7 These reform plans are mostly designed based on Western experience and adopt the same template, known

as the 'political template'. The template mainly covers free and fair elections, the building of government with a balance of power, promotion of civil society (especially including NGOs and media). The whole process is not only designed by Western donors but also manipulated by them. See Carothers (1999: 87, 92, 125–8).

References

Chen Muhua (1982) 'Break new ground in foreign economic relations and trade', *People's Daily*, 20 September.

China Statistical Yearbook (2005, 2006 and 2007) Beijing: China Statistical Press.

China Yearbook of Commerce (2006) Beijing: China Commercial Press.

Chu, S. (2006) 'China's foreign affairs strategy of peaceful development', in Ma Zhengang (ed.), *The New Changes in China's Peaceful Development International Environment,* Beijing: Contemporary World Publisher.

CPC (1982) *Selection of Important Documents since the Third Plenum of the 11th CPC Central Committee*, 1st edn, Beijing: People's Publishing House, August.

Deng Xiaoping (1986) 'Speaking with the president of Mali: China after development shall still belong to the Third World', *People's Daily*, 22 June.

— (ed.) (1993a) *Selected Works of Deng Xiaoping*, vols I, II and III, Beijing, People's Publishing House.

— (1993b) 'Realise four modernisations and never seek hegemony', *Selected Works of Deng Xiaoping*, vol. II, Beijing: People's Publishing House.

— (1993c) 'Some proposals on economic work', *Selected Works of Deng Xiaoping*, vol. II, Beijing: People's Publishing House.

Hu Angang et al. (2005) *Assistance and Development*, Beijing: Tsinghua University Press.

Hu Jintao (2005) 'Promote universal development to achieve common prosperity', Statement by President Hu Jintao of China at the High-Level Meeting on Financing for Development at the 60th Session of the United Nations, New York, 14 September.

Jiang Zemin (1992) 'Accelerate the pace of reform, opening up and modernisation and win greater victory in the building of socialism with Chinese characteristics', Report to the 14th CPC National Congress, *People's Daily*, 21 October.

— (ed.) (2006) *Selected Works of Jiang Zemin*, vols I, II and III, Beijing, People's Publishing House.

Li Anshan (2007) 'Three kinds of changes in China's policy toward Africa since reform and opening up', in Yang Guang (ed.), *Middle East and Africa Development Report 2006–2007 – History and Reality of the Relations between China and Africa*, Beijing: Social Sciences Documentation Press, pp. 13–35.

Li Anshan and Xu Liang (2007) 'China's African strategy: a roundup of the workshop on international image and countermeasures', *International Strategy Studies Bulletin*, 9, 9 October.

Li Peng (2007) *Market and Regulation: Li Peng's Economic Diary*, vols I, II and III, Beijing, Xinhua Publishing House.

Ma Zhengang (ed.) (2006) *New Changes in the International Environment for China's Peaceful Development*, Beijing: World Knowledge Publishing House.

Mao Zedong (1956) 'In commemoration of Dr Sun Yat-sen', *People's Daily*, 12 November.

— (1963) 'Talks of Chairman Mao Zedong during a meeting with African friends', *People's Daily*, 9 August.

People's Daily (2006) 'Document on China's policy toward Africa', 13 January.

People's Net (2005) 'Hu Jintao announces five moves for China to support developing countries', *People's Net*, 16 September, politics.people.com. cn/GB/8198/52409/52414/3702055. htm, accessed 15 November 2011.

Shi Lin (ed.) (1989) *Foreign Economic Cooperation of Contemporary China*, Beijing: China Social Sciences Press.

State Council Information Office (2010) 'The People's Republic of China, China–Africa economic and trade cooperation', Beijing.

— (2011) 'China's foreign aid', *People's Daily*, 22 April.

Wang Nan (2007) 'Experiences and cases of China's aid to Africa', Speech at the Sino-French Dialogue on Technical Assistance to Africa, 15/16 October.

Wang Weiguang (2008) 'China's reform and opening up and China's development path', *Marxism Studies*, May.

Wang Xu (2001) *China's High-Level Policy Decision Taking: Foreign Affairs*, Xi'an: Shaanxi Normal University Press.

Websites of the Ministry of Commerce, the Ministry of Foreign Affairs, the Ministry of Finance and the Import and Export Bank.

Wen Jiabao (2008) Speech at UN High-Level Meeting on MDGs, www. chinaview.cn, 26 September.

Wu Yi (2007) Letter to National Work Conference on Training in Foreign Aid, *People's Daily*, 27 July.

Xu Dunxin (ed.) (2006) *World Trend and China's Peaceful Development*, Beijing: World Knowledge Publishing House.

Yang Guang (ed.) (2007) *Middle East and Africa Development Report 2006–2007: History and reality of China–Africa relations*, Beijing: Social Sciences Documentation Press.

Zhou Enlai (1964) 'Government report

to the First Session of the Third National People's Congress', *People's Daily*, 31 December.

Zhou Hong (ed.) (2003) *Foreign Aid and International Relations*, Beijing: China Social Sciences Press.

Zhou Hong, Zhang Jun and Zhang Min (2007) *Foreign Aid in China*, Beijing: Social Sciences Documentation Press.

Non-Chinese sources

Aho, M. C. and M. Levinson (1988) *After Reagan: Confronting the Changed World Economy*, New York: Council on Foreign Relations.

Bates, G., C.-H. Huang and S. J. Morrison (2006) 'China's expanding role in Africa – implications for the United States', Report of the CSIS Delegation to China on China–Africa–US Relations, 28 November–1 December.

Berger, B. (2006) 'China's engagement in Africa: can the EU sit back?', *South African Journal of International Affairs*, 13(1).

Berger, B. and U. Wissenbach (2007) 'EU–China–Africa Trilateral Development Cooperation. Common challenges and new directions', Discussion Paper 21, Bonn: Deutsches Institut für Entwicklungspolitik.

Brautigam, D. (1998) *Chinese Aid and African Development: Exporting Green Revolution*, London: Macmillan Press.

— (2009) *The Dragon's Gift: The real story of China in Africa*, Oxford: Oxford University Press.

Browne, S. (1990) *Foreign Aid in Practice*, London: Pinter Publishers.

Campbell, H. (2007) 'China in Africa: challenge US global hegemony', in F. Manji and S. Marks (eds), *African Perspective on China in Africa*, Cape Town: Fahamu.

Carothers, T. (1999) *Aiding Democracy Abroad*, Washington, DC: Carnegie Endowment for International Peace.

Cassen, R. and associates (1986) *Does Aid Work? Report to an Intergovernmental Task Force*, Oxford: Clarendon Press.

Davies, M., H. Edinger, N. Tay and S. Naidu (2008) *How China Delivers Development Assistance to Africa*, Johannesburg: Centre for Chinese Studies, University of Stellenbosch.

Davies, P. (2007) *China and the End of Poverty in Africa – towards mutual benefit?*, Sundbyberg, Sweden: Diakonia.

Dos Santos, T. (1999) *Imperialism and Dependence*, Social Sciences Documentation Press.

Draper, P. and G. Le Pere (eds) (2005) *Enter the Dragon: Towards a free trade agreement between China and the Southern African Customs Union*, Midrand, South Africa: Institute of Global Dialogue.

Gaffney, J. (1991) *Political Culture in France and Germany*, London: Routledge.

Galtung, J. (2006) *Peace by Peaceful Means*, Chinese edn, Nanjing: Nanjing Publishing House.

Glosny, M. A. (2006) 'Meeting the development challenge in the 21st century: American and Chinese perspectives on foreign aid', China Policy Series no. 21, National Committee on United States–China Relations.

Grilli, E. R. (1993) *The European Community and the Developing Countries*, New York: Cambridge University Press.

Groves, L. and H. Rachel (eds) (2004) *Inclusive Aid. Changing Power and Relationships in International Development*, London: Earthscan.

Halloran, D. (1993) *Moral Vision in International Politics. The Foreign Aid Regime: 1949–1989*, Princeton, NJ: Princeton University Press.

Hogan, M. J. (1991) *Explaining the History*

of American Foreign Relations, Cambridge: Cambridge University Press.

Hyden, G. and R. Mukandala (1999) Agencies in Foreign Aid – Comparing China, Sweden and the United States in Tanzania, London: Palgrave Macmillan.

Kaplinsky, R., D. McCormick and M. Morris (2006) 'The impact of China on sub-Saharan Africa', Working Paper 291, Institute of Development Studies.

Karumbidza, J. B. (2007) 'Win-win economic cooperation: can China save Zimbabwe's economy?', in F. Manji and S. Marks (eds), African Perspectives on China in Africa, Oxford: Fahamu, pp. 87–105.

Killick, T. (1998) Aid and the Economy of Policy Change, London and New York: Routledge.

Kohler-Koch, B. and R. Eising (1999) The Transformation of Governance in the European Union, London: Routledge.

Large, D. (2008) 'Beyond "Dragon in the Bush": the study of China–Africa relations', African Affairs, 107(426): 45–61.

Le Pere, G. (ed.) (2006) China in Africa. Mercantilist Predator, or Partner in Development?, Midrand, South Africa: Institute of Global Dialogue.

Lewis, A. W. (1954) The Theory of Economic Growth, London: Allen and Unwin.

Managers at Huawei in Ethiopia (2008) Minutes of discussions with author, January.

Manji, F. and S. Marks (eds) (2007) African Perspective on China in Africa, Cape Town: Fahamu.

Manning, R. (2006) 'Will "emerging donors" change the face of international cooperation?', Development Policy Review, 24(4): 371–85.

Marks, G., L. Hooghe and K. Blank (1996) 'European integration since the 1980s. State-centric versus multi-level governance', Journal of Common Market Studies, 34(3): 343–78.

Marks, S. (2007) 'Introduction', in F. Manji and S. Marks (eds), African Perspective on China in Africa, Cape Town: Fahamu, pp. 6–7.

Middleton, N. and P. O'Keefe (1988) Disaster and Development, London: Pluto Press.

Morgenthau, H. J. (1962) Politics in the Twentieth Century, Chicago, IL: University of Chicago Press.

Natsios, A. S. (2006) 'Five debates on international development: the US perspective', Development Policy Review, 24(2): 131–9.

Neumayer, E. (2003) The Pattern of Aid Giving. The impact of good governance on development assistance, London and New York: Routledge.

Noël, A. and J.-P. Thérien (1995) 'From domestic to international justice: the welfare state and foreign aid', International Organisation, 49(3): 523–53.

Obiorah, N. (2007) 'Who's afraid of China in Africa? Towards an African civil society perspective on China–Africa relations', in F. Manji and S. Marks (eds), African Perspective on China in Africa, Cape Town: Fahamu, pp. 38–9.

Payaslian, S. (1996) US Foreign Economic and Military Aid, New York: University Press of America, Inc.

Pronk, J. P., J. Boyce, L. Emmerij, G. Edgren, J. Degnbol-Martinussen, J. Petras, A. Geske Dijkstra, W. Hout, S. Mehrotra, D. Slater, R. Sobhan and J. Hanlon (2004) Catalysing Development: A Debate on Aid, Oxford: Blackwell.

Reference News (2007) 'Zoellick praises China's aid-financed investment in Africa', October.

— (2010) 'China has become a main character outside the EU–Africa summit', 10 December.

Riddell, R. C. (1987) Foreign Aid

Reconsidered, Baltimore, MD: Johns Hopkins University Press.

Rosenau, J. N. and E.-O. Czempiel (eds) (1992) *Governance without Government. Order and Change in World Politics,* Cambridge: Cambridge University Press.

Rostow, W. W. (1960) *The Stages of Economic Growth*, Cambridge: Cambridge University Press.

Schraeder, P. J. (ed.) (1992) *Intervention into the 1990s. U.S. Foreign Policy in the Third World*, Boulder, CO, and London: Lynne Rienner Publishers.

Shelton, G. (2006) 'China and Africa: advancing South–South cooperation',

in G. Le Pere (ed.), *China in Africa: Mercantilist Predator or Partner in Development?*, Midrand, South Africa: Institute of Global Dialogue, pp. 99–122.

South African Institute of International Affairs (2006) *South African Journal of International Affairs – China in Africa*, 13(1).

Stokke, O. (ed.) (1995) *Aid and Political Conditionality*, London: Frank Cass.

Van Ufford, P. Q., A. K. Giri and D. Mosse (2003) 'Interventions in development', in P. Q. Van Ufford and A. K. Giri (eds), *A Moral Critique of Development*, London: Routledge.

7 | INDIA AND DEVELOPMENT COOPERATION: EXPRESSING SOUTHERN SOLIDARITY

Sachin Chaturvedi

Introduction

India's long-standing development cooperation policy, within the framework of South–South cooperation (SSC), has undergone major change. India's rapid economic growth upset the delicate balance between its roles as a recipient of development aid and as a development partner for other developing countries. The origins of the shift are economic in nature. India's foreign exchange reserves have grown significantly in the past two decades. Having stood at $5.8 billion in 1991, they increased gradually to $300 billion by the end of 2009 and $297 billion in 2010 (Reserve Bank of India 2010). The changes in aid policy reflect this accumulation of large foreign exchange reserves, and a resultant, new self-confidence and desire for a larger global role.

This is peculiarly nationalist in nature, following on from the Indian nuclear tests of 1998 that led to wide-scale sanctions imposed by the United States and other major aid donors. However, the 'feel good' factor generated by India's phenomenal economic growth was so strong that it introduced the idea of 'India shining'.

In the process, the economic cost of sanctions was overlooked as it seemed affordable. Indian diplomacy also played its part in softening the hard edges of sanctions and mobilizing counter-pressures (Rana 2000). At the same time Brazil, India and South Africa came together to discuss global economic issues; in 2003 those three major emerging nations formed the IBSA group for the further development of SSC. In the same year, at the Fifth Ministerial Meeting of the World Trade Organization (WTO) in Cancún, Mexico, collective representations by developing world nations resulted in the blocking of various trade proposals from the industrialized nations. This success, although skating over the realpolitik of South–North interdependence, was a major morale-booster for the South and instilled in the minds of the South's leaders an indication of their arrival on the world stage.

At another level, it gave a new meaning to the idea of cooperation between developing nations.

In India, the cumulative impact of these developments manifested itself in widespread commitment to SSC. The ruling nationalistic National Democratic Alliance campaigned for self-reliance and announced new decisions related to aid policy, setting a minimum limit for external assistance; all offers below that limit were to be turned away. At present this limit is of US$25 million. Though in the initial years of planning, aid to India was mostly tied, India's dependence on aid has reduced with time, and it has affirmed its stand on not accepting tied aid. As of February 2003, India no longer accepted any tied external assistance. In 2003 the list of donors was reduced to six (the United Kingdom, the USA, Russia, Germany, Japan and the European Union). This policy was further revised by the subsequent United Progressive Alliance coalition in 2007, eventually allowing all G8 countries on to the list of official donors. This was also a time when Indian foreign policy was moving towards economic priorities as the central policy thrust in a more pragmatic direction than hitherto.[1]

Aid partnerships with other developing countries are an important component of current Indian foreign policy. There is no comprehensive and detailed paper available on the issue, and although several documents have defined the government's economic policy agenda, none articulates its impact on foreign policy (Baru 2006). There have been some efforts to capture the new trends; Raja Mohan (2003), for example, lists five major changes in Indian foreign policy in the 1990s. The first was a move away from socialist ideas towards a modern capitalist approach. Secondly, economic priorities replaced global politics as the central pillar of policy-making. The third and fourth marked shifts from a Third World and anti-West stance to a more self-interested approach; and finally there was a move from idealism to pragmatism.

Rana (2000) brings realism to the changing dimension of India's foreign policy when he observes that economic growth brings with it the capacity to project the country abroad and that it is sound domestic economic policies and effective economic diplomacy which together build a receptive climate for projecting national power. Perceptions matter perhaps more than reality, so India may continue to try to play on the world's conscience, although a more pragmatic school of foreign policy scoffs at any suggestion of global morality (Sikri 2009). This raises the question of whether or not the development partnership policy would also be sacrificed at the altar of realpolitik or shielded under a wider SSC umbrella. It is important to note that a few months before India's independence in August 1947, the Asian Relations Conference in New Delhi brought together the leaders of many independence movements in Asia. It was thus an expression of India's political philosophy of non-alignment that pre-dated its adoption as government policy; as Gujral (1998) points out, at a very early stage it represented India's commitment to addressing imbalances and inequities at the global level.

This chapter discusses some of these issues at greater length. The next section brings together the historical evolution of India's development partnership. The chapter then presents an institutional framework and channels of assistance. The last section draws conclusions and presents policy recommendations.

Historical evolution

From the time of its emergence as an independent state, India saw linkages with other developing countries as an important policy priority. Prime Minister Jawaharlal Nehru was categorical on the question. He laid the foundation for India's SSC policy in 1947 when he said:

the service of India means the service of the millions who suffer. It means the ending of poverty and ignorance and disease and inequality of opportunity. The ambition of the greatest men of our generation has been to wipe every tear from every eye. That may be beyond us, but as long as there are tears and suffering, so long our work will not be over. And so we have to labour and to work ... to give reality to our dreams. Those dreams are for India, but they are also for the world, for all the nations and peoples are too closely knit together today for any one of them to imagine that it can live apart. Peace is said to be indivisible, so is freedom, so is prosperity now, and also disaster in this one world that can no longer be split into isolated fragments. (Government of India 2011)

In 1949 the Indian government established seventy scholarships (increased to 100 in 1952) with the aim of promoting cultural relations with other countries in Asia and Africa, and providing facilities for higher education to students from those countries. There were contemporary instances of India's coming together with other developing countries; for instance, in 1951 India established a maternity home in Addis Ababa with a contribution of Rs10,000 (then $2,000) and Ethiopia returned the gesture with a gift of 500 tons of wheat (Ministry of External Affairs 1950, 1951). This mutually supportive approach continued to define India's SSC. A series of initiatives in line with this stance took place well before the 1955 Afro-Asian Conference in Bandung. Indonesia brought together twenty-nine Asian and African states, many of them newly independent, with the expressed aim of promoting Afro-Asian trade, cultural and political cooperation.

Such exchanges were characterized by a principle of reciprocity. When India provided Rs50,000 ($10,000) of flood relief assistance to the Kingdom of Bhutan in 1954, the Maharaja of Bhutan reciprocated the gesture by donating Rs20,000 ($4,000) to the Prime Minister's Relief Fund in India (Ministry of External Affairs 1955). Similarly, India donated more than Rs25,000 ($5,000) worth of assistance for flood relief in Iraq in 1954 and later received from Iraq a gift of similar value for distribution among its own flood victims. In return for help from India the Iranian government donated forty books on various aspects of Persian literature to the Khodabaksh Library in Patna.

Important pragmatic and rational aspects to India's aid policy emerged in those years. First, India had a very open approach to trilateral cooperation, which in later years seems to have disappeared. India built a 128-kilometre, Rs30 million ($6 million) mountain highway in Nepal, handed over in June 1957. It also entered into a Tripartite Road Agreement with the Nepalese government and the USA for the construction of a further 1,450 kilometres of road. India's contribution came from its Ten Crore Aid Programme to Nepal (Ministry of External Affairs 1958). Similarly, in 1959 the Indian government contributed Rs50,000 ($10,000) from its aid funds towards the cost of freighting 1,000 tons of wheat given by Canada to Nepal as aid under the Colombo Plan, a regional collective aid organization founded in 1950 (Ministry of External Affairs 1959). In June 1958, a tripartite telecommunications agreement between Nepal, the USA and India was signed at Kathmandu; its purpose was to improve telecommunications between Kathmandu and Delhi and Calcutta, and provide Nepal with efficient internal telecommunications (ibid.).

The second major characteristic was transparency in support of non-governmental organizations (NGOs) as channels for assistance, which in later years is not at all evident. In 1959, the government provided $20,000 as an ad hoc grant to a hospital in Rangoon,

Burma (with a subsequent annual $7,000 grant), and gave $5,000 to the Ramakrishna Mission to enable it to disseminate information on social and cultural aspects of Indian life among Indian and Burmese communities in Rangoon (Ministry of External Affairs 1960). The third important feature at this time, no longer evident, was programme-based development assistance. In the history of India's foreign aid, 1959 represented a turning point, because that year India opted for programme-based support for various aid activities in Nepal and Bhutan. In the financial year 1960/61 India agreed to support Nepal's second five-year plan (intended for 1960–65 but in the event beginning only in 1962 owing to the suspension of the Nepalese parliament) with an aid package of Rs180 million ($36 million). This was the first example of support to a neighbouring country's own development plan. In the case of Bhutan it was decided to grant an annual subsidy of Rs0.7 million ($35,000) from 1960 onwards (in addition to Rs0.5 million – $25,000 – already being paid under the 1949 Indo-Bhutanese Friendship Treaty), replacing the ad hoc grants made hitherto. The main aim of the change was to enable the Bhutan government to draw up its development plan on a more systematic basis.

At that time the Colombo Plan was the major avenue for external engagement in aid. In the first decade of the Plan, India provided training places to 1,622 students from various Plan member countries in fields such as health, medicine, aviation, engineering, forestry, statistics and community development, and various graduate and postgraduate courses. India also arranged training facilities for 662 foreign nationals from non-member countries.

Most changes in India's external development cooperation policy have been at the initiative of the Ministry of Finance (MoF). In this regard, 2003 was a landmark. Several policy changes were announced in that year's budget speech, which contained five essential points. First, an 'India Development Initiative', aimed at promoting India as 'both a production centre and an investment destination', was established in the MoF, with an allocation of $46 million for the period 2003/04. This was also intended to leverage and promote India's strategic economic interests abroad (Ministry of Finance 2003/04). Secondly, there was to be a review of India's position as a recipient country, since according to the government 'a stage has [been reached when we] should ... review our dependence on external donors ... extend support to the national efforts of other developing countries

[and] re-examine the line of credit route of international assistance to others' (ibid.). Thirdly, the government planned to provide relief to some bilateral partners, with smaller assistance packages, 'so that their resources can be transferred to specified ... NGOs in greater need of official development assistance ... [T]here will be no more tied aid' (ibid.). Fourthly, in consultation with the Ministry of External Affairs (MEA), the government was to consider a debt relief package for heavily indebted poor countries.

Finally, it proposed to discontinue the earlier practice of extending loans or credit lines to other developing countries. Instead, it would provide grants or project assistance to developing countries in Africa, South Asia and other parts of the developing world under the umbrella of the India Development Initiative.

Discussions following the budget duly produced guidelines delineating various strategies for implementation. The government was to reorient its aid policies mainly by no longer taking aid from several donors and confining itself to a select few, and by itself setting up an agency for consolidating outward flows of aid (Ministry of Finance 2003). It also decided that it would release Official Development Assistance already committed to India, for diversion to developing countries in greater need.[2]

Since, apart from its mandate for fostering techno-economic and intellectual cooperation, the India Development Initiative was also intended to promote India's interests in overseas markets, a new government, which took office in 2004, announced a review of the initiative (Iyer 2004). As a result the budget for 2007/08 contained a proposal for a new entity, the India International Development Cooperation Agency (IIDCA), which is now likely to be renamed the Indian Agency for Partnership in Development (IAPD). It was noted that India had reached a stage of development from which it must assume greater responsibility for assisting other developing countries. The total amount of development aid was already about $1 billion annually, channelled through many ministries and agencies; it was felt that all activities relating to development cooperation should be brought under one umbrella, hence the proposed IIDCA. The ministries of External Affairs, Finance and Commerce, and other stakeholders, were to be represented in the new agency (Ministry of Finance 2007/08).

As yet IIDCA has not begun operating but its potential importance lies in the fact that India has now been a major development partner for various developing countries for several years. It is worth examining, however, the extent to which Indian aid programmes have played any significant part in India's foreign policy and to what extent development cooperation is leveraged to meet foreign policy goals.[3] For many years the focus of development aid was largely on South Asia, but more recently it has extended to other countries and regions. It has also diversified in terms of the financing mechanisms employed, and the nature of activities covered through development programmes. India has entered a phase of domestic development from which cooperation with many developing countries in 'frontier technologies' has advanced at considerable pace. For example, India has established several leading institutions in high technology, such as (with the African Union) the India–Africa Institute of Information Technology, the Ghana–India Kofi Annan Centre of Excellence in ICT, Ghana's first advanced information technology (IT) institute; and in Delhi has extended support to major international institutions including a centre of the Asia and Pacific Institute for Transfer of Technology in Panipat, and the UNESCO Regional Centre for Biotechnology in Delhi.

In expanding its development cooperation linkages in various parts of Africa and Latin America, India has tried to consolidate the flow of funds through effective partnerships. The first India–Africa Forum Summit, held in Delhi in 2008, produced a framework of cooperation that was later translated into an action plan that committed it to the establishment of new cooperative bodies (see Table 7.1). The India–Africa Institute of Foreign Trade was to meet within the next five years in Kampala, Uganda, while Burundi would host the Institute of Education Planning and Administration, which would train professionals to plan and manage higher education across Africa. Ghana hosts the India–Africa Institute of Information Technology, while the Diamond Institute was planned to be located in Botswana.

Delhi hosted a preparatory meeting with least developed countries (LDCs) in preparation for the fourth LDC Summit in May 2011,[4] where it announced an annual grant of another five scholarships for each LDC under the Indian Technical and Economic Cooperation Programme. India has also established a special fund of $5 million over the next five years to help implement programmes arising from the 2011 United Nations LDC IV conference in Istanbul, and a $500 million credit line over the next five years to be used specifically for

TABLE 7.1 Newly established Indian institutes in developing countries

Institute	Purpose	Country
Diamond Institute	Training for diamond polishing	Botswana
India–Africa Institute of Foreign Trade	MBA and related diploma courses in foreign trade	Uganda
India–Africa Institute of Information Technology	Professional courses in ICT	Ghana
Institute of Education Planning and Administration	Training professionals to plan and manage growth of higher education	Burundi
Institute for Telemedicine	Specialized training for doctors	Ethiopia
Entrepreneurship Development Centre	Training in economically active sectors	Senegal
Plastic Technology Training Centre	Designing, tool room, processing division and testing centre for the plastics industry	Namibia
Vocational Training Centre for Small and Medium Enterprises	Training in economically active sectors	Zimbabwe

projects and programmes of LDCs. India had earlier extended a $1 billion credit line for projects in Bangladesh (Bangladesh News 2011). Delhi intends to take a less restrictive approach to LDCs, and is anxious for the private sector to take an active role in this field. Since 2003, private and state-owned companies have invested $35 billion (Rs1.6 trillion) in LDCs and extended $4.3 billion in credit lines, while importing goods worth $10 billion from them (Roche 2011). In particular, the four LDCs commonly referred to as C4 or the 'cotton-growing four' (Benin, Burkina Faso, Chad and Mali) are being helped to develop their cotton sector (Hindustan Times 2011).

India has also made known its wish to participate with other countries to benefit third countries. This trilateral cooperation, which was a feature of early Indian aid programmes (see above), is likely to become more important as professional skills and other necessary resources such as finance and technology are combined in a bid to optimize returns on development expenditure. It has recently been suggested that India might partner with Germany for various infrastructure projects in Africa. The Indian Council of Medical Research and Helmholtz-Gemeinschaft Deutscher Forschungszentren (the Helmholtz Association, Germany's largest scientific organization) have come together in a €4.5 million project to study various infectious diseases that have affected more than seventeen million people across the globe (Alok 2007). Similarly, the UK's Department for International Development (DfID) is exploring possibilities for trilateral cooperation with India (Wall Street Journal 2007). In association with the US-based William J. Clinton Foundation, DfID has embarked on a programme costing up to £9 million between 2009 and 2012 to provide technical support to Indian companies producing and registering new treatments for AIDS and malaria, and negotiate affordable prices for those drugs. The aim is to help more than eleven million people with HIV/AIDS gain access to antiretroviral drugs by 2012 (India PRWire 2008).

Institutional framework and channels of assistance

As noted earlier, the MEA is the key agency for extending bilateral and technical assistance, through its various missions. The Department of Economic Affairs of the MoF is normally approached by MEA with country-specific requests for disbursements. When analysing economic assistance data, therefore, it is important to include both MEA and MoF as there can be differences between recommendations from

TABLE 7.2 Outflow of India's development assistance 1990–2011 (Rs million)

	1990–91	2003–04	2004–05	2005–06	2007–08	2009–10	2010–11
South Asia	1,333	11,000	11,555	12,873	13,725	18,572	18,590
Africa	90	716	1,068	609	500	1,250	1,500
Central Asia	0	52	85	90	200	1,450	400
Latin American countries					15	20	40
Other developing countries	1,091	1,760	7,173	5,168	9,157	1,045	1,443
ITEC	134	330	505	555	600	850	1,000
Loans			2,989	2,784	480	9,146	

Source: Ministry of Finance, Government of India Expenditure Budget, vol. 2; loans from MEA Annual Reports

the former and disbursements by the latter. As Table 7.2 shows, the quantum of development assistance from 1991 to 2010 has shown considerable fluctuations.

Multilateral flows Grants to multilateral institutions comprise almost 1 per cent ($3.6 million/Rs160 million)) of the total outflow. Multilateral institutions receive support through relevant ministries; for example, the Ministry of Commerce and Industry (MoCI) makes available $200,000 (Rs8.8 million) to the UN Industrial Development Organization, UNO is supported by the Ministry of Environment and Forest (MoEF) for Rs6.2 million and the MoF has helped fund a number of organizations, including the African Development Bank ($340,000/Rs15 million), the International Fund for Agricultural Development ($635,000/Rs28 million) and the Afghan Reconstruction Fund ($23,000/Rs1 million). The Ministry of Science and Technology allocates about $170,000 (Rs7.45 million) for international collaboration,[5] while the Ministry of Human Resource Development donates $340,000 (Rs15 million) to UNESCO.

Bilateral flows India's total bilateral aid has expanded from $22 million (Rs1 billion) in 1991/92 to $295 million (Rs13 billion) in 2006/07. These numbers include both grants and loans but exclude credit lines through the Export-Import Bank of India (EXIM Bank), which are recorded separately (see Figure 7.1). They also do not include India's support for multilateral agencies. The main recipients of aid under this programme have been India's neighbouring countries and some major African economies. Among the former, Bhutan is the prime beneficiary of aid and concessional loans, followed by Bangladesh and Nepal. Allocations for African countries increased from $2.4 million (Rs103 million) in 1991/92 to $24.3 million (Rs1,068 million) in 2004/05.[6] The tables show fluctuations across different years in South Asia and (initially) Africa, probably due to exceptional funding for specific large infrastructure projects. Neighbouring countries such as Bhutan, Maldives, Nepal and Sri Lanka have shown consistent increases in development support from India. Assistance takes different forms but includes training, technical advice, fellowships and scholarships at all educational levels, and provision of goods such as medical products. In the recent past, funding related to infrastructural construction and maintenance has also experienced major increases.

Development support from India for 2006/07 was mainly by way of bilateral grants and through Indian Technical and Economic Cooperation (ITEC) programmes which respectively accounted for 44 and 47 per cent of the total. The remaining 8 per cent was mostly made up of credit lines from EXIM Bank.

ITEC programme A brainchild of Prime Minster Nehru, ITEC was launched in 1964 as a vehicle for bilateral assistance, under the control of the MEA. It is supplemented by the Special Commonwealth Assistance for Africa Programme. The involvement of African developing economies in the science and technology sector is hampered by a lack of adequate and trained manpower, and India has made concerted efforts to enhance technical cooperation and capacity-building in this sector. India spends about $11 million (Rs500 million) annually on ITEC activities, with training programmes as the major policy plank, and since its inception has provided more than $2 billion in technical assistance to developing countries[7] (Ministry of Finance 2005/06). It currently provides 5,000 places for trainees in various relevant disciplines to representatives of 158 countries, many of which are LDCs (Hindustan Times 2011).

In twenty years from 1985, government funding for ITEC rose from $4.3 million to $12.6 million (Rs189 million to Rs555 million), while in the subsequent ten years the number of trainees under its auspices increased from 427 to 2,014. Government strategy appears to be to extend ITEC more widely among developing countries: originally trainees from Asian countries accounted for 57 per cent and those from Africa 32 per cent of the total, with the remaining 11 per cent from developing countries elsewhere. By 2005 this had changed: participation of other developing countries was 19 per cent against the same proportion from Africa. The number of participating countries increased from twenty-six in 1995 to forty-eight in 2005, the latter figure including several LDCs from Asia.

ITEC operations fall into five main categories, respectively (ITEC 2009).

- training in India for students nominated by ITEC partner countries (with a growing focus on new issues in trade, investment and technology);
- projects and related activities, including feasibility studies and

consultancy services, also extended to regional programmes under the Economic Commission for Africa, the G77, the Afro-Asian Rural Reconstruction Organization, the G15 and the Southern African Development Community;

- deputations of Indian experts abroad;
- study tours; and
- aid for disaster relief.

Project-related assistance is spread over a wide range of activities. For instance, under the ITEC programme a donation of a US$200,000 solar energy plant was made to Colombia in 2002. As shown in Table 7.2, allocations for ITEC programmes have expanded almost tenfold from 1990 to 2010, although the share of ITEC in total allocations for development assistance has declined. This may be because assistance to other developing countries has greatly increased: for instance, aid to Nepal has risen from $11.8 million in 1990 to $34.3 million in 2010 and assistance to Africa rose from $2 million to $34 million in the same period. In the case of Nepal, India introduced a novel scheme in 2003 called the Small Development Project (SDP). Under a memorandum of understanding between the government of India and the government of Nepal, this programme provided assistance directly to communities to finance small projects for infrastructure development and capacity-building in the areas of education, health and community development. All account-keeping and auditing are undertaken by the local communities themselves. In the period 2003–10, around 405 projects were financed, with a total outlay of $784 million.[8]

Indian industrial organizations are important to this effort. The Confederation of Indian Industry has undertaken several measures for capacity-building and technology transfer. In 2006, for example, it organized an international training programme on IT applications in manufacturing at a new IT hub at Ebene Cybercity, near Port Louis in Mauritius.[9] Its aim was to provide participants with a comprehensive understanding of IT applications in manufacturing, particularly automation and semi-automation in the clothing industry (an important industry in Mauritius); and to equip them to introduce and manage IT applications in their own organizations. Such integration of IT and communications across functions is helping companies in LDCs become more globally competitive.

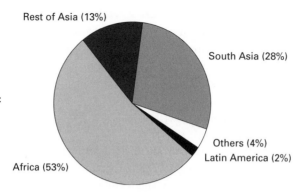

7.1 EXIM Bank's operative lines of credit as of 1 September 2010 source: Export-Import Bank of India (2010)

EXIM Bank is a lead financial institution in financing, facilitating and promoting India's international trade. Among its activities, negotiating credit lines has emerged as a key instrument for supporting small and medium enterprises (SMEs). Since the financial year 2003/04, when the government launched a new scheme for supporting development cooperation, lines of credit are provided on concessional terms for financing exports from India. The Indian government provides repayment guarantee and interest subsidy and equalization support to the EXIM Bank. This scheme was called the India Development and Economic Assistance Scheme (IDEAS). The bank extends credit to foreign financial institutions, regional development banks, sovereign governments and other agencies to enable buyers to import projects, goods and services from India on deferred credit terms. Since most Indian development cooperation takes the form of project aid, EXIM Bank plays a central role in the implementation of various such schemes. Aside from its own credit lines to overseas entities, since 2003 it has been extending credit at the behest of the Indian government to various developing countries. The top five recipients of Indian lines of credit are the Sudanese government ($350 million), Ceylon Petroleum ($150 million), Bank Mellat ($200 million), the Ethiopian government ($122 million) and the ECOWAS Bank for Investment and Development ($250 million).

Its total commitment in credit lines as of September 2010 was $5.2 billion, covering seventy-three separate lines in eighty-three countries in Africa, Asia, the Commonwealth of Independent States, Europe and Latin America. Figure 7.1 shows that EXIM Bank operates mainly in Africa, followed by South Asia and the remainder of

Asia (Export-Import Bank of India 2010). At the 2008 India–Africa Summit in Delhi, India announced an increase from $2.15 billion to $5.4 billion in credit lines to provide further impetus to project aid programmes in other countries. At the second India–Africa Summit in 2011 in Ethiopia, a further $5 billion in credit lines was offered and an additional $700 million to establish new institutions and training programmes in consultation with the African Union. Some of the initiatives announced included an India–Africa Food Processing Cluster, an India–Africa Integrated Textiles Cluster, an India–Africa Centre for Medium Range Weather Forecasting, an India–Africa University for Life and Earth Sciences and an India–Africa Institute of Agriculture and Rural Development.

India also announced support for the development of a new Ethiopia–Djibouti railway line to the tune of $300 million (Singh 2011).

Emerging policy options and the way forward

Policy options As noted earlier, development cooperation is an important tool for meeting strategic foreign policy goals. India, however, has yet to evolve mechanisms for ensuring its effective deployment to those ends. Current development cooperation policy rests on three planks: technical support; training programmes led by ITEC; and project-based support programmes. It is undeniable, however, that not only are there limited ties between foreign policy objectives and development cooperation, but also that linkages between the three planks need strengthening.

An increasing number of traditional donors are trying to decentralize their operations to the local level. Some have succeeded in placing up to 60 per cent of staff in the field. For example, DfID has evolved a business principle called 'closeness to client',[10] which involves placing half of its staff in its sixty-seven overseas offices. Each office puts forward its Country Assistance Plan, which is then submitted to headquarters to ensure consonance with national policy. Reforms at the Japan International Cooperation Agency have ensured greater deployment to field offices, while the Swedish International Development Cooperation Agency has launched three major decentralization projects with the aim of finding a balance between an empowered and strengthened field presence and a supportive organization at headquarters. India already has a highly decentralized development cooperation framework, as most of its projects are implemented through missions. The main challenge is to bring them under a broader programmatic framework to ensure greater coherence, synergy and consistency.

To help bring this about a modified structure may be useful. IIDCA would have to draw on expertise available within MEA and also upon the strengths of various ministries, individual professionals and specialized agencies. However, the fact that IIDCA has not been established yet indicates intricacies within the MEA. For some progress to be made, the MEA would have to see the advantages of a centralized institution to propel development cooperation. In line with the existing structures in the ministry, five regional departments could cover West Asia and North Africa, South-East Asia and Pacific, East Asia, South Asia, and sub-Saharan Africa. Among its departments five major sectors may be defined: social development, infrastructure, economic and technical cooperation (largely covering ITEC), research cooperation, and humanitarian assistance. Since science-based government entities, such as the departments of Science and Technology and of Biotechnology, the Ministry of Commerce and Industry, and other specialized agencies (for example, the Council for Scientific and Industrial Research) already have strong international cooperation programmes, their representatives might be recruited by way of a research council with an attached department of research cooperation. Several Indian NGOs possess established credentials in the field of humanitarian assistance[11] and a future department of humanitarian assistance could work closely with them. Several ministries already work very closely with NGOs within India, but no rules have been clearly defined for replicating this relationship beyond its borders.

In order to avoid a completely 'top-down' approach it has been suggested that the appropriate field units should always become involved when development cooperation programmes for their region are under discussion. Operational lines between field offices and headquarters should be defined from the outset, with systems sophisticated enough to avoid undue systemic delays and reach a balance between foreign policy goals and the desire to meet recipient countries' perceived expectations.

India also needs to respond effectively in the area of disaster relief diplomacy. Chandran et al. (2009) point out that there are certain events in other developing countries that can adversely affect India's economic interests; for example, a major earthquake in the Sichuan region of China in 2008 led to the closure of several silk manufacturing units in India, because Sichuan is a primary supplier of raw silk to several operations in Benares and Bangalore, among others. This affected many hundreds engaged in the sector.

The way forward Liaison between economic diplomacy and development has yet to be addressed in a way that introduces so-called 'pragmatism' to Indian development policy. While it is true that the amount of its own incoming aid is now in decline, India has a wealth of experience to offer developing countries that are aid recipients. This experience and India's own economic development model need to be placed before partner countries. There is an equal need for India to learn from its own long history as a recipient of development aid. In the past couple of years, a detailed and robust database has been created that may help to identify precise areas of concern at various domestic donor agencies. The same information is missing, however, when scrutinizing outgoing development assistance. At best, some details are available either in the annual reports of the MEA or on the websites of various Indian missions, but there is an urgent need to collate these details properly, to facilitate trend analysis.

At some stage, the government may also consider publishing external peer reviews of Indian development projects, which would help to ensure their better delivery in future. Lessons from established aid providers are there to be learned. Several traditional donors have evolved different mechanisms for gathering information, such as DfID's Performance Reporting Information System for Management. The German government's development aid agency, Deutsche Gesellschaft für Internationale Zusammenarbeit (GIZ), has established twenty regional sector centres charged with promoting the exchange of experience between field staff and headquarters, appropriately categorized documentation and the dissemination of cross-sectoral policies.

Once IIDCA begins operating, measures would probably be required for implementing integrated structures for policy planning and formulation, so that India may move gradually from a project- to a sectoral-based approach. If this came about, India might also be able to shed the peculiar colonial mindset that looks to importing raw materials from other developing countries. India's development cooperation projects should rather help set up units that may contribute to added value. For example, India at present imports large quantities of potassium from Senegal, but arguably it should explore the possibilities of supporting construction of a fertilizer plant close to the potassium mines to generate more local employment. Such projects may require the merger of several small schemes into one broad umbrella programme. Identification of strategic goals should be made within the context of India's basic international cooperation policies, in which case the MEA would have to produce a policy statement enumerating those objectives. This in turn would probably demand wide public consultation and detailed discussion on international cooperation. One possibility to accommodate such a debate would be an advisory council to consolidate and institutionalize specialized expertise and policy perspectives.

IIDCA may also play an important part in initiatives related to development cooperation programmes of those emerging economies that may be considering producing global public goods (a case in point is the current cooperation between Brazil and Cuba that could lead to the development of vaccines for meningitis, which could in turn provide African countries with vaccines for mass immunization in Africa at cost-effective prices) (TWN 2006). Similarly, in 2009 India announced the establishment of a pan-African e-network for improving connectivity in various parts of Africa, and committed $117 million to the project. South Africa and Brazil have joined other major economies in supporting the International Finance Facility for Immunization, a British initiative established in 2006 to accelerate the availability of funds for health and immunization programmes through the GAVI Alliance (formerly the Global Alliance for Vaccines and Immunization) in seventy of the world's poorest countries.[12] South Africa has pledged $20 million for this over twenty years and Brazil will do the same.

In sum, future policies and institutional arrangements should be seen against the background of changing requirements involving multiple organizations in partner countries. The future course of development aid is likely to be much more complex than that of the past, since expectations are now so much higher, and global development challenges so much greater. Any past successes of institutional machinery should not be the sole guideline for the future. Institutional innovation is a necessary condition for future performance, and for that reason should not be delayed.

Notes

1 Baru (2006) seems to suggest that Nehruvian policies incorporated pragmatism and ideas of linking economic interests with foreign policy goals but, after him, India followed his policy initiatives but lost the spirit of ideas.

2 Subsequently, the new government in 2004 changed the policy for incoming aid and agreed to accept aid.

3 There are studies like Abraham (2007) which have observed that India has not used this instrument effectively.

4 The first LDC event was held in Paris in 1981; the second again in Paris in 1991; the third in Brussels, Belgium, in 2001. This category of LDCs was first enunciated in 1971 but the preparatory work for it was done by the 2nd United Nations Conference on Trade and Development, which India hosted in Delhi in 1968. At its point of inception there were twenty-five LDCs. Over the years this grouping has grown to include forty-nine – until Maldives graduated recently – and now there are technically forty-eight least developed countries.

5 Technology cooperation has, incidentally, been one of the strongest areas for development cooperation. For a historical account of this, see Banerjee (1982).

6 The subsequent years of 2005/06 and 2006/07, though, show a decline, although there is an abnormal increase in the category of others, such as from Rs3 billion to Rs5 billion in 2006/07.

7 See Kumar (1987) for an early account of the programme. In 2007/08 forty-two institutions offered 200 courses to 4,000 students with different time frames.

8 Based on communication with the Indian Mission in Kathmandu.

9 Personal communication with the Confederation of Indian Industry.

10 DfID has adopted a one-point reference book called the Blue Book to guide on rules and procedures.

11 For instance, the Ramakrishna Mission bypassed government support in Nepal during the recent earthquake.

12 By investing the majority of resources up front – 'front loading' – this innovative funding programme will increase significantly the flow of aid to ensure reliable and predictable funding flows for immunization programmes and health system development during the years up to and including 2015.

References

AAA (2011) *Brief History of External Assistance in India – 2009–2010*, New Delhi: Aid, Audit and Accounts Division, Department of Economic Affairs, Ministry of Finance.

Abraham, I. (2007) 'The future of Indian foreign policy', *Economic and Political Weekly*, 20 October.

Alok, S. (2007) 'Clinical research: growing opportunities, dwindling manpower', *Financial Express*, New Delhi, 31 August.

Banerjee, B. N. (1982) *India's Aid to Its Neighbouring Countries*, New Dehli: Select Books.

Bangladesh News (2011) 'Dhaka champions LDCs' cause at Delhi meet', 18 February.

Baru, S. (2006) *Strategic Consequences of India's Economic Performance*, New Delhi: Academic Foundation.

Braude, W. (2007) 'Emerging powers and their development policies: case of South Africa', Presentation made at a workshop on Emerging Powers and Their Development Aid Policies organized by the South African Institute of International Affairs, Johannesburg, 30 October.

Broadman, H. G. (2007) *Africa's Silk Road: China and India's New Economic*

Frontier, Washington, DC: World Bank.

Chandran, D. S. et al. (2009) 'India's disaster relief diplomacy', *Foreign Affairs Journal*, 4(2), April–June, New Delhi.

Chaturvedi, S. (2006) 'An evaluation of the need and cost of selected trade facilitation measures in India: implications for the WTO negotiations', ARTNeT Working Paper no. 4, Bangkok: Asia-Pacific Research and Training Network on Trade (ARTNeT), United Nations Economic and Social Commission for Asia and the Pacific (UN ESCAP).

— (2007) 'Development aid policies: emerging experience from India', Presentation made at a workshop on Emerging Powers and Their Development Aid Policies organized by the South African Institute of International Affairs, Johannesburg, 30 October.

— (2008) 'The role of emerging powers in development cooperation: issues and future perspectives', Presentation made at the conference on Reshaping the Global Development Cooperation Architecture: The Role of the Emerging Powers, InWEnt and DIE, Bonn, 17 April.

Croft, A. (2011) 'UK gives $1.6 billion of aid to India over 4 years', Reuters, 14 February.

Export-Import Bank of India (2010) *Annual Report 2010–11*, Export-Import Bank of India.

Government of India (2011) Inaugural address delivered by the external affairs minister of India on 'Harnessing the positive contribution of South–South Cooperation for development of least developed countries (LDCs)', at the India–Least Developed Countries (LDCs) Ministerial Conference, New Delhi, 18 February.

Gujral, I. K. (1998) *A Foreign Policy for India*, External Publicity Division, Ministry of External Affairs, Government of India.

Hindustan Times (2011) 'South–South cooperation a new phenomena', 17 February.

India PRWire (2008) 'UK government and Clinton Foundation to help Indian companies produce cheaper aids drugs', 17 November.

ITEC (2009) 'Indian Technical and Economic Cooperation, 2009–10', Civilian Training Programme, Indian Technical and Economic Cooperation (ITEC), Ministry of External Affairs.

Iyer, P. V. (2004) 'Chidambaram shelves aid initiative', 26 June, rediff.co.in/cms/ print.jst?docpath=/money/2004/jun/26bud.htm, accessed 7 July 2008.

Kumar, N. (1987) 'India's economic and technical cooperation with the co-developing countries', in Agrawal et al., *South–South Economic Cooperation*, New Delhi: Radiant Publishers.

Kumar, N. and S. Waslekar (1994) 'Developing countries in the international division of labour in design engineering and construction services: the case of India', RIS Occasional Paper no. 45, Research and Information System for Developing Countries.

Menon, S. (2010) 'Cut in DfID aid not a concern for India', *Business Standard*, 16 July.

Ministry of External Affairs (1950) *Annual Report*, New Delhi: Ministry of External Affairs.

— (1951) *Annual Report*, New Delhi: Ministry of External Affairs.

— (1955) *Annual Report*, New Delhi: Ministry of External Affairs.

— (1958) *Annual Report*, New Delhi: Ministry of External Affairs.

— (1959) *Annual Report*, New Delhi: Ministry of External Affairs.

— (1960) *Annual Report*, New Delhi: Ministry of External Affairs.

— (2007) 'ITEC: civilian training programme 2007–08', Indian Technical and Economic Cooperation, Ministry of External Affairs.

Ministry of Finance (2003) 'Finance Ministry to formulate new guidelines for bilateral aid in consultation with development partners', Press release, Ministry of Finance, Government of India, 6 June, pib.nic.in/archieve/lreleng/lyr2003/rjun2003/06062003/r060620039.html, accessed 15 November 2011.

— (2003/04) Speech of Jaswant Singh, Minister of Finance, 28 February 2003.

— (2005/06) Annual Report, Government of India.

— (2007/08) Speech of P. Chidambaram, Minister of Finance, 28 February 2007.

Ministry of Foreign Affairs (2007) *Japan's Official Development Assistance White Paper 2007, Japan's International Cooperation*, Tokyo: Ministry of Foreign Affairs.

Parthasarathi, A. (2000) 'India's experience with TCDC', *Cooperation South*, 1, New York: UNDP.

Raja Mohan, C. (2003) *Crossing the Rubicon: The Shaping of India's New Foreign Policy*, New Delhi: Viking Penguin.

Rana, K. S. (1997) 'Promoting India's economic objectives abroad: the main tasks ahead', in L. Mansingh et al., *Indian Foreign Policy Agenda for the 21st Century*, vol. I, New Delhi: Foreign Service Institute and Konark Publishers.

— (2000) *Inside Diplomacy*, New Delhi: Manas Publications.

Reserve Bank of India (2010) *Report on Foreign Exchange Reserves*, Mumbai: Reserve Bank of India, November.

Roche, E. (2011) 'India may offer loans to poor nations to develop infrastructure', *Mint*, 16 February.

Sharma, S. N. (2006) 'India finally agrees to Paris Declaration on aid', *Economic Times*, 3 December.

Sikri, R. (2009) *Challenge and Strategy: Rethinking India's Foreign Policy*, New Delhi: Sages.

Singh, M. (2011) Address at the Plenary Session of the 2nd Africa–India Forum Summit, Addis Ababa, 24 May.

Srinivas, G. (2007) 'Ministry keen to create agency for providing development aid', *Hindu Business Line*, 31 December.

TWN (2006) 'Cuba: conquering vaccines – and their markets', *TWN Info Service on Health Issues (December 06/06)*, Third World Network.

Wall Street Journal (2007) 'As world cuts aid to India, UK pledges £252 mn more', 14 June.

World Bank (2001) 'India: the challenges of development – a country assistance evaluation', Washington, DC: World Bank Operation Evaluation Department.

8 | MEXICO: LINKING MESOAMERICA

Maximo Romero[1]

Introduction

International development cooperation exists to promote the dissemination of ideas, programmes and initiatives leading to real exchanges of best international practices.

In a 2007 report the United Nations General Assembly High Level Committee on South–South Cooperation noted a significant intensification of SSC. This was due to three main factors: the excellent economic performance of several developing countries; the positive results of efforts to achieve regional and sub-regional integration; and a focus on poverty reduction as part of the Millennium Development Goals (MDGs).[2] The report acknowledged significant progress in SSC since the adoption of the Buenos Aires Plan of Action (BAPA) in 1978, notably in regions such as Latin America.

After BAPA, regional and international organizations, such as the UN Economic and Social Council (ECOSOC), the UN Development Programme (UNDP), development banks and the Organisation for Economic Co-operation and Development (OECD), focused on the precise results and general effectiveness of the assistance. After the 2000 New York Millennium Summit, in which the development of a global partnership was agreed as one of the MDGs, participants moved forward through the Rome Declaration of 2003 to considering harmonization of cooperation efforts. The declarations and actions that followed (including Paris, Accra and the Doha Declaration on Financing for Development) serve to highlight an unprecedented global situation in which diverse mechanisms of international cooperation for development are becoming increasingly important, and where structures of cooperation, including SSC, meet with international support for their continuation and renewal. This understanding is a key element in the development of Mexico's cooperation policies.

Concepts such as triangular cooperation highlight the fact that principles change with time. Traditionally triangular cooperation was understood as a system whereby two donors – one developed and one developing economy – address cooperation with a third, less developed, country. Today non-traditional donors undertake triangular cooperation without the participation of a developed country. There are, however, no international rules to guide this process except, possibly, those principles applicable under the Paris Declaration.[3] This chapter focuses on Mexico and its dual cooperation role. It discusses, first, Mexico's current policy on cooperation, followed by new trends of cooperation implemented by the Mexican government. Finally, it analyses four case studies: (a) regional integration programmes with SSC; (b) triangular cooperation from traditional donors; (c) Mexico and Central America; and (d) one example of South–North cooperation.

Mexico's current international development cooperation activities: an overview

International cooperation is a key component of Mexico's foreign policy. Indeed, Article 89, section X of the United Mexican States Constitution mandates that Mexico will apply principles such as international development cooperation to its foreign policy.

As an upper-middle-income country Mexico operates an international cooperation policy with two facets, donor and recipient. As donor, it offers cooperation within the traditional structures of SSC and is also engaged in innovative schemes such as trilateral cooperation. As recipient, it is classed as a low-aid-dependent developing country. Mexico also recognizes that international cooperation, provided it is properly aligned with national development efforts, can make an important contribution to meeting domestic needs in certain economic and social sectors and regions of the country.

As donor, the strategic objectives of Mexico's cooperation are in line with both the international consensus and its own international commitments, in accordance with its constitutional mandate. It also pursues the MDGs. Mexico maintains excellent relations with countries in the western hemisphere, especially the Latin American and Caribbean countries (LAC). Its leadership and participation in several regional forums and summits are widely acknowledged, and deepening communications and relationships with its LAC partners has become one of the Mexican government's priorities. Mexico is also open to cooperation with countries from Africa and Asia. At the same time, given its comparative advantages in terms of culture, language, geographical positioning and so on, and its defined national interests, it has tended to concentrate on Latin America, especially neighbouring regions of Central America and the Caribbean. It is also fair to say that in line with the principles of alignment and appropriation, Mexico's main field of cooperation is shaped by the specific demands of its partner countries.

Responsibility for Mexico's cooperation policies and project implementation lies mainly with the Ministry of Foreign Affairs, through its Unit for Economic Relations and International Cooperation (URECI). The Office for Technical and Scientific Cooperation (DGCTC) is its main executive arm.

Most international cooperation projects offered by the Mexican government, along with those of other developing countries, are under the banner of technical cooperation. URECI and DGCTC are responsible for planning, disseminating, negotiating, coordinating and evaluating technical and scientific cooperation initiated by experts from ministries, agencies and the private sector. Those agencies are also the coordinators of those negotiations through which Mexico agrees its cooperation programmes within the framework of bilateral, regional and multilateral relationships. These negotiations are based on cooperation agreements that include technical, scientific, economic, cultural, educational and financing matters.

Mexico has formal cooperation agreements with some fifty countries. The government carries out its agenda for international development through joint commissions, bilateral meetings and cooperation programmes. Relevant projects are identified according to costs and shared benefits; and depending on the partner country, Mexico appears either as donor, recipient or both. Some of the more common criteria for current cooperation projects are:

- short internships, technical courses and training;
- feasibility and previous feasibility studies;
- development of human resources;
- exchange of experts;
- joint research;
- prospecting and diagnosis missions; and
- meetings, workshops and seminars.

Mexico has partnerships with both developed and developing countries. This kind of cooperation is considered 'horizontal', because it is designed to share responsibilities between parties, each of which will benefit from the other's capacities. Through their cooperation agencies or their foreign ministries, Mexico has established bilateral cooperation agreements with traditional donors such as Japan, Spain and Germany; as well as arrangements with regional and international groupings such as the European Union and the Organization of American States.

As a donor country, Mexico cooperates on a bilateral basis. Coordination and communication are established through local representations and embassies of recipient countries, and through Mexican embassies in association with the appropriate ministries of foreign affairs. Where cooperation agencies are available, such as in Peru, Ecuador and Colombia, Mexico works directly through them.

Given Mexico's limited resources, its bilateral schemes must be complemented by trilateral operations. The most important partner countries in this regard are Germany, Spain and Japan. Mexico's contribution by way of local knowledge, financial resources and the exchange of experts, taken with the developed countries' financial cooperation and/or technical assistance, has become an important means of achieving changes in the region's infrastructural development. In addition, Mexico's strategic geographical location, language and culture make a significant contribution to the success of trilateral projects.

Mexico's international development cooperation has recently been relaunched. In December 2009, after spending two years on its design and construction, the government completed its international cooperation registry system. Prior to this, Mexico had encountered difficulties in arriving at estimates of expenditure for each area of cooperation for all the relevant working regions. Mexico has now become one of the first developing countries to implement transparency programmes for the financial aspects of its cooperation programmes. (The legislative branch of government, the Congress of the Union, has approved legislation to establish a formal cooperation agency.)

The cooperation registry not only incorporates data concerning activities or projects but also tries to consolidate information with respect to direct and indirect costs. These might include costs related to joint research, exchange of experts, travel expenses, per diem expenditures and, more importantly, the cost related to the time and other commitments of its own personnel.

A new policy of international development cooperation

For Mexico the promotion of cooperation policy is paramount. As noted, Mexico is in the middle of a profound reorganization of its international cooperation system. A new cooperation law, approved by the Congress[4] and published by President Calderón's administration, entered into force on 16 April 2011.[5] It is an important step for Mexico, after four years of negotiations in Congress. This initiative was presented in 2007 by former minister of foreign affairs and current senator Rosario Green. The new legislation provides for the creation of the Mexican Agency for International Development Cooperation (AMEXCID).

Fifteen years ago, as other agencies of cooperation in the region were being created (e.g. the ABC in Brazil and ACCI in Chile), Mexico incorporated its Institute of Cooperation, by executive order. After the end of President Zedillo's administration in 2000, the new government of President Fox decided to dissolve the Institute and transfer its powers and obligations to the Ministry of Foreign Affairs. Mexico has learned from past experience and intends to establish its cooperation policies in a global context; aspiring to a major long-term role in international aid structures despite its limitations as an emergent economy. As its second attempt to consolidate a long-standing policy on cooperation, AMEXCID will operate as the leading agency, responsible for coordinating all federal institutions and research centres within Mexico and with its partners abroad.

AMEXCID will be created as an independent entity, part of the Ministry of Foreign Affairs, with its own budget and technical autonomy. AMEXCID's scope includes Mexico as donor and recipient in the areas of technical, scientific, educative, cultural, economic and financial cooperation. Mexico is the first developing country to pass a law which was drafted from the start with this dual function of being responsible for both incoming and outgoing aid in mind (the Brazilian and Chilean agencies of cooperation, as well as others, such as those of Peru and Colombia, were created initially as exclusive agencies for receiving cooperation).

The law is based on three pillars:

- a new international cooperation agency (AMEXCID) as an independent body within Mexico's Foreign Affairs Ministry;
- a trust fund for cooperation; and
- a Consolidation of Cooperation Registry.[6]

The law made provision for AMEXCID to be established by no later than 4 August 2011 and for the Cooperation Plan and the trust fund to be ready by early December 2011. Mexico's National Registry would begin operations by 31 March 2012.

Challenges The creation of AMEXCID reflects worldwide practice. Mexico is an important player in SSC, and as such further changes are expected in its foreign policy over the next decade, in particular as the cooperation law comes into force. The law is applicable to all federal institutions and research centres, and local governments such as state and municipal administrations.

Mexico's new law incorporates bilateral, regional, multilateral and triangular cooperation, as well as humanitarian aid. It emphasizes the need to cooperate with Central America and the rest of the Latin American countries and the Caribbean.

Congress will allocate budgetary resources that can be complemented by foreign governments, international organizations or local governments.

Statistics on Mexico–South cooperation

The new cooperation law will affect Mexico's current cooperation framework as the country embarks upon an institution-building process leading to the creation of AMEXCID. This task will represent a challenge for Mexico, which is a member of the OECD but not of the Development Assistance Committee (DAC).

In the past Mexico has provided only limited information regarding international development cooperation. The new cooperation law, however, establishes an international development cooperation registry that takes account of the country's dual role as donor and recipient. In that respect, it should be noted that over the past two years the Ministry of Foreign Affairs has worked with the OECD, the UN Development Programme (UNDP) and its own national statistics offices to create an information system that holds data concerning international cooperation activities. The Information System of Mexico's International Cooperation for Development (SIMEXCID) includes a formula to estimate the economic value ('real cost') of those Mexican experts involved in cooperation projects and activities. The formula covers the total participation costs of those officials, over and above administrative expenses such as transportation, travel and accommodation. The table below shows the most recent (2009) valuation of Mexican technical and scientific cooperation.

TABLE 8.1 Cost and economic value of Mexico's technical and scientific cooperation, 2009 (cost and value in US dollars: cost/value as percentage)

	Cost	Economic assessment	Economic value	Cost/ value
Chile	817,219	3,461,358	4,278,577	19.1
Costa Rica	1,144,804	2,844,067	3,988,870	28.7
Guatemala	316,458	1,193,231	1,509,689	21.0
El Salvador	270,537	820,473	1,091,011	24.8
Bolivia	492,573	544,752	1,037,325	47.5
Colombia	168,921	629,660	798,580	21.2
Ecuador	212,314	686,664	898,978	23.6
Uruguay	119,137	530,037	649,174	18.4
Cuba	184,129	276,872	461,001	39.9
Honduras	56,080	260,635	316,715	17.7
Argentina	81,800	185,203	267,002	30.6
Panama	50,648	185,730	236,378	21.4
Nicaragua	30,686	155,979	186,665	16.4
Dominican Republic	59,645	86,940	146,585	40.7
Peru	27,071	68,640	95,711	28.3
TOTAL	4,032,021	11,930,240	15,962,260	25.3

Note: The cost represents the share of expenses assumed for the development of the activity (T+G). The assessment is the value assigned to the agent/expert [(X*(1+A)*(1+E) plus operating costs (FC)]. The economic value is the result of adding the first two.

Source: Ibero-American General Secretariat (SEGIB), based on data from the Technical and Scientific Cooperation Bureau of the Foreign Ministry of Mexico

Mexico, as an upper-middle-income country, is a marginal beneficiary of international development cooperation. It continues, however, to receive important support from international cooperation agencies for specific projects. The main strategic donors in this field are the USA, Japan, Germany, France and Spain. It may be anticipated that as its economy develops Mexico will receive less support of this kind and will be compelled to consolidate its international development

Over 10.1%
7.6–10.0%
5.1–7.5%
2.6–5.0%
Less than 2.5%

8.1 Distribution of cooperation initiatives executed by Mexico

Note: The map shows the geographic distribution of Mexican cooperation in the region, measured by percentages according to the number of actions implemented in each recipient country.

Source: Ibero-American General Secretariat (SEGIB), *Report on South–South Cooperation in Ibero-America*, Segib, Madrid, 2008, p. 42

policy. In 2008 the UNDP 'graduated' Mexico,[7] so other countries and international organizations will probably follow suit.

Mexico's active participation in SSC has been recognized by different regional organizations, including the Ibero-American General Secretariat (SEGIB). As a donor, Mexico has demonstrated an important level of stability; according to SEGIB's 2009 *Report on South–South Cooperation in Ibero-America*, Mexico was the second-largest regional donor in 2008, and the third in 2009.

As Figure 8.1 shows, priority countries for Mexican cooperation are in Central America, and less importantly South America and the Caribbean. This situation is likely to change, however, given the cooperation that Mexico provided during 2010 to Haiti and the Dominican Republic, among other Caribbean countries.

Triangular cooperation in Latin America and the Caribbean SEGIB has carried out various studies to quantify its activities in Latin America and the Caribbean; seventy-two activities or projects were identified and registered in 2008. In that year, Chile and Mexico were the major new participants in triangular cooperation initiatives, respectively accounting for 35 and 25 per cent of total projects.

In its latest report (2010) SEGIB states that in order to harmonize cooperation criteria a more precise distinction is to be made between activities and projects. In that respect, Mexico has been one of the

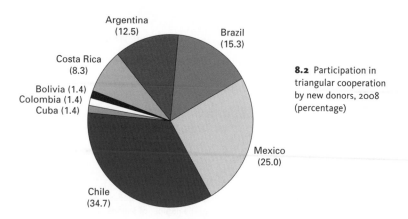

8.2 Participation in triangular cooperation by new donors, 2008 (percentage)

Source: Ibero-American General Secretariat (SEGIB), *Report on South–South Cooperation in Ibero-America*, Segib, Madrid, 2009, p. 87, Segib.org/publicaciones/files/2009/12/South-South_.pdf

RECIPIENTS

		LMIC											UMIC							
PROVIDERS		Bolivia	Colombia	Colombia	Cuba	Ecuador	El Salvador	Guatemala	Honduras	Nicaragua	Paraguay	Peru	Dominican R	Argentina	Chile	Costa Rica	Mexico	Panama	Uruguay	Venezuela	TOTAL
LMIC	Bolivia		1																		1
	Brazil	10	7	14	4	4	3		2	15	8	2	9		6	7	5	10		15	121
	Colombia	1		8		8	12	8	3	1	3	7	1		6	8	8	2		1	77
	Cuba	13	7	5		4	3	11	4	6	2	5	3	9	5	2	7	8	5	106	205
	Ecuador									1										14	15
	El Salvador																				
	Guatemala		1																		1
	Honduras																				
	Nicaragua																		1		1
	Paraguay		2																		2
	Peru																				
	Dominican R																				
UMIC	Argentina	12	10	7	14			3		2	18	2	2			3	4	3		9	89
	Chile	3		2	2	2	2	18			2		5			7	10	1	1		55
	Costa Rica			5													1				6
	Mexico	3		7	4	15	11	27	4	2		2	4	5	12	20		3	7		124
	Panama																				
	Uruguay													1		1	1			2	5
	Venezuela	25	8	1	103	4	1	1			24	2		4		1		1		4	179
	TOTAL	67	25	38	145	29	29	75	16	39	41	21	27	24	18	43	39	28	29	148	881

8.3 Bilateral horizontal South–South cooperation projects, 2009 (in units)

Note: Countries classified by income level according to World Bank GNI per capita criteria: lower middle income – LMIC (US$936–US$3,705); upper middle income – UMIC (US$3,706–US$11,455)

Source: Ibero-American General Secretariat (SEGIB), Report on South–South Cooperation in Ibero-America, Segib, Madrid, 2010, p. 29, segib.org/publications/files/2010/12/sur-sur-ingles.pdf

few countries able to offer relatively comprehensive information on its activities. Given the clear differences between different countries' progress on cooperation in the region, some of their data were misleading. It is worth noting that, for several periods, Cuba stands as SSC's main donor country. Despite detailed analysis of its actions, however, the methodology used to arrive at this conclusion remains

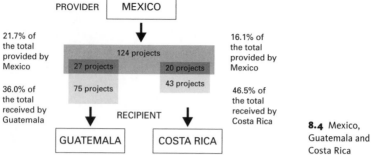

8.4 Mexico, Guatemala and Costa Rica

Source: Ibero-American General Secretariat (SEGIB), *Report on South–South Cooperation in Ibero-America*, Segib, Madrid, 2010, p. 39, Segib.org/publicaciones/files/2010/12/sur-sur-ingles.pdf

unclear. Figure 8.3 shows how, with 124 projects, Mexico stands as one of the three main SSC donor countries.

The SEGIB report shows that Mexico executed projects in fifteen countries. More than one third of them were concentrated in Guatemala and Costa Rica (see Figure 8.4), indicative of the priority Mexico applies to the Central American region.

Case study: the Mesoamerica Project

The Mesoamerica Project, formerly called Plan Puebla Panamá,[8] is a proposal launched by the Mexican government in 2001 that aims to improve the quality of life of inhabitants of the territory that includes Mexico's south-south-east region and seven Central American countries,[9] a geographical region known as 'Mesoamerica'.[10] It represents one of Mexico's most ambitious initiatives in terms of regional integration and development cooperation. This case study shows how, through the Mesoamerica Project, Mexico provides development assistance to Central America, and how the mechanisms used for the Project are an effective means of promoting dialogue, integration and joint projects between SSC partners.[11]

In explaining the aims, activities and results of the Project, the study also analyses how it is informed by the principles of the Paris Declaration, such as: ownership, alignment, harmonization, management of results, and mutual accountability. Mexico has endorsed those principles as well as those of the Accra Agenda for Action (AAA).

The Mesoamerica Project is a cooperative initiative focused on

Central America, a key area of Mexico's development cooperation. The project presents an overall framework for economic and human development in the region, and for continuous development. Mexico also contributes significant resources for the implementation of the project, both financially and through technical assistance. Although the Mesoamerica Project precedes the Paris Declaration, it complies with many of the Declaration's principles.

One of Mexico's priorities is to build a strategic alliance with Central American nations which seeks to enhance the Mesoamerican region's human and environmental capital within a framework of sustainable development that respects cultural and ethnic diversity, and is open to Mesoamerican civil society and the international community. In June 2001 in San Salvador, the presidents of Belize, Costa Rica, El Salvador, Guatemala, Honduras, Nicaragua, Panama and Mexico approved the text[12] that launched the plan. This original proposal was formulated by Mexico in order to promote social and economic development in Mesoamerica.[13] The Mesoamerica Project comprises nine initiatives along three strategic lines of action (also called development lines). These are:

- Human Development and Its Context: further subdivided into four initiatives: human development; sustainable development; national disaster prevention and mitigation; and climate change.
- Competitiveness and Productive Integration: formed by five initiatives: energy; competitiveness and trade facilitation; telecommunications services integration; transport; and tourism.
- Institutional Strengthening: this strategy constitutes a transversal issue around which the plan is structured. Its purpose is to assure continuity in state policy, followed by coordination, planning and follow-up mechanisms – primarily the Presidential Summit and the Executive Commission – and the Technical Commissions and Groups for each initiative. It also includes transversal civil society and indigenous population information, and consultation and participation programmes.

Within the Mesoamerica Project, finance for public investment projects is derived mainly from participating countries' national budgets, together with credits granted to the specific country or project. These credits mainly centre on infrastructure projects such as roads, electricity and telecommunication networks. International organizations also offer significant non-refundable cooperation at the formulation, management and implementation stages of the projects. This aid is always within the appropriate cooperation areas and structures of the plan. Examples might be projects which require technical assistance and skills training, among other needs; cooperation is also promoted by development institutions such as the Inter-American Development Bank (IDB) and the World Bank.

Mexico's contribution to implementation of the Mesoamerica Project Mexico contributes to the Mesoamerica Project through a range of instruments. These include technical assistance provided by Mexican experts, as well as specific financial contributions to individual projects. It is important, however, to mention a particular aspect of Mexico's support related to the resources available under the Energy Cooperation Programme for Central American and Caribbean Countries, also known as the San José Agreement (SJA). The SJA was signed in 1980 by the governments of Mexico and Venezuela and renewed annually until November 2005.[14] It assured supplies of oil, financing of trade-related activities, and public and private sector studies and projects between Costa Rica, El Salvador, Guatemala, Honduras, Nicaragua, Jamaica and the Dominican Republic. Belize joined in 1988 and Haiti in 1991.[15]

The accord has fallen away since Venezuela began pursuing its interests through other instruments.

President Chávez of Venezuela has shifted the country's policy to new and diverse modalities away from Mexico and Central America, preferring its alliances with partners such as Cuba and Bolivia. Unfortunately, no further approaches to discuss SJA have been recorded so far. It is clear that Venezuela's administration has taken a different strategy, including its termination of its Free Trade Agreement with Mexico and Colombia.

For Mexico, however, the SJA remains a priority and is still used to support cooperation programmes; some development assistance to the Mesoamerican Project has been provided by Mexico through its legal and institutional frameworks. Under the SJA system 20 per cent of revenues accruing to Mexico from its oil sales to Central American countries is deposited in a fund that may be used for public or private research and development projects (e.g. road construction, other infrastructure, feasibility studies and so on) in any of the beneficiary countries. The fund is administered by the Central American Bank for Economic Integration (Cabei), and Mexico's Foreign Trade Bank (Bancomext).

Consistent with DAC recommendations on untying certain ODA to the least developed countries (LDCs) and in order to facilitate the use of resources from the SJA to finance activities under the plan, Mexico introduced important changes and amendments to the SJA in 2001. These included greater granting of credits, a reduction of the share of joint resources from 61.5 to 55 per cent of the total, and a broadening of uses permitted under the agreement. In consequence 45 per cent of those resources can now be used by partner countries for local expenditures. In 2003 a total of $684.7 million was assigned to countries participating in the Mesoamerica Project, of which $275.5 million (40.2 per cent) was committed to thirty projects and $409.2 million (59.8 per cent) remained available for financing feasibility studies, development projects and trade.

In 2005, Mexico introduced further flexibility and allowances into the SJA. In particular, interest rates for participating LDCs (i.e. Honduras and Nicaragua) were further lowered to 2 per cent, thus bringing the Mesoamerica Project into conformity with the joint IMF–World Bank Heavily Indebted Poor Countries (HIPC) protocols. The duration and grace period of credits were extended for credits in both public and private sectors.

In Honduras and Nicaragua, those resources were applied to infrastructure projects that are part of the Mesoamerica Project. So far, $22.8 million has been allocated to the Honduras Puerto Cortés–Frontera highway at the Guatemalan border, while $19.5 million is being spent in Nicaragua for repairing and building the Chinandega–Guasaule highway. Both these schemes are part of the Mesoamerica Project.

Results of the Mesoamerica Project The original portfolio represents an investment of about $8 billion, with progress on thirty-three regional projects that absorbed a total of $4.5 billion. Among these projects are:

- *Moves towards a regional electricity market in Central America through harmonizing the regulatory framework.* The most significant project within this scheme is the start of construction to integrate a Central American Countries Electrical Power Inter-connection

(Siepac) with 2,000 kilometres of electricity transmission lines. These include the Mexico–Guatemala energy interconnection and feasibility studies for a Panama–Colombia interconnection. Apart from extending electrical power to remote areas, completion of this project will effect savings of 15–20 per cent in electricity costs for those regions. The Mexico–Guatemala interconnection (*Los Brillantes*) was inaugurated during the visit to Guatemala of Mexico's President Calderón in October 2009. Currently Mexico can trade electricity only with Guatemala, but in future it will be able to do so with the whole of Central America.[16]

- *Creation of the Mesoamerican Integration Energy Programme*, which focuses on development of a hydrocarbon market, interconnection of energy grids, renewable energy, biofuels and energy efficiency.

- *Rural electrification* benefiting 300,000 new users in Guatemala and Honduras.

- *Improvement of the International Network of Mesoamerican Highways (Ricam)*, including the modernization and construction of international bridges that will contribute to the accessibility of the region. Funds have been allocated to rehabilitate 13,000 kilometres of roads, and for the construction of two main highways in the Atlantic corridor that will be completed by 2012. According to a 2009 report published in the Economic Commission for Latin America and the Caribbean *FAL Bulletin*, 6,629 kilometres of the road work had been completed by that date.

- *Conclusion of a technical and financial feasibility study for the Mesoamerican Information Highway (AMI)*, a fibre-optic telecommunications network to be built using Siepac infrastructure; as well as cooperation programmes with Mexico and Colombia to support *telecentros*. These are digital community centres that provide Internet access for services such as education, business development and health.

- *Public and private sector participation in the Mesoamerican Competitiveness Council*, which guides the establishment of priorities to improve competitiveness in areas such as logistics, technological and scientific development, trade facilitation, elimination of non-tariff barriers and transportation services.

- *Implementation of a pilot epidemiological observation programme*, with special reference to malaria, dengue, haemorrhagic fever, Chagas', tuberculosis and HIV/AIDS.

• *Conclusion of the first stage of the Mesoamerican Risk Map*, to identify areas in Mexico and Central America that are vulnerable to natural disasters, and methods of prevention.

Mexico's support through the SJA: International Network of Meso-american Highways (Ricam) One concrete achievement of the Mesoamerica Project, through the mechanisms of the SJA, is financial and cooperation aid for infrastructure, especially the extension and improvement of highways and roads that connect Mesoamerica. The Rehabilitation and Improvement of the Chinandega–Guasaule Road project involves reconstruction of 71.8 kilometres of road for the Mesoamerican Pacific Corridor. This road is in northern Chinandega, itself the extreme north-western region of Nicaragua, in the coastal zone of the Pacific Corridor. It will link the cities of Managua, Leon, Chinandega and Guasaule, the last sited at the border with Honduras. Cabei provided $19.5 million for this project.

Rehabilitation and upgrading of the Chinandega–Guasaule road will enhance regional capacity in terms of movement of people and the flow of trade. International carriers and other users will enjoy reduced transport costs, faster travel and improved security.

The project belongs to a series of initiatives that aim to benefit regional integration and the sustainable integrated development of the Mesoamerican region. Specifically, the road integration programme is aimed at the construction, improvement, rehabilitation and main-tenance of main roads. It will have a beneficial effect on health services and education capacity, and will improve the competitiveness of Central American economies by making transport more efficient.

Key factors leading to favourable results for the Mesoamerica Pro-ject Given the ancient Mesoamerican cultures' common traditions and history, it is to be expected that modern Mesoamerica shares regional and national development aims and interests. The challenges that these countries face make for relatively smooth cooperation.

Ownership. After the Mexican proposal was launched, all member countries' governments committed themselves to strengthening the plan, not only through regular meetings (the Presidential Summit, the Executive Commission and Technical Commissions and Groups), but also by taking into account the part played by civil society organiza-tions and the private sector. These are regarded as key participants in development assistance structures. The attitude of the indigenous people of the region is a further significant factor. Through a range of social programmes the Mesoamerica Project is intended both to contribute to eradication of poverty and through joint programmes to promote better integration of these groups into the wider society.

Alignment. The Mesoamerica Project takes into consideration each country's different financial policies and practices, in order to ensure the effectiveness of their projects within each national context. Nevertheless, all member countries are committed to an attempt to align some at least of their national activities and initiatives with the main goals of the plan. Hence, within the framework of the SJA, partner countries submit proposals for specific projects to an evaluation committee. Once a proposal is approved it is implemented by partner countries using their own domestic systems and procedures.

Two aspects must be factored in when considering assurances of support under the SJA. The first is that the availability of SJA resources of itself makes for a degree of predictability. Aside from meeting basic eligibility criteria, there are no conditions attached to the use of SJA funding. As member countries accumulate SJA resources, therefore, they can decide for themselves how to use them. Secondly, the level of resources to be made available is linked to each individual member country's oil imports. Fluctuations in those imports affect the total amount of funds available for development. This factor is still relatively predictable, however, since the SJA also contains provisions under which the share of available resources is linked to the price of oil.

It is important that, as noted, 45 per cent of these resources can now be used by member countries for domestic purposes. Thus through technical and scientific cooperation with many Mesoamerica Project partner countries, Mexico also contributes to strengthening each beneficiary country's institutions and systems. Examples include cooperation with Costa Rica to strengthen citizens' participation and accountability for municipalities; cooperation with El Salvador for capacity-building of local authorities; and capacity-building for various ministries and government agencies in Guatemala.

Harmonization. The Mesoamerica Project is an important instrument for regional development. It provides a platform for coordinated support from various sources, including national governments, multilateral development banks and bilateral donors. One eligibility criterion for new schemes under the Project is that they should be harmonized with other regional projects, to avoid duplication.

A further step towards harmonization is the involvement of institutions such as Cabei, which, especially within the mechanism of the SJA, is vital to the plan's implementation. Support from the Inter-American Development Bank (IADB) and the Organization of American States is also critical to its success.

Management of results. The Mesoamerica Project has been in operation for some time and its results can now be measured and taken into account in the annual planning and budgeting of each participant country. Coordination between all members on monitoring and agreed evaluation of recent results is important to the regional execution of the Project over the following year. The project administration's evaluation of its past performance is also part of the decision-making process for each year's implementation.

Mutual accountability. Since the Mesoamerica Project is a regional mechanism and involves the government participation of eight countries, transparency and mutual accountability are vital. One important means of providing information and receiving requests is through the plan's web page, www.planpuebla-panama.org/index.htm. This site may be regarded as the main channel of information and communication for all the countries involved, and especially for citizens interested in the development of the plan.

Results and lessons One of the most important results of the Mesoamerica Project is the creation of regional initiatives for specific areas. These initiatives involve contributions from all participant countries, and focus on a specific issue that affects the region as a whole and is therefore best addressed from a regional perspective.[17] Such initiatives include:

- Mesoamerican Initiative for National Disaster Prevention and Mitigation;
- Mesoamerican Initiative for Energy; and
- Mesoamerican Initiative for Transportation.

Among the main lessons arising out of the Project is an innovative scheme through which Mexico plays a dual role as recipient from bilateral or multilateral donors, and a donor to neighbouring countries. A number of lessons have emerged.

First, development assistance and capacity-building require working with resources provided by the beneficiary country that best respond to its own domestic needs. The process is not a one-way street from North to South. Instead, development assistance involves mutual learning between all stakeholders, particularly, and increasingly, from South to South (and sometimes from South to North).

Secondly, ODA from traditional donors, combined with technical cooperation from emerging donors, enhances mutual understanding and learning among all development partners. In addition, triangular cooperation has great potential, combining as it does financial resources, such as ODA from traditional donors, with the knowledge and experience accumulated by emerging donors. In itself it can also be considered a learning instrument for practising 'equal partnership', which makes ODA projects more efficient and sustainable over time.

Thirdly, partner countries' 'ownership' and leadership in managing and coordinating related projects are essential elements for successful development projects.

In addition, international organizations and agencies such as the UNDP, the IDB or the World Bank play an important part in identifying relevant experience and creating linkages between the participants. The IDB is the largest single investor in the funding of the Mesoamerica Project, providing 21 per cent of the total of $8 billion from participant countries and the private sector. The president of the IDB acted as coordinator for the Puebla-Panama Plan Promotion and Financing Committee, established in Miami in 2008. As such, the Bank serves as the primary vehicle for allocating financial and knowledge resources in the Mesoamerica Project as a whole (which comprises almost one hundred separate projects).[18]

Other cooperation projects effected by Mexico

Many DAC countries are dissatisfied with the results generated by years of North–South technical cooperation, which they see as contributing little to capacity development in partner countries. This view was, for example, reflected in the first draft of the AAA, which stated that 'technical cooperation efforts remain largely uncoordinated and supply driven' and went on to suggest that these flaws have 'hampered capacity development'.

As noted earlier, Mexico's technical cooperation stems from its comparative advantage as a regional donor. It is demand-driven, naturally aligned with the priorities of partner countries and therefore designed to help develop endogenous capacity among recipients. As a developing country, Mexico is in the same position as its recipient partners. Its assistance programmes are not conceived in universities or research centres detached from Southern economic, political and social realities. They are technical cooperation schemes that in many instances have been applied on a large scale and in a socio-economic context very similar to that of most of its partner countries. Mexico's technical cooperation in social policy, for example, is backed by its own experience, which has also proved relevant in a developed country context.

It appears that in many respects, where South–South cooperation (i.e. funding) fails, North–South cooperation excels. The converse also applies. Dialogue between traditional and non-traditional donors is therefore necessary. Both need to evolve synergies to exploit trilateral cooperation, to achieve the common goals of alleviating poverty, meeting the MDGs and avoiding duplication.

Triangular cooperation: Mexico–Japan with Latin America and the Caribbean Triangular cooperation by Mexico and Japan with third parties arose from the need for joint efforts combining Mexico's experience in technical cooperation for development with that of Japan in providing ODA.

In order to formalize the mechanisms of SSC, to regulate collaborative actions within its framework and to exploit the two nations' capacities to benefit third countries through the diversification of existing channels of cooperation, Mexico and Japan signed a Joint Programme of Cooperation (PCCMJ) in October 2003. Each party established an executive and a technical group, charged with creating a coordination mechanism to achieve better communication, monitoring and scrutiny of the programme's activities.

The executive and the technical group establish strategies of joint cooperation. The former assembles and approves the annual working plan and the budgets. The latter organizes strategies and areas of cooperation; establishes the basis for collaboration with third countries; proposes mechanisms of evaluation and scrutiny for cooperative projects; and finally, manages the links between the Mexican institutions that execute activities established by the PCCMJ.

Triangular cooperation: Mexico and Germany with Guatemala
CASE STUDY: SOLID WASTE TREATMENT Mexico and Germany are promoting triangular cooperation both to foster regional integration and to strengthen their bilateral relationship. Together, they instituted a project for solid waste management on a municipal scale in Guatemala. The outcome was the creation of the Guatemalan network of environmental promoters of control and integrated management of solid waste. Institutions involved in the project included: Mexico's Ministry of Environment and Natural Resources, its National Institute of Ecology, and the National Centre for Investigation and Ambient Capacity Building; and the German Agency for Technical Cooperation. The beneficiary institution was the Ministry of Atmosphere and Natural Resources of Guatemala.

As a result a committee was created from the institutions supporting the network. In order to achieve project sustainability, the committee evolved a working plan which guaranteed the application of better practices for disposal of solid waste in Guatemala.

Currently, Mexico and Germany are evaluating the implementation of a second phase of the programme in Guatemala, while similar projects are planned for El Salvador, Ecuador and the Dominican Republic.[19]

In late 2009 and early 2010, Mexico, together with Germany and Guatemala, as well as with El Salvador and Japan, carried out independent evaluations of its triangular cooperation programmes. The purpose was to monitor the results and to present successful case studies at the High Level Event in Colombia in March 2010. The Task Team on South–South Cooperation (TT-SSC) listed both cases above as successful projects.[20]

IMPROVEMENT OF TECHNOLOGY FOR CONSTRUCTION AND DIFFUSION OF LOW-INCOME EARTHQUAKE-RESISTANT HOUSING IN EL SALVADOR This project was triggered by a seminar held in January 2001, on reconstruction in El Salvador following a violent earthquake in January of that year. Initially a management committee was established that included government institutions, public universities and NGOs. The project aimed at creating a laboratory to carry out tests on earthquakes; the laboratory was constructed in the University of El Salvador with the help of the José Simeón Cañas Central American University in San Salvador.

As a result thirty-one Mexican experts have offered technical assistance and have participated in meetings of the project's Joint Coordinating Committee. As part of Mexico's cooperation, some 450 Salvadoreans have received technical training. The project has transmitted to Central America technical knowledge related to earthquake-resistant construction technologies. Based on the results of the project, El Salvador is reformulating its laws and regulations on the construction of domestic housing. There is also the intention to establish a Central American regional laboratory for large structures responsible for monitoring activities related to earthquake-resistant construction and promoting the use of improved and more earthquake-resistant materials in low-income housing construction.

South–North cooperation: Oportunidades programme as a model for New York City With the aim of helping some of its poorest people out of poverty traps that in some cases are multigenerational, the New York City authorities are using Mexico's *Oportunidades* conditional cash transfer programme as a model. Some 5,100 families in the Bronx, in Harlem and in the Brownsville sections of Brooklyn will participate in 'Opportunity NYC', the first conditional cash transfer in the USA. Under the scheme these families will receive annual cash transfers ranging from $4,000 to $6,000, provided they meet certain education, health and employment targets. In 2007 New York mayor Michael Bloomberg led a team of New York officials to rural areas in Tepoztlan and Toluca to observe the operation of the *Oportunidades* programme in those regions. *Oportunidades* benefits 25 million low-income Mexicans, representing about a quarter of the country's population. Costing $2.5 billion annually, it is similar to other conditional cash transfer programmes in Latin America, such as *bolsa familia*, a scheme that reaches 46 million low-income Brazilians (see Chapter 5).

'Opportunity NYC' was a two-year, $53-million programme, launched in December 2007. To speed its start-up it was privately funded by the Rockefeller Foundation and other donors. The first cash payments, averaging $524, were made in December 2007 to 1,431 families. Payments include $25 or $50 per month to reward 95 per cent school attendance for elementary, middle and high school students; $25 for attending parent–teacher conferences; and $50 for obtaining a library card. Improvements in test scores can increase payments to $300–$600. High school students can share $600 with their parents for annually accumulating eleven credits, with a $400 bonus for graduating. In addition there are sets of incentives for healthcare and for maintaining employment.

With reference to the new South–North route for conditional cash transfers, World Bank Vice-President for Latin America and the Caribbean Pamela Cox stated:

> Development cooperation goes well beyond the traditional concept of aid or assistance, and … it is not a one-way process limited to financial flows from the rich world to developing countries, but a truly mutual learning process, where innovative ideas, and state-of-the-art knowledge, are part of our shared resources to build a better world.[21]

Conclusion

Mexico's international role as an emerging economy and non-traditional donor is increasing in importance. Its differing methods and the departure from previous international practice that they represent demonstrate that in addition to traditional donor structures, upper-middle-income economies can also provide efficient technical and scientific assistance to other similar economies, even those of the North. For this to work effectively, however, global forums on development cooperation must be strengthened, promoted and extended, in this way becoming frames of reference for the creation of international agreements and commitments in the field.

The entry into force of Mexico's law for international development cooperation generates new expectations, especially for the establishment of its agency, AMEXCID.

In terms of triangular cooperation, it is important to note that it is not only donor countries which invest financial resources in these initiatives. Mexico, as an upper-middle-income country, provides technical assistance and capacity-building, and also financial resources, in order to carry out effective triangular cooperation. In addition, Mexico is considering more of these projects in association with other Latin American emerging economies, such as Chile and Brazil, in order to build the capacities of less developed third countries from the region.

For Mexico, international development cooperation represents a major challenge. As part of the OECD, but constrained by the framework of SSC, Mexico is looking to structure a long-term policy for cooperation taking into consideration its own capacity and potential. The difficulties inherent in this process, however, are not easy to overcome. Mexico's adoption of a more aggressive cooperation stance reveals the same reality that traditional countries faced in the past: that SSC can only be based on capacity development.

When Mexico provides aid, it uses its own officials. South–South cooperation is based on drawing capacity development directly from the personnel in charge of implementing national programmes, rather than providing funding for recruitment of experts from other countries. Mexico is, however, reaching a point where its national pool of expertise is overloaded. It can therefore either reduce its international cooperation agenda or modify its mode of cooperation, accepting the necessity of providing finance in order to retain outside experts to achieve agreed aims. Obviously, this will not be an easy decision. But it will certainly represent a critical point in new aid architecture for countries promoting SSC.

Notes

1 The views expressed are the author's alone and should not be taken to be those of the government of Mexico. Any errors are his alone.

2 See SSC/15/1, 15th session period, New York, 29 May–1 June 2007, Theme 2 of the provisional programme, southsouthconference.org/wp-content/uploads/2009/10/A6239_Eng.pdf, accessed 17 September 2009.

3 In 2010, Spain and Mexico carried out a study in order to consolidate a triangular cooperation policy, including a manual. This is the first attempt to provide clear guidance to users.

4 In March 2007, Senator Rosario Green Macias submitted the bill entitled 'International Cooperation for Development Law'. On 13 December the same year, the Senate approved the initiative. It was approved by the House of Representatives on 13 April 2010. In light of some reservations the initiative was returned to the Senate, where it was issued again on 29 April and redirected to the Executive. On 1 September 2010 the opinions of the president were received. In October the Senate approved the decree through which the International Cooperation Law for Development was issued, welcoming all the observations made by the Executive. On 28 October 2010 the law was returned to the House of Representatives, where it was approved on 15 December and re-sent to the Executive for constitutional processing.

5 See dof.gob.mx/nota_detalle.php?codigo=5184958&fecha=06 per cent2F04 per cent2F2011, 7 April 2011.

6 Mexico is the only OECD member that does not provide figures for the aid that it disburses; see Article XIV, 'National Registry: National registry of international cooperation actions and participant experts and institutions', of the new law in Congress, www.senado.gob.mx/gace.php?sesion=2007/12/13/1&documento=53.

7 Graduation within the UN

system means that the host country is committed to guarantee permanence of UN organizations in its territory. The host country then ceases to receive financial support from the UN headquarters, and shares the administrative and operational costs of UN agencies and programmes. It should be noted that Mexico ranks second in the world as the nation with the largest representation of UN agencies and programmes (twenty-three).

8 During the preparation of this chapter, there was an official announcement changing the name of Plan Puebla Panamá to 'Mesoamerica Project' (*Proyecto de Integración y Desarrollo de Mesoamérica*).

9 Plus Colombia and the Dominican Republic.

10 The term Mesoamerica refers to an ancient geographical area where common culture, architecture and tradition were represented by the pre-Columbian populations and cultures that lived there. Mesoamerica would then have been located where part of modern Mexico and other Central American countries now extend. Modern Mesoamerica can be understood as the region that extends across Mexico's south-south-east to the border between Panama and Colombia. It extends over more than one million square kilometres with a population of 64 million.

11 In addition to the Mesoamerica Project, the Mexican government carried out other regional and bilateral cooperation programmes, such as the Mesoamerican Programme of Technical and Scientific Cooperation and the bilateral Commissions of Technical, Scientific, Cultural and Educative Co-operation. The Mesoamerica Project promotes alternative ways of cooperation that complement bilateral and other regional initiatives.

12 *Joint Declaration of the Tuxtla*

Agreement and Dialogue Mechanism – Member Countries' Extraordinary Summit, San Salvador, El Salvador, June 2001, www.planpuebla-panama.org/documentos/decl_1166_3_14102005.pdf.

13 Mexico's south-south-east region comprises the following states: Campeche, Chiapas, Guerrero, Oaxaca, Puebla, Quintana Roo, Tabasco, Veracruz and Yucatan. All are important to the Mesoamerica Project.

14 Vautravers Tosca Guadalupe, *Encuentros y desencuentros. Relaciones entre México y Venezuela* [Meetings and misunderstandings: relations between Mexico and Venezuela], pp. 755–7, www.juridicas.unam.mx, accessed 11 February 2011.

15 The Energy Cooperation Programme for Central American and Caribbean Countries (also known as the San José Agreement) has been also used de facto as a multilateral cooperation agreement.

16 See www.proyectomesoamerica.org.

17 As mentioned earlier, in addition to the Mesoamerica Project Mexico supports and participates in the Meso-american Cooperation Plan, designed to execute technical and scientific cooperation projects for the region, as well as to promote bilateral cooperation with each of the members of the Mesoamerica Project.

18 See 64.202.170.137/index.php?option=com_docman&task=search_result&Itemid=28.

19 It is important to note that in addition to this successful triangular programme, Mexico offers technical and scientific cooperation on a bilateral basis complementary to other triangular cooperation schemes at a national level.

20 See evaluation reports published by the TT-SSC for 'El Salvador–Mexico–Japan – TAISHIN (Earthquake-resistant popular housing)

project' at www.impactalliance.org/ ev_en.php?ID=49124_201&ID2=DO_ TOPIC; and 'Guatemala–Mexico– Germany – Managing solid waste' at www.impactalliance.org/ev_en.php? ID=49240_201&ID2=DO_TOPIC.

21 'The South teaches the North how to break poverty cycle', web. worldbank.org/WBSITE/EXTERNAL/ NEWS/0,,contentMDK:21642718~pag PK:64257043~piPK:437376~theSitePK: 4607,00.html.

9 | SOUTH AFRICA: DEVELOPMENT, INTERNATIONAL COOPERATION AND SOFT POWER

Elizabeth Sidiropoulos[1]

In the eyes of many observers the continent of Africa is the last economic frontier, where socio-economic development is both desirable and necessary in its own interests and those of the wider world. This perception has transformed Africa into a terrain for heightened activity and competition between many global diplomatic, economic and military interests. While this is potentially a positive development for South Africa as sub-Saharan Africa's most developed economy, it poses two main sets of challenges. The first requires South Africa to develop a means to deploy its regional economic power and influence, and its development aid diplomacy, in such a way as to ensure that it is not left behind in the race for development 'partnerships' in Africa. The second requires South Africa to decide how to maintain its competitive advantage over the medium term. This is especially important at a time when its relative economic power may be on the wane (some projections indicate that Egypt will overtake South Africa by 2014 as the continent's largest economy, and Nigeria will overtake it in 2026) (Cilliers et al. 2011: 82). The development and implementation of 'soft' power[2] – which might be defined as the accomplishment of political aims through attraction rather than coercion – will be crucial to success in tackling these problems. Development cooperation can play an important role in this.

Since the elections in 1994 that ushered in constitutional democracy to the country, South Africa has demonstrated its willingness diplomatically to engage outside its geographical borders and beyond narrow domestic political imperatives. While its relative economic size is an asset in this process it is not a sufficient condition for success, and various institutional initiatives are also necessary. Some of these, however, have now been put in place. Perhaps the most important is the establishment of a development partnership agency that offers a vehicle for soft power projection through the effective championing and implementation of continental developmental programmes.

In fact, South Africa has been in a position to project a measure of 'soft' power for the past seventeen years. This essentially has come about from the way in which the country moved from apartheid state to universal suffrage. Other factors helped in the process, not least an espousal of the values of human rights and democracy, and a willingness to assist in bringing peace to conflict-racked African states and in building continental institutions that would advance Africa's development and its place in the world. South Africa's soft power may also derive from a multilateral engagement that has focused on contributing to global public goods, especially with regard to Africa. These range from public sector capacity-building in the Democratic Republic of Congo (DRC) and the newly created South Sudan, to mediation in the civil war in Côte d'Ivoire in 2006, and playing a key role in establishing the African Union. Yet many countries (including African regional powers) view South Africa's involvement in Africa and the projection of its continental vision with only grudging acceptance, often coloured by unease and resentment (Adebajo et al. 2007: 21, 92–104).

More effectively to promote this vision and advance its own domestic economic priorities (neither of which is mutually exclusive), South Africa announced that it would establish the South African Development Partnership Agency (SADPA), as a channel for its international cooperation efforts. Due to be launched by mid-2012, this institution offers an opportunity for more effective 'development diplomacy', defined here as actions in the international domain that focus on promoting regional integration, help institutionalize accountable governance regimes, and resolve conflicts in a way that accrues both material and less tangible soft power benefits.

South Africa's current development cooperation originated in normative drivers of promoting peace, security and economic development on the African continent, but debate within government circles now is about the correct mix of self-interest and normative imperatives. As its development cooperation evolves, South Africa's objectives (as are those of many in countries of the North) are reflecting more openly this dichotomy, which to some extent is informed by ideological underpinnings rooted in solidarity with national liberation movements and former supporters of the anti-apartheid movement.

Much of South Africa's international development cooperation is said to occur in the context of South–South cooperation (SSC),

which, some argue, differs from the traditional development cooperation model. South Africa has been an arch proponent of this type
of cooperation, considering its Africa agenda and SSC as foreign
policy priorities.

A coherent and streamlined development cooperation policy is a
vital component of South Africa's desire to play a more central and
leading role in Africa and the world. It will, however, require adroit
diplomatic navigation around some of Africa's stereotypical perceptions of South Africa as a hegemon in the continent.

'Development cooperation' is regarded here as broadly inclusive of
the various developmentally focused initiatives South Africa is now
engaged in, whether at regional or continental level. They include,
first, support for regional integration and projects related to the New
Partnership for Africa's Development (NEPAD); secondly, South
Africa's conflict resolution initiatives, including peacekeeping and
support for the continent's institutional architecture; and thirdly,
technical assistance in state capacity-building.

Development cooperation has been one of the tools used, albeit
initially in an ad hoc fashion,[3] to advance what the Department of
International Relations and Cooperation (DIRCO) calls the government's 'Africa agenda'. Some Africans see South Africa's involvement
as driven by selfish economic interests (Grobbelaar 2008). Yet while
South Africa is often at pains to argue that it does not carry out the
programme for selfish reasons, a number of senior officials consider
that its conflict resolution efforts are not sufficiently appreciated
by other Africans; nor have they brought direct rewards to South
Africa; they have, rather, benefited other countries which have received
contracts, or access to resources, after hostilities ended.

Development cooperation in diplomacy

In her budget speech of April 2010 South Africa's minister of
international relations and cooperation, Maite Nkoana-Mashabane,
announced that the department would present a bill to parliament
to establish SADPA (see above). Its remit would be to 'give legal
framework to the execution of our foreign policy and facilitate more
effective cooperation' (Department of International Relations and
Cooperation 2010). Her announcement had been preceded by the
May 2009 nominal transformation of the Department of Foreign
Affairs into the DIRCO:

The name change moves from the premise that foreign policy is based upon and is indeed an advancement of our domestic priorities at an international level. ... South Africa recognises that its destiny is inextricably linked to that of the developing world in general and the African continent in particular. Consequently as South Africa seeks to attain its foreign policy objectives it should simultaneously pursue a developmental agenda both in the continent and the developing world.

This developmental agenda can only succeed to the extent to which strategic and mutual developmental cooperation is built with countries of the continent, the developing and the developed world ... [T]he renaming of the Department as the Department of International Relations and Cooperation is a deliberate decision on the part of government to ensure a holistic approach to foreign relations which reflects on developmental agenda. (Nkoana-Mashabane 2009)

The name change clearly set out the government's aspiration that South Africa's external relations should be driven by both domestic and foreign developmental factors. This is most apparent in the emphasis on the part of the administration of President Jacob Zuma that all state departments should work towards the goal of creating more jobs and improving access to health and education at home. In the Ministry of International Relations and Cooperation (MIRCO) this has translated into more overt commercial diplomacy. While the two objectives ought not to be contradictory, they unquestionably require more careful articulation if they are to be pursued in such a way that they do not become tools in the hands of a narrow commercial diplomacy.

A 2005 International Monetary Fund (IMF) paper (Arora and Vamvakidis 2005: 4) estimated that a one percentage point growth in South Africa's economy had a positive impact of 0.5–0.75 percentage points on sub-Saharan Africa's regional growth. This putative role as catalyst for regional development was also captured in the government's document on a *New Growth Path* published in 2010 by the Economic Development Department. The paper argued that:

support for regional growth is both an act of solidarity and a way to enhance economic opportunities ... South Africa should be the driving force behind the development of regional energy, transport and telecommunications infrastructure. Government will work with South African development finance institutions (DFIs) and state-owned enterprises (SOEs) to address backlogs in regional logistics, water and electricity infrastructure. Government will launch an appropriately structured Africa Development Fund to assist in financing this kind of infrastructure, and at the same time play the role of a sovereign wealth fund in helping to achieve a more competitive rand. (Department of Economic Development 2010: 25)

Of course, the aim of the 'new growth path' is first and foremost to create decent work based on a 'new growth path founded on the restructuring of the South African economy to prove its performance in terms of labour absorption as well as the composition and rate of growth' (ibid.: 1). It does, however, recognize a symbiotic national–regional relationship in achieving that objective.

South Africa's development cooperation pre-1994

South Africa's international development assistance can be traced to efforts – largely ineffectual – by the apartheid regime to bolster support in a few African countries (Lesotho, Gabon, Côte d'Ivoire, Equatorial Guinea and Comoros) and in Paraguay, as part of attempts to overcome diplomatic isolation, win friends and buy votes at the UN. Development assistance was also primarily designed to support the so-called 'homeland' enclaves within South Africa's borders, essentially government creations to serve the fiction that black South Africans were citizens of their own 'states'.

The Development Assistance Programme was located within the Department of Foreign Affairs and provided direct project-related development assistance to the homelands.

As the political context changed the Development Assistance Programme was wound down; at the end of 2000 it was replaced by the African Renaissance and International Cooperation Fund ('African Renaissance Fund': ARF).

The Development Bank of Southern Africa (DBSA), established in 1983, formed part of the edifice of grand apartheid. Its original purpose was to act as a regional bank through a multilateral agreement between South Africa and its four 'independent' homelands. In 1988 the DBSA also became involved in Lesotho and Swaziland. Subsequent to the 1994 elections it became an important regional development financing institution.

Development partnership in the democratic state

Apartheid South Africa always considered itself part of the developed North and an outpost of 'European' or 'white' civilization in the 'dark continent'. This perspective, however, reflected only one element of its composition, the First World economy of white South Africa, and ignored the poverty and underdevelopment of the rest of the population, which closely resembled those of a developing African state.

On its accession to power in 1994 the African National Congress (ANC) government wished to affirm both its African identity and its 'developing South' identity. The concept of an 'African Renaissance', of which President Mbeki became the architect and which culminated in NEPAD, came to represent the apogee of this thinking. The African Renaissance was nothing less than a vision aimed at the holistic reinvigoration of Africa in all aspects of human affairs – economic, cultural, political and social. These aims include the reclamation of Africa's right to chart its own destiny, the promotion of political democracy, the eradication of neocolonial relations, and the advancement of 'people-centred' economic growth and development. South Africa's involvement in conflict resolution and institution-building on the continent formed part of this vision (Sidiropoulos and Hughes 2004). The fact that the country had itself gone through a transformation from apartheid state to constitutional democracy without the bloodbath that had been widely predicted itself carried soft power impact in terms of both South Africa's leadership role on those issues and a firm belief in the 'demonstration effect'.

The 2010 UN Conference on Trade and Development (UNCTAD) publication *Economic Development in Africa Report 2010: SSC: Africa and the New Forms of Development Partnership* noted: 'SSC is a much broader concept than either technical cooperation among developing countries or economic cooperation among developing countries. The former focuses on the cooperative exchange of knowledge, skills, resources and technical know-how and the latter refers mainly to cooperation in trade, investment and finance' (UNCTAD 2010).

South Africa's development cooperation, especially at the continental level, is for the most part susceptible to analysis against this broader definition of SSC. South Africa is one of Africa's biggest trading and investment partners.[4] It has played a key role in spearheading infrastructural initiatives aimed at creating economic and commercial opportunities, the most successful to date being the Maputo Development Corridor, which connects the deep-water ports of Mozambique with the South African industrial and agricultural heartland. South Africa's trade relations with other African states, however, tend to display North–South characteristics, i.e. South African exports mainly manufactures to its neighbours and imports largely commodities. To break this mould Draper and Khumalo argue that South Africa should open its markets to imports from Africa and introduce a generous preferential access scheme (Draper and Khumalo 2005) to stimulate trade within the Southern African Development Community (SADC).

The focus of this chapter, however, is not on trade and investment, important as these may be in terms of SSC, but rather on two other main issues. The first is aspects of regional integration that date to the establishment of the Union of South Africa in 1910 and the creation in the same year of the Southern African Customs Union (SACU).[5] The second is assistance channelled through the ARF, various government departments and state agencies, which takes the form of support for conflict resolution initiatives, financing infrastructure, running elections and offering technical assistance in state capacity-building. (It should be noted that South Africa also channels much of its assistance, including funds for humanitarian support, through multilateral forums including the UN, the African Union and SADC.)

SACU SACU comprises South Africa and its neighbours Botswana, Lesotho, Namibia and Swaziland (BLNS). Members share the revenues accruing from customs and excise duties, although South Africa accounts for much the largest volume flowing into the pool while the BLNS states derive proportionately the most income from it. A Common Monetary Area (CMA) also exists between South Africa, Namibia, Lesotho and Swaziland; the CMA is based on the South African rand and the currencies of the other members are pegged to it.

Under the terms of the renegotiated 2002 SACU Agreement, customs revenues are divided according to a formula based mainly on trade within SACU. South Africa currently receives about 10 per cent of the intra-SACU customs pool, and the others around 90 per cent. The smaller, excise, pool is divided differently; about 85 per cent of it goes to South Africa, and the remainder to the other states. A development fund is financed from 15 per cent of the excise

TABLE 9.1 Trends in SACU revenue shares among member states (in billion rands), 2005/06–2008/09

	2005–06	% of CRP	2006–07	% of CRP	2007–08	% of CRP	2008–09	% of CRP
Botswana	4.008	16.0	5.549	16.4	8.330	19.1	9.473	17.8
Lesotho	1.984	7.9	2.784	8.2	3.822	8.8	4.901	9.2
Namibia	3.228	12.9	5.394	15.9	6.015	13.8	8.502	16.0
SA	13.027	52.0	16.478	48.7	20.796	47.8	24.264	45.7
Swaziland	2.795	11.2	3.654	10.8	4.591	10.5	6.009	11.3
Total payment out of CRP	25.042		33.859		43.553		53.150	

Note: CRP = common revenue pool
Source: Southern African Customs Union, Annual Report 2008/2009, p. 40

revenue and is allocated according to each country's per capita gross domestic product (GDP). These monies, however, are merely allocated as recurrent revenue in member states' budgets.

The revenue-sharing agreement compensates the BLNS to offset the trade distortions they suffer as a result of the overwhelming economic dominance of South Africa within the customs union. South Africa's disproportionate regional economic influence means that trade and investment flows are naturally drawn to it rather than to its neighbours, and South African exports crowd out other members' manufactures. Hence the compensation mechanism is designed to allow BLNS states to reduce their reliance for development assistance on other external donors such as the EU. Transfers to the BLNS make South Africa their largest foreign donor (in 2008 they amounted to R27 billion, equivalent to 1.15 per cent of South Africa's GDP) (Qobo 2010). The South African government's *Budget Review 2011* reported that SACU revenues make up between 20 and 70 per cent of total government income for South Africa's SACU partners (National Treasury 2011a: 52).

The SACU revenue distribution formula is very sensitive to changes in trade policy. If external tariffs decline, trade preferences enjoyed by South Africa decrease and the amount of compensation from South Africa to the BLNS falls, in line with the relative size of the customs pool. Table 9.1 on page 223 shows trends in SACU revenue from 2005 to 2009.

Some officials and observers within the establishment in South Africa argue quite strongly for an end to an arrangement under which South Africa subsidizes the public accounts of BLNS states. They contend that it is a throwback to the apartheid system, when there were reasons of realpolitik for such an arrangement; and that South Africa cannot remain indebted to those countries for what were destabilization policies pursued by the country under apartheid (Qobo 2010). Equally, the impact of the 2008/09 international banking and financial crisis on South Africa's own economy (e.g. the loss of more than one million jobs since 2009) means that the country cannot afford 'indefinitely [to] carry the fiscal burden imposed by the revenue-sharing formula' (Draper and Dube 2010).

Currently, in the jargon of the EU, the manner in which funds from the common revenue pool are channelled to the BLNS can be characterized as a form of budget support. Qobo argues that there is no accounting for how these resources are utilized; nor is there any assessment of their real development impact, or of the extent to which the funds improve the lives of the people. The renegotiated 2002 SACU Agreement also limits South Africa's ability to enter into free trade agreements with other countries or regions, since it now negotiates as part of a customs union. Qobo asks: 'Why does South Africa prop up an institution that runs counter to its fundamental foreign economic objectives? What is so significant about SACU that it is worth preserving even at the risk of sacrificing economic sovereignty?' (Qobo 2010).

The SACU Council of Ministers has decided to review the revenue-sharing arrangement to find 'a more equitable distribution of revenue and to enhance economic integration'. An independent study has recommended the following formulaic and funding reforms:

> An entitlement based on the taxes that each country generates through customs and excise duties, combined with an adjustment based on the extent to which a member state benefits or is disadvantaged by its membership of SACU; and
> A fund to support infrastructure and trade projects which promote regional integration and development. (National Treasury 2011a: 52)

Any argument to discontinue SACU, however, has to be seen in the light of its potentially deleterious impact on the economies of the two weakest member states, Lesotho and Swaziland, and South Africa's regional soft power potential through this compensatory mechanism. The global economic crisis has had a negative impact on transfers from the common revenue pool. Projections by the IMF in a 2001 report indicated that Lesotho and Swaziland were expected to have SACU revenue shortfalls over the next three fiscal years of 23 per cent and 16 per cent of GDP respectively (Mongardini et al. 2011: 5). Swaziland was the worst hit in 2011, having to request financial assistance from South Africa. South Africa agreed to provide a loan amounting to $355 million, but linked it to democratic and governance reforms, which by late 2011 the Swazi monarch had not acceded to (Southern Africa Report 2011). Draper and Dube have proposed that SACU consider a regional development agenda which factors in the different development priorities of each member country, in order to create sustainable economies and thus reduce dependency on the common revenue pool. The SACU development fund would be tied to investments in public goods in underdeveloped regions (including South Africa) and multilateral partners would be asked to assist in capitalizing it (Draper and Dube 2010).

As the biggest economy in the region, South Africa has a responsibility to underwrite the region's economic and political stability, which clearly is in its own long-term interests as well. The more radical views of SACU as an anachronism need to be considered against that background. A reformed SACU, with a greater emphasis on revenue transfers for development projects (rather than for recurring expenditure), would help underscore South Africa's role as a regional power and benign hegemon, while acting as a key factor in driving regional development and economic diversification. Such reforms would not necessarily exclude some EU-style budget support, but the weighting should favour developmentally oriented projects identified through SACU institutions such as its Council.

The African Renaissance Fund The ARF is the most visibly structured component of South Africa's development cooperation. Regulated by the African Renaissance and International Cooperation Fund Act of 2000, its aim is to enhance cooperation between South Africa and other countries, in particular in Africa, through the promotion of democracy and good governance, socio-economic development and integration, humanitarian assistance and human resource development, and the prevention and resolution of conflict. Start-up funding was $30 million in 2001.

In financial terms, however, the ARF takes up only a small proportion of South Africa's overall assistance – around 3.8 per cent in 2002 and 3.3 per cent in 2004, according to a survey by the National Treasury in 2006.[6] The bulk of the government's development cooperation since 2000 has been conducted by various government departments, it having been estimated that almost half of all departments support a range of projects on the continent in their separate capacities. The ARF is held within the DIRCO (formerly the Department of Foreign Affairs) and falls under the NEPAD Directorate, a reporting line reflecting the Fund's alignment with the implementation of NEPAD projects. The Fund utilizes both concessionary loans and grants, although the latter make up the bulk of its operations.

South African support to Africa takes the form not of general core budgetary support, but cooperative projects and direct assistance to specific sectoral initiatives. Examples include funding for two infrastructural projects in Lesotho, the South African Top–Mokhotlong Road, a major trading link between Lesotho and the port of Durban, and the Metolong Dam project in the Maseru district of Lesotho (for sustainable utilization of water resources); a donation of R6.6 million to geochemical and hydrological projects of the Lesotho Ministry of Natural Resources; R10 million to help Zimbabwe in its 2007/08 local, parliamentary and presidential elections; R31 million to train Comorian armed personnel to provide security during the presidential elections, and a technical team of electoral experts to assist the electoral commission in the same year; R22 million for a water supply scheme in Katanga province in the DRC; and R172 million for trilateral cooperation with Vietnam on efficient rice production in Guinea (National Treasury 2009: 15).

Further examples of the ARF's broad focus on African renewal are its funding of cultural activities such as the preservation of manuscripts in Timbuktu in Mali, and its writing off of almost R44 million in unrecoverable long-term loans made to various (mainly African) developing countries in previous decades, which could be seen in one sense as South Africa's own contribution to Heavily Indebted Poor Country debt relief[7] (African Renaissance and International Cooperation Fund 2004/05, 2005/06).

While its engagement is largely in Africa, in December 2010 the government announced that it was writing off Cuba's debt of R1 billion for diesel engines it had bought from South Africa in the 1990s. At the same time President Zuma announced a R40 million contribution to Cuban agriculture for seed and fertilizer purchases after a devastating hurricane in 2008, and a further R100 million from the ARF for purchases of South African goods.[8] Ranging from R330 to R630 million ($47–90 million), total annual expenditure of the ARF has been relatively small. Table 9.2 on pages 228 and 229 shows the value of funds provided for various activities from 2007/08 to 2010/11 and includes projections to 2014.

When SADPA becomes operational in 2012/13 the ARF will be subsumed into the new body. The ARF was quite forcefully criticized by the opposition in the parliamentary portfolio committee on international relations and cooperation in August 2010, in particular for its lack of means to monitor expenditure and for using its funds to

TABLE 9.2 African Renaissance and International Cooperation Fund

Indicator	Programme/activity	Past			Current	Projections		
		2007–08	2008–09	2009–10	2010–11	2011–12	2012–13	2013–14
Number of projects approved (per year)	Bilateral and other projects*	6	9	9	10	15	17	15
Total value of projects approved	Bilateral and other projects	Rm 352	Rm 476	Rm 631	Rm 401	Rm 450	Rm 464	Rm 495
Funds approved for promoting democracy and good governance (per year)	South Africa's participation in the observer missions in the continent	Rm 96	Rm 4	Rm 394	Rm 141	Rm 110	Rm 86	Rm 91
Funds approved for the prevention and resolution of conflict (per year)	Bilateral projects related to post-conflict, reconstruction and development in particular in the Great Lakes Region	Rm 8	Rm 10	Rm 100	Rm 90	Rm 80	Rm 110	Rm 116
Funds approved for humanitarian assistance and disaster relief (per year)	Funding, humanitarian and technical assistance to countries in need of disaster relief	Rm 22	Rm 300	Rm 10	Rm 10	Rm 15	Rm 15	Rm 15

Funds approved for cooperation between South Africa and other countries, in particular African (per year)	Bilateral projects related to socio-economic development in Africa	Rm 35	Rm 42	Rm 72	Rm 70	Rm 130	Rm 155	Rm 163
Funds approved for human resources development (per year)	Technical assistance to identified countries; and training Congolese public service officials	Rm 176	Rm 20	Rm 25	Rm 80	Rm 55	Rm 49	Rm 55
Funds approved for socio-economic development and integration (per year)	Bilateral projects	Rm 15	Rm 100	Rm 30	Rm 10	Rm 60	Rm 50	Rm 53

Note: * Bilateral projects include support in areas such as agriculture and health services
Source: National Treasury (2011b: 82)

'prop up rogue states and countries [with] a history of human rights abuses'. The latter reference was to the Fund's support of Guinea Conakry (R172 million) and Zimbabwe (R300 million for water and agriculture) during 2008 and 2010.[9] Some of its activities are clearly puzzling, an example being the R29 million it spent on the financial rescue of the African Cup of Nations football tournament held in Mali in 2002. It is certainly true that more clarity is required on the strategic intent and the developmental impact of the ARF, while its potential developmental benefits for South Africa also need to be considered. In an interview in January 2011 the director-general of international relations and cooperation intimated that the tracking of funding had not been optimal under the ARF, but that SADPA would have the administrative capacity to correct this problem (IRIN 2010).

Aside from the ARF two other groupings, respectively government departments, and parastatal bodies, government agencies and other statutory bodies, implement development cooperation projects. The 2006 Treasury study found that ARF contributions were dwarfed by the activities of other government departments, but it is very difficult to present an overall picture of development cooperation funding from those departments and agencies, given that their expenditure is not individually captured.

Other government departments and agencies Almost a dozen South African government departments run a diversity of projects. A number of departments can be identified that according to research conducted for the National Treasury (National Treasury 2006)[10] together account for 'most ... interventions in Africa by major line function stakeholders'. They include: Defence; Education; the South African Police Service; Trade and Industry; Justice and Constitutional Development; Arts and Culture; Public Service and Administration; Public Enterprises; Science and Technology; and Agriculture.

Development cooperation through these ministries is regulated by memorandums of understanding or treaty agreements and is funded out of their own budgets. Some examples of support rendered include training and technical assistance to Namibia, Botswana, Zambia, Sudan and the DRC through the Department of Justice and Constitutional Development; schools as centres of a care and support pilot programme with Swaziland, Zambia, Sudan, Rwanda, Burundi, Mali and Lesotho among others through the Department of Education; operational police training in the DRC by the Department of Police's criminal asset recovery account fund; and support through the Department of Public Service and Administration for the DRC's public service census project, anti-corruption initiatives and the establishment of a national public administration training institute. (Some of these schemes are funded by the ARF.) Since 2005 the South Africa government, acting through the University of South Africa, has trained more than a thousand Southern Sudanese officials on diplomacy, public service administration, public financial management and legal affairs, among other disciplines (Langeni 2011). The Department of Agriculture works with other African countries on capacity-building projects, often around phyto and sanitary measures. The South African Reserve Bank has trained central bank officials from the DRC and the National Treasury trains treasury officials in the DRC and other African states (SAIIA 2008).

In addition to the departments identified above, a number of parastatals and other statutory bodies have played, or are playing, significant roles in extending assistance to other African countries. Two of South Africa's key development finance institutions, the DBSA and the Industrial Development Corporation (IDC), each have units charged with support for NEPAD. These institutions are capable of playing a significant part in Africa, especially in infrastructure development, a function that would reflect global trends in development finance (World Bank 2008). Against the background of discussions in Africa concerning greater domestic (i.e. African) resource mobilization (either regional or national), the role that the DBSA and the IDC may play becomes significant (African Development Bank and OECD 2010: 79ff.).

The DBSA's mandate was expanded in 1997 to include funding of projects in SADC. About one third of its funding is now for projects outside South Africa, largely in infrastructure (between 2006 and 2009 the DBSA supported projects totalling some R60 billion), energy, telecommunications, mining, transport, water, manufacturing and health. Most SADC countries have taken part in these schemes (DBSA 2006, 2007, 2008, 2009).[11] In January 2011, the Bank concluded a loan agreement of $262 million with the Zambian Road Development Fund Agency for the rehabilitation of five priority roads, three of which form part of the UN-sponsored Trans African Highways network, specifically the route from Cape Town to Katanga province in the DRC and onwards to Kinshasa. The rehabilitation of these roads would open economic trade routes between Angola, Botswana, DRC and Namibia. In 2010, under a special agreement with the Common Market for Eastern and Southern Africa, SADC, the East African Community and the UK government as lead donor, the DBSA established a new infrastructure trust fund in excess of $100 million to support infrastructure development projects along Africa's north–south corridor (DBSA 2011). In 2011 DBSA's annual Africa investment approvals are expected to exceed $1 billion while more than two-thirds of its international development financing will be in the sector of transport infrastructure, including that of Zimbabwe (ibid.).

The IDC, which was established in 1940 to foster industrial development in South Africa, also had its mandate extended in 2001 'for the benefit of the Southern African region specifically and the rest of Africa generally' (Government Gazette 2001). Its expansion was in line with the 'national thrust to support Nepad'. Its areas of particular interest include mining and beneficiation (i.e. adding value to raw materials prior to export), agro-processing, infrastructure (telecommunications, energy, water and sanitation, transport), tourism, public–private partnerships, healthcare, education and manufacturing among others. The IDC also has a cooperation agreement with the Banco Nacional de Desenvolvimento Econômico e Social, the Brazilian Development Bank, which includes joint financing of projects on the African continent. Its schemes include a R361 million investment in a Namibian cement plant in 2010; a R850 million majority stake (together with the Mozambican government, the South African power utility Eskom and the DBSA) in the Cahora Bassa hydroelectric plant on the Zambesi river in Mozambique in 2008; and collaboration with Healthshare Health Solutions in funding a new private hospital in Lusaka, Zambia, in 2009.

Conditionality Because democratic South Africa has emphasized its differentiation from the North and identification and alignment with the South, it has eschewed both the terminology (donor) and some of the practices (conditionality) of the Northern development aid community. Its aversion to applying conditionality to its cooperation is also an outcome of a heightened sensitivity to its economic dominance in Africa and 'big brother' characterizations. It is clearly averse to applying political conditionalities of democracy and good governance. The exception was the manner in which the South African Treasury handled the request from Swaziland in 2011 for a loan to help it through its acute fiscal difficulties after a contraction of the common customs pool (see above). Two key premises of the loan guarantee were that the kingdom undertake:

- confidence-building measures to broaden the political dialogue process among all stakeholders in Swaziland, including allowing the parties to the dialogue to determine the appropriate reforms needed; and
- fiscal and related technical reforms as required by the IMF.

(National Treasury 2011c)

The Swazi king has been reticent in implementing these measures and at the time of writing the first tranche had not been disbursed by South Africa.

Assistance has also not been conditional on the use of South African experts in project implementation. The ARF specifically notes that its projects do not contain provisions 'tying' recipients to South African specialists.

Such conditionalities should not, however, be confused with conditions laid down for financial, evaluative and reporting standards. These are likely to be an essential feature of SADPA and a response to the challenges presented by the need to monitor and evaluate the impact of development assistance.

Nevertheless, the debate around conditionality may in time manifest itself in discussions around the ultimate objective of development cooperation, i.e. that South Africa should derive some economic and political value from the assistance it provides. This continues to be a sensitive issue within government circles and may well rear its head as SADPA evolves, and if commercial diplomacy becomes increasingly pivotal to the country's economic relations.

Triangular cooperation Triangular cooperation is an area in which South Africa, together with traditional donors, has been experimenting. It essentially comprises partnerships between South Africa and another donor (usually a Northern partner), with a third country receiving either funding or technical assistance. Since the first projects of this kind in 2000, triangular cooperation has grown. South Africa now has partnerships with Canada, the Netherlands, Switzerland,

Sweden, Norway, Belgium, Germany, France and the UK. These partnerships are almost entirely in Africa and focus largely on post-conflict rebuilding.

For example, using funding from the Canadian International Development Agency, South Africa's Public Administration Leadership and Management Academy (Palama) runs a five-year (2008–13) programme on building public sector capacities in post-conflict countries. Partners include Rwanda's Institute for Administration and Management (RIAM), Burundi's École National d'Administration (ENA) and South Sudan's Capacity Building Unit (CBU). There are plans to make the project's existing office in the Rwandan capital Kigali a hub for continued collaboration, sharing of resources and capacity-building in the region. Palama managers of the regional capacity-building project point to a number of protocols that would determine the success of the programme. They include, first, acknowledging that Palama does not possess the particular knowledge and insights enjoyed by ENA, RIAM and CBU in regard to their respective locales; secondly, avoiding the 'big brother' approach; thirdly, incorporating their skills as co-designers and co-researchers; fourthly, conducting capacity-building in the partner country; and finally, utilizing participants as teachers rather than 'specimens' (Muthayan and Pangech 2009).

IBSA One concrete area of triangular cooperation among Southern partners is the India, Brazil and South Africa Facility for Poverty and Hunger Alleviation (IBSA Trust Fund), which was created out of the IBSA Dialogue Forum held in New Delhi in March 2004. Its purpose is to identify small projects in the fight against poverty and hunger that can be implemented quickly in interested developing countries.[12] The fund is managed by the UN Development Programme's Special Unit for SSC and managed by a board of directors against a set of project guidelines.[13] Each IBSA member contributes $1 million a year to the fund. Individual grants may not exceed $50,000. Proposals are evaluated on ten criteria that include:

- national ownership and leadership (alignment with the priorities of the country concerned);
- SSC (mutual exchange of experiences between developing countries, in particular best practices in reducing poverty and hunger);
- use of IBSA country capacities;
- strengthening local capacity;

- sustainability;
- innovation (new ways of approaching development issues with emphasis on replicating innovative experiences in other developing countries).

The IBSA Fund could become the springboard for increased development activities not only in Africa, but also in Asia and Latin America, using a pure South–South model. Although evaluation systems of South Africa's cooperation are at an early stage, lessons have been derived from a number of the projects. It is crucial that as South Africa moves into the next phase, these lessons are incorporated into the planning of subsequent projects. Longer-term success of these initiatives will be dependent on the systematization of goals, monitoring and evaluation.

Institutional frameworks and their challenges Since it has lacked an overarching development agency, the South African government has had limited ability to coordinate, track and evaluate its overall development cooperation. Nor are there separate structures or personnel specifically trained for 'development'. For example, the ARF had no dedicated personnel, being completely supported and administered by the DIRCO. ARF's budget was earmarked entirely for the funding of projects (National Treasury 2011a: 84). Although formal financial reporting structures exist for all expenditure within all government departments, development cooperation expenditure is hard to track as there are no separate budget lines for such expenditure within departments (funds are often used from other budget lines to fund these activities). A very well coordinated structure does, however, exist for tracking and monitoring inward development assistance. Run and maintained by the National Treasury, this Development Cooperation Information System could form the basis for a similar system for tracking and monitoring external development assistance.

Many of the problems outlined above have already been identified by the government (specifically, by the Treasury and the DIRCO). Thus it can be expected that once the SADPA starts work, its operations and the system will be more streamlined. It will, however, require clear criteria against which to select projects that are transparent and form part of South Africa's overall international relations vision. At the time of writing, the SADPA Bill had not been tabled yet. However, from a DIRCO parliamentary briefing, it is clear that SADPA will focus on Africa, regional integration, SSC and attaining the Millennium Development Goals, all encompassed in the government's foreign policy goals of addressing poverty, underdevelopment and the marginalization of Africa and the global South. Using SADPA as a tool for creating opportunities for South African investments was also noted, while it would also work with other donor agencies to coordinate development programmes mainly in Africa, including with the private sector (Parliamentary Monitoring Group 2011).

Conforming with international criteria

Like all Southern partners, South Africa has an ambivalent relationship with the body of protocols and principles on aid effectiveness that have emerged in the North over the past decade, specifically through the OECD's development assistance committee (OECD-DAC). South Africa is a signatory (as an aid recipient) to the OECD 2005 Paris Declaration on Aid Effectiveness; in fact the National Treasury wants all incoming aid (whether from North or South) to adhere to Declaration principles.

So far, however, there has been no debate in DIRCO around the Paris Declaration as a guidance framework for outgoing aid. South Africa's reticence in adopting this and other principles around aid effectiveness developed by and in the North is because these have been crafted by the North and reflect a particular world view that often does not take cognizance of global shifts in power and influence over the past two decades. A key element of South Africa's foreign policy has been the need to work actively to create a multilateral rules-based global order that is more fair and equitable than hitherto (Landsberg 2010; Sidiropoulos 2006). Many people in South Africa's government departments believe that a rethinking of global discourse on the aid–development nexus and the instruments required to achieve development in poor countries is now necessary.

In Southern eyes, what differentiates SSC from the Northern modalities of cooperation is that it is cooperation among equals driven by mutual benefit, and for that reason falls outside the donor–recipient mould. Clearly, while this is the rationale and perhaps the aspiration, reality does not always jibe with it, especially where global power shifts have elevated developing countries such as China and India to the top of the global table, while the poorer, smaller developing economies continue to be politically and economically marginalized. SSC is not inherently good for beneficiaries, or more power-symmetrical, simply because it comes without some of the historical baggage of the North. It is equally important to recognize that SSC is driven by specific interests of the funding country. It may have overt political aims just as much as does traditional development aid in the North, notwithstanding the Paris Declaration and other pronouncements on aid effectiveness. The current debate within South Africa's foreign policy establishment on what might colloquially be termed 'what's in it for us?' illustrates the paradox between mutual benefit and pure national interest.

Undoubtedly there is value in better coordination and harmonization among partners in development, not least because it reduces transaction costs and guards against project overlap. Nevertheless, the OECD's drive to persuade 'new donors' to comply with Paris principles is regarded by many countries of the South as a means of locking them into a specific framework, not determined by them, which in turn might constrain their relations with other developing countries.

Since the Accra Agenda for Action was formulated in 2008 to 'accelerate and deepen' the Paris principles the aid effectiveness debate has been overtaken by a broader discourse on SSC and development effectiveness. It is meant to encompass a larger set of initiatives that may have the desired developmental outcome and also reflects the different way in which countries such as China are handling development cooperation programmes. At a global level this trend is reflected most notably by South Korea's initiative in the G20 group of major economies to establish a development working group, of which South Africa is the co-chair. The Seoul Development Consensus for Shared Growth, adopted at the G20 summit in that city in November 2010, emphasizes the need for 'strong, sustainable, inclusive and resilient growth' [because] 'consistently high levels of inclusive growth in developing countries and [low-income countries] in particular, are critically necessary, if not sufficient for the eradication of extreme poverty' (G20 2010).

The outcome reflects Korea's own developmental experience and also chimes with South Africa's thinking on the need for stronger state-driven development, in which the state is a 'developmental' one and industrial policy a key element of economic development. South Africa's perspective is that for too long the debate on development has been steered by the G8 group of the North's leading economies, which in practice often means that it is seen through the narrow prism of 'aid'. Instead there is a strong argument to be made for a shift from equity- to growth-oriented development policies (Hallet 2011), a debate accelerated by the 2008/09 financial crisis. The greater confidence of developing countries such as South Africa is shown by their contributing to and strongly articulating a change in developmental debate at the global level, in turn indicative of their desire to shape international norms on development rather than simply accede to existing global frameworks.

Challenges for South Africa's regional development cooperation

South Africa faces three major challenges: the first is institutional and technical, the second political and the third financial.

Regarding the first, given that the driving objective is to develop a system of partnership that is coherent, focused and systematized, attention will have to be given to the question of managing interdepartmental dynamics around priorities and processes. Political primacy of development cooperation should lie with the DIRCO while the National Treasury has a vital technical and public financial management function. Crucially, if South Africa wishes to optimize its partnership and alliance-building in Africa through development cooperation, it must ensure a greater degree of intra-governmental coordination on regional initiatives.

The second challenge relates to the continental politics of South Africa's development cooperation and diplomacy: how to manage its development partnership in a way that assuages some of the prevalent concerns with South Africa's motives on the continent while advancing both its normative objectives of peace, stability and development, and a more interest-driven agenda that includes leverage in its political as well as its commercial interests. Clearly a more rigorous, performance-related evaluation of its development projects, however small they may be, will be essential. Neither can South Africa escape difficult decisions about prioritizing funding allocations, in the process deciding which countries *not* to support; decisions that in turn may affect its diplomatic relations. These are unavoidable and it will be necessary to construct mechanisms to manage them.

Finally, there is a financial challenge arising from material constraints on South Africa's development cooperation in Africa, given the limited capacity of its economy and its own, significant socio-economic problems. Recognizing this is crucial to the integration of soft power strategies into the development, political and economic framework; other states, especially some in the North, have mastered this skill rather well. Lacking a large sovereign wealth fund and with an economy that has been growing annually at about 3 per cent (compared to the high growth rates of other emerging economies), South Africa must be both ruthless in prioritization and narrowly focused in its regional developmental objectives, factors that also necessitate cooperation with other 'donors' in the public and private sector. The correct selection of aid projects will have to be more tightly evaluated against potential tangible benefits if the charge that some of the ARF's projects reflect 'random spending' is to be avoided (Games 2010). Some important elements of an institutional framework are, however, now in place. Given appropriate controls and the necessary allocation of resources and expertise, they offer opportunities for further and more ambitious integration initiatives. Development diplomacy may therefore prove a critical element if South Africa wants to play a significant role on the broader global political stage, well beyond the boundaries of its immediate neighbourhood. The success of such a programme may help Africa as a whole to create more autonomous productive economies, rather than those that can survive only by external transfers – crumbs from the fine linens on the tables of the more developed nations.

Notes

1 The author would like to thank Alexis Assimacopoulos for poring over numerous government and agency annual reports, and Wolfe Braude and Pearl Thadrayan for earlier work they conducted on South Africa as an emerging donor for the IDRC: *Emerging Donors in International Development Assistance: The South African Case*, IDRC, January 2008.

2 Nye (2004) defines soft power as the 'ability to get what you want through attraction rather than coercion or payments. It arises from the attractiveness of a country's culture, political ideals, and policies.' Soft power is enhanced when a country's policies are regarded as legitimate.

3 In recognition of the need to monitor more effectively what is disbursed and its impact, the Treasury undertook a survey in 2006 to inform a White Paper on development cooperation.

4 For a detailed discussion on the impact of South Africa investment on the African continent, see Grobbelaar and Besada (2008).

5 For more on the history of the SACU, see Gibb and Treasure (2011).

6 The Treasury has not conducted a further study of development assistance,

the discussion having shifted to setting up an agency (the South African Development Partnership Agency) that will manage this activity. There are therefore no more recent figures on the sum of South Africa development cooperation.

7 The reports note that R42,886 million in non-recoverable long-term loans was converted to grants, i.e. written off. These loans had been extended to Comoros, Gabon, Lesotho, Mozambique, Malawi, Paraguay, Central Africa (Central African Republic) and Swaziland in previous years.

8 Sapa, 'South Africa cancels R1.1bn Cuba debt, unveils credit package', *Engineering News*, 8 December 2010, www.engineeringnews.co.za/article/cubas-r11bn-debt-cancelled-2010-12-08-1.

9 See pmg.org.za and C. Goko, 'SA's funding rogue states – DA', *Daily News* (Harare), 12 August 2010, www.dailynews.co.zw/index.php/news/53-topstory/397-sa-funding-of-rogue-states-sa.html.

10 This research, completed in March 2006, was commissioned to shed light on current development assistance practice within the South African government.

11 Various annual reports of the DBSA (Development Bank of Southern Africa), 2006, 2007, 2008, 2009.

12 In September 2010 the three governments were recognized by the Millennium Development Goal Awards, in partnership with the UN Development Programme's Millennium Campaign and the Office for Partnerships, for 'their leadership and support of the IBSA Facility for Poverty and Hunger Alleviation (IBSA Fund) as a break-through model of South–South Technical Cooperation'.

13 The directors are the accredited representatives of the three countries to the UN.

References

Adebajo, A., A. Adedeji and C. Landsberg (eds) (2007) *South Africa in Africa: The post-apartheid era*, Pietermaritzburg: University of KwaZulu-Natal Press.

African Development Bank and OECD (2010) *African Economic Outlook 2010*, Special theme on 'Public resource mobilization and aid'.

African Renaissance and International Cooperation Fund (2004/05, 2005/06) *Annual Financial Statements*.

Arora, V. and A. Vamvakidis (2005) 'The implications of South African economic growth for the rest of Africa', IMF Working Paper WP/05/58, March.

Berger, A. and S. Grimm (2010) 'SSC and Western aid: learning from and with each other?', *The Current Column*, 6 September.

Cilliers, J., B. Hughes and J. Moyer (2011) *African Futures 2050*, Monograph 175, Pretoria: Institute for Security Studies and Pardee Centre for International Futures.

DBSA (Development Bank of Southern Africa) (2006–09) Annual Reports, Midrand: DBSA.

— (2011) 'DBSA and Zambian RDFA sign a historic road development loan', Media release, Johannesburg: DBSA, 26 January, www.dbsa.org/(S(fndr1a3dsfvwe545s10axdu3))/Mediaroom/Pages/DBSAandZambianRDFASignaHistoricRoadDevelopmentLoan.aspx, accessed 12 April 2011.

Department of Economic Development (2010) *The New Growth Path*, www.info.gov.za/speeches/docs/2010/new-growth-path.pdf.

Department of International Relations and Cooperation (2010) Interview with the author, 22 September.

Draper, P. and M. Dube (2010) 'Scoping

the future of SACU – a hundred years on', 12 July, www.saiia.org. za/economic-diplomacy-opinion/ scoping-the-future-of-sacu-a-hundred-years-on.html, accessed 15 March 2011.

Draper, P. and N. Khumalo (2005) 'Friend or foe', in P. Draper (ed.), *Reconfiguring the Compass: South Africa's Trade Diplomacy*, Johannesburg: SAIIA.

G20 (2010) Seoul Development Consensus for Shared Growth, G20 Seoul Summit, media.seoulsummit.kr/ contents/dlobo/E3._ANNEX1.pdf.

Games, D. (2010) 'Renaissance Fund's random spending should be more strategically focused', 13 December, www.africaatwork.co.za, accessed 27 April 2011.

Gibb, R. and K. Treasure (2011) 'SACU at centenary: theory and practice of democratising regionalism', *South African Journal of International Affairs*, 18(1).

Government Gazette (2001) *Industrial Development Amendment Act of 2001*, www.thedti.gov.za/thedti/idc.htm, accessed 7 July 2011.

Grimm, S. (2011) 'South Africa as a development partner in Africa', *ECD 2020, Policy Brief*, 11, March.

Grobbelaar, N. (2008) 'Experiences, lessons and policy recommendations', in N. Grobbelaar and H. Besada (eds), *Unlocking Africa's Potential: The role of corporate South Africa in strengthening Africa's private sector*, Johannesburg: SAIIA, pp. 94–104.

Grobbelaar, N. and H. Besada (2008) *Unlocking Africa's Potential: The role of corporate South Africa in strengthening Africa's private sector*, Johannesburg: SAIIA.

GTZ (German Technical Cooperation) (2010) 'Trilateral Cooperation Fund: German/South African partnership to support development of African countries and organisations',

Document provided by the German embassy in South Africa.

Hallet, M. (2011) 'The economic foundations of growth-oriented development policies', Keynote speech presented at the IWH/INFER-Workshop on Applied Economics and Economic Policy on 'The empirics of imbalances and disequilibria', Halle (Saale), 14 February.

IRIN (2010) 'South Africa: aid agency to be launched', 17 January, www. irinnews.org/report.aspx?reportid= 91651, accessed 1 July 2011.

Landsberg, C. (2010) *The Diplomacy of Transformation: South African Foreign Policy and Statecraft*, Johannesburg: Macmillan.

Langeni, L. (2011) 'Southern Sudan referendum in spotlight', *Business Day* (Johannesburg), 5 January.

Minister of International Relations and Cooperation (2010) Budget speech, South African Parliament, 22 April.

Mongardini, J., D. Benicio, T. Fontaine, G. Pastor and G. Verdier (2011) *In the Wake of the Global Economic Crisis: Adjusting to Lower Revenue of the Southern African Customs Union in Botswana, Lesotho, Namibia, and Swaziland*, Washington, DC: International Monetary Fund African Department.

Monyae, D. (2011) 'The role of South African DFIs in regional infrastructure development in Africa', Policy Brief no. 2, Development Bank of Southern Africa, March.

Muthayan, S. and J. Pangech (2009) 'Regional capacity building project: innovations through South–South partnerships', PowerPoint presentation (event undisclosed), 30 September.

National Treasury (2006) 'South Africa as a partner in Africa: a review of South Africa's development assistance to Africa', Presentation to South African Institute of International

Affairs workshop, Johannesburg, December.

— (2009) *Estimate of Expenditure 2009/10*, Pretoria: Government Printer.

— (2011a) *Budget Review 2011*, Pretoria: Government Printer.

— (2011b) *Estimates of National Expenditure 2011*, Pretoria: Government Printer.

— (2011c) 'Media statement on an agreement to provide financial assistance to the Government of the Kingdom of Swaziland', 3 August, www.treasury.gov.za/comm_media/press/2011/2011080301.pdf, accessed 5 November 2011.

Nkoana-Mashabane, M. (2009) 'Statement by Minister Maite Nkoana-Mashabane on the name change to Department of International Relations and Co-operation', 14 May.

Nye, J. S. (2004) *Soft Power: The means to success in world politics*, New York: Public Affairs.

Parliamentary Monitoring Group (2011) *Minutes of the Briefing by Department of International Relations & Co-operation on Legislation for Establishment of SADPA, Select Committee on Trade and International Relations*, 3 August, www.pmg.org.za/report/20110803-department-international-relations-co-operation-legislation-establish, accessed 2 October 2011.

Qobo, M. (2010) 'Why South Africa should kiss the Southern African Customs Union goodbye', 30 May, www.politicsresearch.co.za/archives/472, accessed 15 March 2011.

SAIIA (South African Institute of International Affairs) (2008) *Emerging Donors in International Development Assistance: The South African Case*, Ottawa: IDRC.

Sidiropoulos, E. (2006) 'A new international order? Multilateralism and its discontents: a view from South Africa', in South Africa Institute of International Affairs (SAIIA), *South African Yearbook of International Affairs 2005*, Johannesburg: SAIIA.

— (2011) 'India and South Africa as partners for development in Africa?', Chatham House Briefing Paper, March.

Sidiropoulos, E. and T. Hughes (2004) 'Between democratic governance and sovereignty: the challenge of South Africa's Africa policy', in E. Sidiropoulos (ed.), *Apartheid Past, Renaissance Future: South Africa's Foreign Policy 1994–2004*, Johannesburg: SAIIA.

Southern Africa Report (2011) 'Swaziland: Mswati back in Pretoria – for a no-strings bailout', 13 October.

UNCTAD (United Nations Conference on Trade and Development) (2010) *Economic Development in Africa Report: SSC: Africa and the New Forms of Development Partnership.*

World Bank (2008) *Global Development Finance 2008: The Role of International Banking*, Washington, DC: World Bank.

10 | CONCLUSION: TOWARDS A GLOBAL CONSENSUS ON DEVELOPMENT COOPERATION

Thomas Fues, Sachin Chaturvedi and Elizabeth Sidiropoulos

Introduction

It is clear from the viewpoints expressed in this volume that the intentions, concepts and modalities of traditional and Southern providers of development cooperation differ widely. It is also obvious that 'donors' from North and South act differently in their international practices of dialogue, policy coordination and norm creation. It is safe to conclude from the comprehensive evidence presented here that advanced countries and rising powers from the South, at this point in time, see little common ground that might inform their bilateral interactions with recipient countries. This raises a critical question: To what extent can the existing or evolving international frameworks play a role in guiding and harmonizing the policies of all countries involved in providing development assistance? The analysis arising from this consideration is of interest not only from a narrow sectoral point of view; it also has bearing on broader issues of international affairs. Here, we can gain insight into the dynamics that drive the ongoing transformation of the global system. Will rising powers tend towards integration into the existing institutional architecture cum norms or will they rather seek to establish their own edifice of principles and standards for policy coordination? A third option exists: traditional and Southern providers, acting in unison with recipient partner countries, could agree on a new global framework that would emanate from the diverse experiences, resources and intentions of all sides.

James Mackie's contribution to this volume points to the fact that industrialized countries tend to feel more secure and self-assured than others in the contested arena of development cooperation. For more than five decades they have built up a considerable bank of practical knowledge, specialized expertise and capable institutions in this area. Having made substantial investments in international coordination and harmonization, mostly through the Development Assistance Committee (DAC), the industrialized states now want to safeguard agreed principles and well-tested standards against any erosion resulting from the entry of new, powerful actors, be they private donors or Southern governments. By contrast, most rising powers find themselves at the beginning of the learning curve; they tend to defend their autonomy in shaping cooperation with peer developing countries as a core area of foreign policy and national sovereignty, especially as they also tend to frame and define such cooperation differently from traditional Western concepts.

This divergence of interests, motivations and perspectives does not necessarily imply that either side is opposed in principle to cooperative international efforts that might bring together a wide range of providers and beneficiaries. It seems reasonable to assume, however, that differences between traditional and Southern providers are currently much more pronounced than any shared understandings. While acknowledging the considerable divisions in current approaches from North and South, the editors of this volume see promising gains from enhanced convergence in international development cooperation. Progress in this policy field could also help to propel the implementation of an inclusive global governance system which is apt to meet the challenges of the twenty-first century.

In a long-term perspective it would seem that traditional and emerging providers could each benefit from common frameworks in development cooperation, since this would enhance the provision of global public goods (e.g. stability, prosperity and poverty alleviation). At the level of intergovernmental decision-making, however, national short-term interests usually work against a universal consensus. No matter how convincing arguments in favour of greater harmonization may be, such dynamics will not come about automatically; they will rather require political will and deliberate efforts by all parties. Progress seems feasible only if the existing aid architecture is fundamentally redesigned on the basis of fairness, global justice and equitable burden-sharing.

This concluding chapter first highlights the diverging perspectives of traditional donors and Southern providers that characterize the current international process. The next section looks at the potential and the limitations of existing avenues for dialogue and mutual learning. Finally it ventures into the area of possible common approaches which may enhance human security and inclusive growth in developing countries.

Divergent positions of traditional and Southern providers

In both formal and informal discussions, traditional and Southern aid providers seem to emphasize the normative dimensions of their cooperation with developing countries. These include the consensual positions of all member states of the United Nations on basic principles of global justice and social progress, such as the Millennium Declaration of 2000 and the Millennium Development Goals (MDGs) derived from it. In real life, however, the donor practices in development cooperation are generally determined not by lofty international pronouncements but by national economic and geopolitical interests, historical context and domestic pressures, including the involvement of non-state actors from civil society and the business sector. The variance of such contributing factors helps explain the considerable gaps between traditional and emerging participants in the aid system.

One important aspect is that traditional and Southern donors differ in their balance of self-interest and humanitarian concerns. Many advanced countries are burdened by a history of direct or complicit involvement in colonialism, imperialism and the slave trade that morally compels them to compensate developing countries for past injuries. Western societies are also driven by a centuries-old tradition of Christian proselytizing and charity when they support the use of public funds for poverty alleviation around the globe. After the Second World War, when development cooperation became an established field of public policy in the North, the bipolar world order motivated governments to use external assistance as an instrument to lure partner countries into their respective orbits. Today, vibrant civil societies and influential non-governmental organizations in the West push their governments towards compassionate foreign policies, often finding themselves in competition with nationalist voices that demand cuts in foreign aid. Generally speaking, advanced countries are more adept at concealing their self-interest and would prefer to emphasize altruistic motives in their support for low-income countries.

In contrast, based on a shared experience of colonial domination, Southern providers are less inhibited in articulating their self-interest and framing international cooperation in terms of mutual gains: the proverbial 'win-win situation'. Their line of argument builds on the motives of political solidarity and economic progress rather than human compassion, except in cases of emergency assistance. Southern governments commonly refer to the collective objective of strengthening the negotiating power of the developing world and building up an equitable global economy. A distinctive characteristic of Southern development cooperation is the integrated approach that packages commercial transactions in trade, investment and loans with unidirectional support – for example, in education, health and infrastructural aid programmes.

A further dividing line between traditional and Southern providers can be found in their attitudes on political conditionality and external interference. Industrialized countries are guided by the conviction that governance criteria such as protection of human rights, rule of law and popular participation play an essential part in determining development outcomes. However, policy-makers and academics in the West have, in the recent past, become more sensitive to the charge of imposing culturally biased values. Departing from traditional mindsets, many now support locally adapted manifestations of good governance and political self-determination. Southern providers, by contrast, insist on the primacy of national sovereignty in all aspects of international relations. There are also indications on this side that principled positions may be softened by a more pragmatic, interest-based understanding of non-interference. As the 2011 upheavals in the Middle East and North Africa have demonstrated, authoritarian government can easily lead to political instability, and hence threaten outside economic interests. It is in this line of thought that Southern providers of assistance are beginning to promote broad-based, inclusive development trajectories in partner countries in order to safeguard their long-term interests.

Traditional and Southern development actors also follow different logics with regard to key principles of transparency and accountability. Advanced countries are under growing pressure from their domestic constituencies to account for the impact of public funds spent abroad. These governments have voluntarily established comprehensive rules for transparency and public reporting on multiple dimensions of their development cooperation programmes through the DAC. They are committed to an aid effectiveness agenda enshrined in the 2005 Paris Declaration and the subsequent Accra Agenda for Action of 2008, although implementation efforts are somewhat halting and incomplete.

By contrast, some emerging powers are unable to provide a comprehensive overview of their cooperation programmes owing to a lack of centralized oversight and obvious gaps in data collection as well as inadequate command of evaluation methods; while in other instances they may be reluctant to open details of their cooperation programmes to public scrutiny. This may be ascribed partly to fear of a domestic backlash in the face of severe social disparities at home. Another reason may be the inexperience and unease of Southern providers with elaborate statements of intent and principle that are generally informed by a Western world-view. Guided by their own experiences of dynamic growth, the cooperation approaches of Southern donors have been distinguished by hands-on pragmatism and project-based progress on the ground.

On a more principled level, rising powers criticize the traditional Western concept of aid as a vertical, paternalistic relationship that undermines the potential for self-reliance in recipient countries. Development cooperation by Southern providers, it is claimed, instead focuses on mutual gains while promoting the emancipation of fellow developing countries. Despite these divisions between traditional and new providers, international forums for dialogue and policy exchange have emerged in recent years. Some of them hold promise for helping to bridge the North–South divide in the global aid architecture.

International platforms

Three prominent venues for dialogue between traditional and emerging donors deserve a closer look. The first one has been established within the summit architecture which until recently referred to the club of leading industrialized countries, the Group of Eight (G8). The G8 outreach effort towards certain rising powers was unexpectedly swept aside by the global financial crisis of 2008, at which point the G8 leaders had come to the realization that management of the global economy could not be achieved without the emerging economies. This prompted the transformation of the previously established G20 of finance ministers and central bankers into a steering committee of heads of state and government, with the first meeting in November 2008. Since then the G20 at leaders' level has adopted a development agenda. The second venue for international development cooperation has been set up by the OECD's DAC, which has successfully wooed many developing countries, particularly the beneficiaries of external support. The rising powers, however, have so far chosen to stay on the sidelines. Finally, a third dialogue platform was established in 2005 by the United Nations under the Economic and Social Council. Little of substance has been achieved up to now under this umbrella owing to a lack of interest and commitment by member states, but the process continues.

G8 outreach and G20 development agenda A pioneering step towards institutionalized dialogue and mutual learning on development policy came about as a result of an outreach effort of the G8 that was directed towards five pivotal emerging powers: Brazil, China, India, Mexico and South Africa. It was initiated at the 2007 summit in the German resort of Heiligendamm (Cooper and Antkiewicz 2008). One of its four pillars addressed development cooperation with low-income countries, with special focus on Africa. According to participating officials, the informal dialogue seems to have fostered an atmosphere of trust and understanding with regard to the motives, interests and modalities which each country pursues in its cooperation programmes (see Maximo Romero's chapter). The outreach effort was extended in 2009 for two further years, but was effectively sidelined by the rise of the G20.

Since the G20 includes the five outreach partners on an equal footing with advanced countries, they saw no further value in the Heiligendamm initiative and the process collapsed before the G8 summit in 2010. The initiative, however, produced some symbolic results by way of joint declarations that largely draw on the G8's terminology and agenda, such as the emphasis on aid effectiveness, good governance and triangular cooperation. Participating Southern countries had allowed this to happen by opting for a mainly defensive attitude and by insisting on the singularity of South–South cooperation (SSC). Thus, they succeeded in ring-fencing their relations to low-income countries as separate from North–South interaction. A major unintended consequence of the Heiligendamm process was the temporary emergence of a new collective identity of the outreach countries that had jointly begun to articulate their positions in the international system as the 'G5' group of large Southern economies.

However, the process of alliance-building among rising powers did not stop at this point. From a G7 perspective, the undesired side effect was amplified by the later metamorphosis of the Heiligendamm

Five into the BRICS formation (Brazil, Russia, India, China and – since early 2011 – South Africa), which meant replacing Western-leaning Mexico (a member of the OECD and the North American Free Trade Agreement) with Russia. The former Eastern superpower seems to have switched its affinities from the G8, where it was never fully accepted, to the new alliance of rising powers, thereby de facto shrinking the G8 to its original size of six leading Western economies plus Japan. The BRICS group is rapidly forging a common political identity and is seen by many as growing into a powerful counterweight to Western dominance of the global political system. It remains to be seen how rising powers will capitalize on their new-found economic strength and what use they will make of the G20 for dialogue and policy coordination among equals.

At South Korea's urging, the G20 summit of November 2010 established a permanent working group on development and adopted key documents on enhanced support to low-income countries: the Seoul Development Consensus and a related Multi-Year Action plan with time-bound deliverables. The declared mission of the G20 in this field is oriented towards the framework conditions of the world economy rather than becoming another pledging circle for operational programmes (Fues and Wolff 2010). Contradicting the professed focus on global regimes, the G20 development working group has initiated a wide range of rather detailed work streams which are clustered into nine pillars, from food security to private investment and job creation. G20 progress on these tasks is supported by joint analytical efforts of numerous international organizations, such as the multilateral development banks, the OECD, the World Trade Organization (WTO) and the UN Educational, Scientific and Cultural Organization (UNESCO). Inter-agency consortia of different composition have presented issue-specific reports to the 2011 Cannes summit, such as that on responsible investment standards led by the UN Conference on Trade and Development (UNCTAD) and that on social protection spearheaded by the International Labour Organization (ILO).

As it is still too early to assess the G20 development agenda, a few observations must suffice here. The commitment of the G20 to development challenges can be interpreted as an indication that the group is ready to accept responsibility for global well-being and poverty alleviation. By orchestrating the work of international organizations, the self-selected group of global leaders has made a noticeable contribution to the objective of greater coherence of the international development system. However, while it is still early days, the development working group is falling short of its determination to address structural imbalances in the world economy that work against low-income countries. There is also reason for concern that the underlying paradigm of the Seoul Consensus places too much emphasis on quantitative growth as the most effective tool for poverty reduction while underplaying the relevance of environmental sustainability and social equity for human livelihoods. So far, the G20 has not articulated any intent to work on universal frameworks for development cooperation, perhaps owing to the resistance of rising powers. Recognizing the presently irreconcilable divisions among member states, the G20 limits its ambition to non-committal knowledge sharing, as emphasized in the report of the working group to the 2011 Cannes summit: 'We embrace diversity and encourage different approaches based on each country's situation and specificities. As the G20 gathers countries with distinct experiences, we know that a "one size fits all" approach is not the answer to the development challenge. We will mainstream these rich and diversified experiences through knowledge sharing platforms and networks' (G20 Development Working Group 2011: 13).

Triangular cooperation is mentioned as a possible avenue for sharing the technical experience and know-how of emerging countries, but, as yet, the G20 does not actively promote efforts of member countries in this field. By contrast, common standards and triangular programmes are key concerns of the DAC.

DAC Working Party on Aid Effectiveness The DAC is generally recognized as having produced the most coherent and refined body of standards, guidelines, principles, definitions and data on development cooperation. Its membership of twenty-two industrialized countries plus the European Commission has, as of 1 January 2010, been enlarged to include an advanced developing country, the Republic of Korea. A country wishing to join must comply with the catalogue of DAC rules (which, for example, cover tied aid and credit financing), and must accede to its recommendations and guidelines. Members are also required to provide detailed aid statistics and an annual report on their development policy, and allow regular peer reviews to be carried out.

A significant DAC contribution to international development efforts is the Paris Declaration on Aid Effectiveness, adopted in March 2005. At present, over ninety countries from Africa, Asia, Central and South America, including some rising powers like Brazil, China, India and South Africa, have, in a limited way, endorsed the document. Southern donors insist that their adherence to the Declaration refers solely to their role as beneficiaries of external assistance, and does not affect them as aid providers. The follow-up document, the Accra Agenda for Action (AAA) of 2008, has become the accepted frame of reference for most members of the international development community.

The growing support for the aid effectiveness agenda from low- and middle-income countries has given a boost to the DAC-hosted Working Party on Aid Effectiveness. One of its task teams, which is largely energized by developing countries, focuses on South–South cooperation. It played a major role in organizing a March 2010 conference on its focal interest in Colombia, which undercut the impact of an UN conference with the same topic in Kenya, a few months earlier. According to participants, rising powers, particularly Brazil, India and China, blocked the adoption of a common declaration at the DAC meeting, driven by the fear that their political spaces in South–South cooperation might be restricted in the future. In frustration, the steering committee, comprising numerous developing countries such as Colombia, Egypt, Ghana, Mozambique, Peru and Vietnam, issued an independent statement that gives scant recognition to the role of the UN (TT-SSC 2010). Such a dynamic seems to confirm the trend that a growing number of developing countries want to cultivate horizontal links with their peers and that the interests within the camp of new providers are diverging. In contrast to the 'first league' rising powers, the 'second league', consisting of Southern middle-income countries like Chile, Indonesia and Turkey, may be ready to embrace the frameworks offered by DAC.

Still, major contributors to development cooperation from the South continue to shy away from closer interaction with the DAC. Not considering themselves to be 'donors', they do not recognize the Paris Declaration as a normative or operational framework for SSC. Consequently, they reject the quality standards which have become part and parcel of the Paris process, which they see as having been defined unilaterally by Northern donors. The guarded stance does not imply that Southern providers are against the principles of aid effectiveness as such, but they rather want to see those dimensions embedded in the broader context of 'development effectiveness' which has emerged as the new paradigm since Accra. They also insist that future metrics for quality assessment must reflect the particular modalities and context of SSC.

UN Development Cooperation Forum Under the umbrella of the UN, the international community has, over more than six decades now, adopted an impressive body of normative principles and objectives for poverty eradication and universal development. Though they have no force in law, these resolutions represent the collective will of world society, and commit member states to adopting appropriate domestic and foreign policies. At a special session, the UN General Assembly passed the 2002 Monterrey Declaration on Finance for Development, which emphasizes the primary responsibility developing countries must bear for mobilizing domestic resources, and attaches great importance to private capital flows and trade as engines of development. However, the assembled heads of state and governments also underlined the essential complementary role of external aid. Recipient and donor countries as well as international institutions were called upon to harmonize operational procedures and to reduce transaction costs in order to make development cooperation more effective. The Monterrey conference furthermore adopted a number of key principles which should be observed in support to low-income countries, such as the untying of aid and promoting budget support. While these criteria were thought to apply to Western donors only in 2002, today the programmes of Southern aid providers would also fall under the provision of the Monterrey Consensus.

In 2005, as part of the UN reform summit, member states established the Development Cooperation Forum (DCF) as a sub-organ of the Economic and Social Council (ECOSOC). The Forum's biennial sessions are intended to bridge an institutional gap in the international aid architecture by providing an inclusive platform for dialogue and mutual learning that would be open to all development actors (South Centre 2008a, 2008b). While governments dominate the process, organizations from the private sector participate through an advisory group and consultative round-table events. The declared purpose of the DCF is to act as a focal point for the evolution of universally accepted principles, definitions and norms in development cooperation; facilitate solid analysis of information on implementation; and ensure comprehensive transparency in the allocation and spending of development funding.

The DCF has made little measurable progress since its inception, as the member states that voted for its creation have proved unwilling to generate the political will and financial support necessary to make it operational. While Western reluctance may be explained by a general distrust of the UN, the indecisive attitude of Southern providers is more difficult to understand. In principle, they should feel attracted to the DCF, since developing countries command a majority of votes in the UN according to the 'one-country-one vote' principle of sovereign equality. With the exception of China, however, no influential player from the South has yet taken a public stand on the DCF. Their reluctance may partly be explained by the dislike of public attention. With a functioning DCF, development activities of Southern providers would be subjected to external monitoring and evaluation, as UN Secretary-General Ban implied in his 2008 DCF report:

> South–South development cooperation is subject to relatively little evaluation beyond scrutiny of the timeliness and completion of projects. This reduces missions and studies, lowering the transaction costs of the Governments of programme countries, yet it also means that there will be a reduced longer-term perspective on the sustainability or wider development impact of the project. This cooperation is also subject to much less evaluation with respect to environmental and social impact, particularly in the case of infrastructure projects. (UN 2008: 26)

For the moment, the DCF looks more like a dead-end street of UN reform than a suitable platform for policy coordination between traditional and Southern providers and their development partners. Nevertheless, on a technical level the process continues. After the 2010 DCF meeting, the UN Department of Economic and Social Affairs for the first time published an International Development Cooperation Report, which includes comprehensive statistics on emerging donors and their cooperation modalities with low-income countries (UNDESA 2010). This publication seems like a purposeful step by the UN secretariat to bolster the DCF's reputation as a repository of specialized knowledge, emulating the well-established DAC.

While the evolving mechanisms for North–South dialogue in

development cooperation, such as practised by the DAC and anticipated by the DCF, are welcome steps in the right direction, they have yet not matured to the point of bridging the cleavages among donors. Advanced countries would like to commit rising powers to the principles that they have themselves established in order to maintain their leadership and prevent the erosion of normative standards. Rising powers themselves, however, approach the development of global norms in a manner that may not reflect Western perspectives. Fearing that they might have to abide by rules they had no part in shaping, they continue to interact with low-income countries individually without much international coordination or transparency.

Present trends seem to evolve into a constellation of two distinct international aid regimes. The first, emanating from the OECD'S DAC, is solidly supported by industrialized countries and enjoys growing support from low-income and middle-income countries acting in their role as beneficiaries but also as providers. The other, yet rather embryonic, regime is represented by the DCF under the umbrella of the UN, which has not been able so far to attract significant backing from member states. The parallel nature and latent rivalry of DAC and DCF present considerable challenges to the global governance of aid. Rising powers within the G20, so far, have not given any indication of where they stand on the issue. They seem determined to continue rejecting the DAC as a Western-dominated organization. At the same time, they have not come out in full support of the DCF nor given any inkling of which other international institutional arrangements would meet their interests. It seems unlikely that rising powers can continue with this passive behaviour for an indefinite time. Owing to their increasing prosperity and political clout, rising powers are likely to experience growing pressure from developing as well as industrialized countries in asking for adequate contributions to a new global aid architecture and universal norm creation.

A new international framework for development cooperation

The underlying assumption of this volume is that policy coordination in international development cooperation that leads to global frameworks is both desirable and feasible. Several arguments point to the benefits of common principles. The coherence of global governance regimes across a wide range of policy fields is a prerequisite for the effective and efficient provision of global public goods. If, for example, development cooperation programmes are not aligned with global climate policies, external efforts can be undermined and public resources squandered. In the converse case, integrated support packages to low-income countries can generate synergies between poverty alleviation and ecosystem resilience. Considering the enormous efforts needed to achieve the MDGs and to build broad-based prosperity in poor countries, lower transaction costs are an overriding concern. Policy dialogue and a rational division of labour among donors can bring about significant gains in this regard. In considering the potential for enhanced coordination, the international community needs to face up to the growing relevance of SSC, and to take into consideration the shifting environment of a highly integrated and networked world. In addition to targeted support for low-income countries, reforms of global economic governance must systemically address the special needs of poor countries and the global poor.

South–South cooperation

The contributions by Manmohan Agarwal and Sachin Chaturvedi to this volume point to the growing relevance of SSC in many areas of economic, political and cultural relations. The volume of SSC has risen sharply, from $8.6 billion (6.9 per cent of total global development aid flows) in 2006 to $15.3 billion (9.5 per cent of the total) two years later (UNDESA 2010: 72). Over the course of the recent decade, the share of SSC in total development flows has doubled, reaching an estimated $20 billion in 2010. Most of these resources are channelled through bilateral programmes and come in the form of project funding rather than budget or sector support. In 2008, Saudi Arabia ($5.56 billion), China ($3.96 billion) and Venezuela ($2.33 billion) took the lead among Southern providers. The rather incomplete amounts given on India ($785 million) and Brazil ($437 million) are significantly lower. As the authors of the UN report caution, available data on SSC are underestimates of actual figures, owing to weaknesses in tracking and evaluation systems.

A major challenge for a future global framework will be to accommodate the special nature of SSC while striving for functional principles that build on the experience of both traditional and Southern providers. From the perspective of rising powers, it is clear that the search for appropriate institutional forms could not focus on the OECD but rather on the UN or a similar institution free from

Western dominance. So far, emerging donors have not articulated clear preferences on the institutional or substantive characteristics of a new global system. Emphasizing the responsibility of developing countries to take an active part in setting out collective rules, a UN report urges that 'non-DAC providers should be encouraged to contribute their own ideas for targets to improve aid quality' (ibid.: xvi).

An important feature of SSC that should be considered in global standards is the multidimensional nature of economic exchanges between provider and beneficiary country, going beyond the narrow approach embodied in DAC definitions. Also to be considered is the fact that the current proliferation of objectives, participants and instruments in development cooperation undermines the international community's ability to address key global challenges. Against this background, development experts have called for a fundamental re-structuring of the international aid system (Severino and Ray 2009). They propose a new mandate for leading multilateral institutions which, as trustees of global well-being, should no longer design and implement their own operational projects or programmes, but rather concentrate on creating binding frameworks for the collective provision of global public goods which bilateral donors and non-state actors would need to observe. In the authors' view, resources for external support should no longer be designated as Official Development Assistance (ODA), but rather as 'global public finance', indicating the binding nature of such transfers according to the internationally accepted principle of 'common but differentiated responsibilities'. According to this concept, the creation of global regimes that promote the special interests of low-income countries would include, but not be limited to, the traditional field of development cooperation.

Any progress in such a direction depends on global agreements in intergovernmental negotiations. At present, there seems to be no generally accepted platform for consensus-building. A consistent focus on low-income countries and their specific requirements for exter-nal assistance could be helpful in bringing about a convergence of views between traditional and emerging donors. The well-established UN process on least developed countries (LDCs) could serve as a productive entry point for both industrialized countries and rising powers. On this platform, they could develop shared perceptions with regard to bilateral relations as well as systemic reforms in the international system.

New international development architecture

Leading up to the 2011 UN conference on LDCs, the UN Conference on Trade and Development presented its vision of a new international development architecture, which encompasses far-reaching reforms in global policies over a wide range of areas such as finance, trade, commodities, technology and climate change (UNCTAD 2010). The agency advocates a three-pronged approach: the first would consist of changes to global regimes; the second would concern the design of targeted international support mechanisms for the LDCs; and the third would be enhanced SSC for the benefit of LDCs. Selected examples of UNCTAD's agenda for action are presented in Table 10.1, with a focus on finance, trade, commodities, technology and climate change.

Key measures to support domestic resource mobilization in LDCs include international controls on illicit capital flight and transfer pricing coupled with comprehensive debt relief. The G20 could become a prime mover in these fields. In trade, UNCTAD speaks in favour of selective, development-friendly agreements to be implemented ahead of an overall consensus in the Doha round; this may be significant insofar as it would mean breaking away from the concept of 'single undertaking', which implies that 'nothing is agreed until everything is agreed'. The most radical change promoted by UNCTAD lies in the field of commodities. The agency calls for a return to the 1970s through financing and price stabilization schemes, and suggests combating speculation by the introduction of a specific transaction tax on derivative instruments. By contrast, reform proposals for technology and climate change follow a more gradualist approach.

UNCTAD recommendations on international support mechanisms for LDCs are mainly addressed to advanced countries and call for changes in their ODA policies as well as for development coherence in other relevant policy fields. These ideas deserve international attention, particularly from the G20 as it sets out to reshape regulatory frameworks in support of low-income countries and poverty reduction. The current climate in Western countries does not, however, seem very favourable to such a reform agenda given that, in a time of dire crisis, domestic issues have moved to the centre of popular concerns.

With regard to SSC, UNCTAD's proposals offer substantive guidance for rising powers as they aim to expand their relations with fellow developing countries. It is not clear, however, why UNCTAD neglects

TABLE 10.1 Key components of UNCTAD's new international development architecture

	Global regimes	South–South development cooperation	LDC-specific support
Finance	Domestic resource mobilization through global financial and tax cooperation; debt relief	Scale up financial flows Regional financing schemes Increase development impact of FDI	Increase LDC share in DAC ODA New funding sources such as Special Drawing Rights (SDRs)
Trade	'Early harvest' without completion of Doha round	Deepen regional integration Duty-free, quota-free access for LDC exports	100% duty-free, quota-free access for exports to advanced countries Simplify accession to WTO
Commodities	Counter-cyclical financing facility Commodity price stabilization Transaction tax for derivative markets		Enable resource-based industrialization
Technology	Global intellectual property rights (IPR) regime development friendly	Regional research and development (R&D) hubs SSC on technology	Technology licence bank for LDCs IPR-related technical assistance to LDCs
Climate change	Enhance climate change financing Accountable and representative climate finance governance	Share knowledge in mitigation and adaptation SSC on renewable energy	Reform of the Clean Development Mechanism (CDM) to promote LDC access to renewable energy technology and finance

Source: UNCTAD (2010: xvii–xviii)

the importance of SSC in commodities markets, since emerging powers have become strong forces on the demand side. Emphasis on regional arrangements in all policy fields could play a key role in support of LDCs – for example, by introducing special and differential treatment in regional trade agreements. UNCTAD also wants South–South political forums to provide for special representation of LDC interests, such as those announced by China at meetings of the Forum of China–Africa Cooperation and by blocs such as IBSA (India, Brazil and South Africa), whereas the BRICS still have to formulate a common position on how to cater to the specific needs of low-income countries.

UNCTAD's reform template demands a high level of solidarity and material support from emerging economies for their fellow developing countries – for example, in reference to duty-free, quota-free market access. Both China and India have taken steps in this direction over the past few years, but it still has to be seen whether SSC with low-income countries will differ substantially from traditional patterns of interaction between North and South. Aileen Kwa from the South Centre, a leading Geneva-based intergovernmental think tank of developing countries, points out that South–South trade as such 'is no magic panacea if conducted on exactly the same terms as North–South trade' (Kwa 2010: 9).

Accordingly, the author speaks out for the regulation of South–South trade to ensure its positive impact on low-income countries. It will be interesting to observe the extent to which the new power-houses of the South will follow the advice of prominent forums in the developing world, such as UNCTAD and the South Centre, that advocate qualitative changes in South–South relations. If rising powers are receptive to such policy recommendations, advanced economies will, undoubtedly, feel more pressured to take similar steps.

Conclusions and outlook

In this context, Rathin Roy of the International Policy Centre for Inclusive Growth, a Brasilia-based joint initiative of the UN Development Programme and the Brazilian government, raises a crucial question: 'Will the rise of the emerging economies portend just a broadening of the "great game" … Or will the global South seize this opportunity to forge a new and more inclusive paradigm that secures faster and more sustainable development for all citizens?' (International Policy Centre for Inclusive Growth 2010: 2).

In development cooperation, the greater number of providers reduces the oligopoly of traditional (mostly Western) donors and increases the leverage of beneficiary countries in pursuing national and regional development objectives. On the other hand, such proliferation may mean that the international aid architecture becomes more fragmented and unaccountable. The key conclusion to be drawn from the contributions to this volume is that cooperation and coordination among providers beyond the historical North–South divide is desirable, both as regards the development impact in partner countries and the supply of global public goods. Obviously, this does not imply that rising powers and middle-income countries should abide by the standards and practices that have evolved over five decades under the aegis of the DAC. Traditional and Southern providers of development cooperation need to jointly develop new principles and operational frameworks oriented towards the priorities and needs of their partner countries, particularly the LDCs and other low-income countries. They must also agree on an international burden-sharing formula to guide and monitor the allocation of public resources from middle- and high-income countries to the poorer segments of world society.

A key factor for the future shape of SSC and a fundamental rebalancing of North–South relations will be the position of broad-based alliances in the developing world, particularly the Non-Aligned Movement and the loose coalition of developing nations known as the Group of 77 (G77). Will they act in support of converging principles and practices, nudging emerging powers into a more conciliatory attitude towards traditional donors, or will they rather press Southern providers to deepen the North–South divide and to create a separate universe of SSC? Low-income countries will have a major role in shaping the evolving global dynamics, as they will in regard to the normative substance of the international aid regime. Further analytical work is needed to identify the key characteristics of the new development paradigm in a multipolar world no longer dominated by Western values, perceptions and interests.

An important institutional factor for the evolution of a new global aid regime is the relationship between the UN, particularly the embryonic DCF, and the DAC, with its well-established aid effectiveness agenda. Both frameworks can be understood as progeny of the Monterrey conference on Financing for Development in 2002. Marrying their respective strengths under the leadership of the UN, rather than driving them farther apart, seems to be the single most critical step towards an inclusive and effective global aid architecture. Despite its limited success, the DCF enjoys legitimacy as a universal platform, while the DAC can point to its practical achievements in harmonizing the procedures of traditional donors. In a future integrated architecture, the DCF could assume the function of an intergovernmental platform for political consensus-building while the DAC would continue as technical secretariat by supporting and supervising the operational implementation of guidelines handed down from the DCF. A recent UN publication points out the merits of linking DCF and DAC: 'Such a solution would maximise legitimacy and effectiveness at all levels, and allow everyone to focus on results rather than architecture' (UNDESA 2010: 115).

In any new global aid architecture, the resources and working procedures of the DCF as well as the DAC would require adjustment to permit them to fulfil their revised mandates, and help create the desired synergies. The DCF would have to develop an effective leadership structure that balances the interests of providers and beneficiaries, and it should be granted additional resources for analytical support. In parallel, the DAC would need to establish a more inclusive governance structure to allow for the equal participation of all country groups. Both institutions should move beyond the confines of the conventional aid paradigm by conceptualizing international development cooperation as an indispensable building block for the cooperative provision of global public goods ('beyond ODA') while being ready to operate in a multi-stakeholder mode that embraces the concerns and resources of a wide range of non-state and governmental participants. The editors hope that the contributions to this volume can provide some guidance for scholars and practitioners alike, thus supporting the ongoing political process towards an effective and inclusive global aid architecture.

References

Cooper, A. F. and A. Antkiewicz (eds) (2008) *Emerging Powers in Global Governance: Lessons from the Heiligendamm Process*, Waterloo: Wilfrid Laurier University Press.

Fues, T. and P. Wolff (eds) (2010) *G20 and Global Development: How can the new* summit architecture promote pro-poor growth and sustainability?, Bonn: German Development Institute.

G20 Development Working Group (2011) *2011 Report of Development Working Group*, Cannes: G20

International Policy Centre for Inclusive

Growth (ed.) (2010) 'South–South cooperation: the same old game or a new paradigm?', *Poverty in Focus*, 20, Brasilia: United Nations Development Programme.

Kwa, A. (2010) 'The challenges confronting South–South trade', in International Policy Centre for Inclusive Growth (ed.), 'South–South cooperation: the same old game or a new paradigm?', *Poverty in Focus*, 20, Brasilia: United Nations Development Programme, pp. 9–10.

OECD (Organisation for Economic Co-operation and Development) (2010) *Shifting Wealth*, Paris: OECD.

Severino, J.-M. and O. Ray (2009) *The End of ODA: Death and Rebirth of a Global Public Policy*, Working Paper no. 167, Washington, DC: Center for Global Development.

South Centre (2008a) *Reshaping the International Development Cooperation Architecture:Perspectives on a Strategic Development Role for the Development Cooperation Forum (DCF)*, Analytical Note SC/GGDP/AN/GEG/9, Geneva: South Centre.

— (2008b) *Developing Country Perspectives on the Role of the Development Cooperation Forum: Building Strategic Approaches to Enhancing Multilateral Development Cooperation*, Analytical Note SC/GGDP/AN/GEG/10, Geneva: South Centre.

TT-SSC (Task Team on South–South Co-operation) (2010) *Bogotá Statement: Towards Effective and Inclusive Development Partnerships*, Paris: OECD.

UN (United Nations) (2008) *Trends and Progress in International Development Cooperation*, Report of the Secretary-General, UN document E/2008/69, New York: United Nations.

UNCTAD (United Nations Conference on Trade and Development) (2010) *The Least Developed Countries Report: Towards a New International Development Architecture for LDCs*, Geneva: UNCTAD.

UNDESA (United Nations Department of Economic and Social Affairs) (2010) *Development Cooperation for the MDGs: Maximizing Results*, UN document ST/ESA/326, New York: United Nations.

AFTERWORD

The new role of emerging economies in global governance has sparked a debate on the effectiveness of old and new approaches to development cooperation. This debate, however, is not merely academic. It is about different approaches to economic development and varying historical and cultural ties. At the centre of the discussion lies the question of how developing countries can benefit from and contribute to growth in a globalized economy.

Emerging economies and industrialized countries have chosen the political club of the Group of Twenty (G20)[1] as a platform to address the challenges of global governance. Since the G20's first meeting in 2008, the international community has placed considerable hope in the ability of the G20 to bring about economic and financial stability. One aspect of this new responsibility for global development is the economic inclusion of the least developed countries (LDCs). The long-established donor relations of the OECD countries are now being challenged by a variety of emerging economy approaches to trade, credit and infrastructural development.

The G20 is by no means a homogeneous group. There are not only differences between the G8 countries and the eleven emerging economies in the G20, but there are also disparities in GDP and economic development among the emerging economies themselves. The diversity of interests and potentials could be the strength of the G20. But not much is known about the actual policies and the effectiveness of the new approaches to development cooperation.

In this book, *Development Cooperation and Emerging Powers: New Partners or Old Patterns?*, the approaches of emerging powers and traditional donors to development cooperation are analysed. The focus is on five major emerging powers from the G20, namely Brazil, China, India, Mexico and South Africa. The authors come from seven

---

1 Argentina, Australia, Brazil, Canada, China, the European Union, France, Germany, India, Indonesia, Italy, Japan, Mexico, Russia, Saudi Arabia, South Africa, South Korea, Turkey, the United Kingdom, the United States of America.

different countries and are part of a network of think tanks and universities that collaborate through the Managing Global Governance programme (MGG). All contributors share the belief that the new role of emerging powers in global governance processes calls for new thinking on North–South and South–South paradigms and new administrative and political structures in the respective countries. These new studies show that emerging economies take highly disparate approaches in implementing their development assistance and foreign trade instruments. After decades of largely ideologically motivated policies, they began in the late 1990s to adopt a more strategic approach to external relations both regionally and globally. This has led to improved linkages between aid, trade and financing. Each of these countries has developed its own formats and forums for trade and aid with LDCs. The diversity of systems and methods makes it hard to compare them. Researchers are faced with the challenge of measuring political effectiveness – both for the donor and the recipient country. This unique approach to comparative research reflects in itself a new dialogue between scholars from seven different countries.

Over 170 junior researchers and government officials from nine countries have participated in MGG since 2007. It started as a training programme for young professionals from Brazil, China, India, Mexico and South Africa. Institutions from Egypt, Indonesia and Pakistan are also part of the MGG network. Today over sixty government organizations and policy-oriented research bodies send their staff on MGG courses.

MGG is funded by the German Federal Ministry for Economic Co-operation and Development. It is jointly implemented by the Deutsche Gesellschaft für Internationale Zusammenarbeit and the German Development Institute.

Over the years MGG has not only created a strong alumni network but has also facilitated collaboration between institutions from different countries and continents. Working on similar questions of global development, MGG partner institutions from Africa, Asia, Europe and Latin America have established close South–South ties and met for MGG partner conferences. The 2010 conference provided the impetus for the present publication.

Previous research of the MGG partners network led to the publication in 2011 of the book *Power Shifts and Global Governance: Challenges from South and North*, edited by Ashwani Kumar and Dirk Messner. In 2010 the MGG partners closely followed the preparations for the G20 summit in Seoul, Korea, and contributed their ideas on the role of the 'G20 and global development'. This first volume of MGG partner debates was edited by Thomas Fues and Peter Wolff from the German Development Institute.

I would like to thank Sachin Chaturvedi from the Research and Information System for Developing Countries, India, Thomas Fues from the German Development Institute, and Elizabeth Sidiropoulos from the South African Institute of International Affairs, for initiating this collaborative research into new forms of development cooperation from emerging powers, as well as for editing this volume. My thanks also go to the authors of this book for stimulating debate and discussion on the role of development cooperation in global development.

Adolf Kloke-Lesch

Managing Director, Deutsche Gesellschaft für
Internationale Zusammenarbeit (GIZ)

ABOUT THE CONTRIBUTORS

Manmohan Agarwal is currently senior visiting fellow at the Centre
for International Governance Innovation (CIGI) in Waterloo,
Canada. He served as an economist at the World Bank and senior
economist with the International Monetary Fund. He has taught at
the Centre for International Trade and Development at the School
of International Studies, Jawaharlal Nehru University (JNU), India,
and served as dean of JNU's School of International Studies. In the
late 1980s he was a visiting professor at the University of Western
Ontario, researching the Uruguay round of trade negotiations. Since
joining CIGI, he has focused his research on the growth of emerging
economies, and their role in the global economy and international
development. In 2009, he edited a book on India's economic future,
and he has also contributed numerous papers, policy briefs, and
commentaries on the role of developing countries within the G20.

Ross Herbert is currently a PhD candidate at the Johns Hopkins
School of Advanced International Studies (SAIS). He was previously a senior research fellow and head of the Governance and
African Peer Review programme at the South African Institute of
International Affairs. He has worked for Independent Newspapers
in South Africa on its foreign desk, covering Africa. He has travelled
extensively through Africa and has written widely on African developmental issues, conflict and governance.

James Mackie is a specialist on EU development policy and a senior
adviser at the European Centre for Development Policy Management
(ECDPM). Since joining ECDPM in 2002, he has served as one of
the centre's heads of programme, and is a member of the management team. He is a visiting professor at the International Relations
and Diplomacy Department of the College of Europe in Bruges and
has served as Secretary-General of the EU-NGO Liaison Committee
(now CONCORD).

Maximo Romero is head of the Council for Science and Technology in the State of Puebla, Mexico, and was general director for technical and scientific cooperation at the Ministry of Foreign Affairs, Mexico, where he was responsible for policy on international development cooperation. He has been president of the board of the Interamerican Agency of Cooperation of the Organization of American States (OAS) and president of the Special Fund of Cooperation in the Association of Caribbean States. He has also served as Mexico's representative on issues related to international development cooperation to the OECD, UN and OAS. He is a member of the Mexican Bar Association and member and former president of the Academy of International Private Law.

Enrique Saravia is senior consultant and project coordinator at Getulio Vargas Foundation, Rio de Janeiro, where he was a professor before retirement in 2010. He is visiting professor at the Federal University of Rio de Janeiro and at the Andean University Simon Bolivar, Ecuador. He is a member of the Center for Advanced Studies in International Cooperation in the 21st Century, and of the scientific committee of the International Association of Arts and Cultural Management, Paris/Montreal. He has been vice president of the International Association of Schools and Institutes of Administration, Brussels. He is a member of the editorial boards of *International Journal of Arts Management*, Montreal, *DICE Dossier/ACRONIM Database*, London, and *Droit et Économie de la Régulation*, Paris.

Zhou Hong is the director of the Institute of European Studies at the Chinese Academy of Social Sciences (CASS) and chairs the Chinese Association for European Studies. She is a member of the Academic Division of CASS and is serving as deputy chair of the Academic Division for International Studies of CASS. She is a standing member of the China Economic and Social Council and is vice president of the Chinese Association for International Relations. Her recent publications include: *Chinese Views of the World* (editor), *EU as a Power* (editor), *EU Governance Model* (co-editor), *China-Europe Relations* (editor), *Donors in China*, *Whither the Welfare State* and *Foreign Aid and International Relations* (co-editor).

INDEX